Emmett Lee

Witness for

AID

WITNESS FOR
AID

FRANK M. COFFIN

HOUGHTON MIFFLIN COMPANY BOSTON
The Riverside Press Cambridge
1964

FOREWORD

THIS IS NOT a book about the dark side of the moon. It is a book about a relatively unknown side of the United States — a side far more visible to two thirds of the world than to its citizens at home. For this is about our already historic and bold venture in helping the peoples of the developing nations.

No fewer than eleven Congresses and five Presidents have made the same basic commitment to economic aid as an instrument of national policy. After twenty-one years, one might expect aid to have come of age, to be an accepted program, and to be administered by an agency beginning to be called "old line." Not so with overseas economic assistance. It has undergone the plastic surgery of reorganization so often that its scar tissue has scar tissue. And it is still "foreign aid," a label luminous with an alien glow. It has the dubious distinction of being at once the least understood, the most widely misjudged, the most hotly controversial, and yet one of the most critical major strands in the fabric of national policy.

A democracy thrives on controversy if it is based on some hard core of national consensus and leads somewhere. Aid policies and programs should by all means be constantly subjected to debate. But the perennial controversy on aid is far too strident and sterile. Each year protagonists and antagonists throughout the land, like aging knights in rusting armor, enter the lists and make the same thrusts and parries.

As a nation, we have not yet reached a basic and broadly shared understanding of the what, why, and how of aid. I know of no other major national policy which has endured so long without such a consensus. True, opinion polls reflect that a majority support the idea of aid. But what people mean by aid, how they view its purposes, what they think it costs, what results they think have been achieved, how high a priority it is — on these questions there is a vast diversity of opinion.

One major reason for this failure of consensus has been an almost complete lack of perspective. We have only fragmentary notions of what aid is. We have not been aware of the record we have written. We have not developed a clear idea of our national interest or objectives. We have failed to recognize either the limitations within which we must work or the opportunities within reach. We have exaggerated our failures and discounted our successes. We have been all too unmindful of, and impatient with, the efforts of those who are joined with us in this striving world — the nations linked with us in a free world aid movement and the developing nations who are not only receiving assistance from without but are increasingly mobilizing their resources from within in a determined drive for a better way of life. Finally, we have not faced up to the kind of role our nation ought to be equipped to play on the world stage in the closing decades of this century.

In this most exciting and complex of times, our greatness as a nation and, with greatness, our leadership and durability will be largely measured by our effectiveness in helping other nations move rationally and with increasing pace toward the goals of prosperous, responsible, and free societies. On the success of this effort, in harness with other industrialized nations, depends our ultimate freedom and security, if by security we mean living in the kind of world we want to see and being the kind of nation we want to be . . . not only today and tomorrow, but in the generations to come.

In the years ahead, the United States needs to profit from both its successes and its failures. Remote activities which cost tax dollars are difficult for a representative democracy to sustain. But to a large extent our willingness to make this kind of commitment will fix the boundaries of our achievement. There are still no simple answers to complex questions; there are no neat ways to manage revolutions in development. If we avoid misplaced utopianism and easy despair, we can learn to do better. We can enhance our achievements and reduce our frustrations. In short, we can marry idealism to competence and reconcile short-term necessities with long-term hopes.

These are the links in the chain: a sense of perspective that makes possible a consensus; and a basic consensus that makes possible a sustained policy carried out with competence. The purpose of this book is to help forge this chain.

My indebtedness is far-flung. To my former colleagues on the Committee on Foreign Affairs of the House of Representatives, I owe four years of useful apprenticeship in the intricate art of aid legislation. For my apprenticeship during the past three years in the equally complex art of aid administration, I am indebted to my colleagues in the executive branch — principally in the Agency for International Development. Although they all are responsible for my tutelage, I absolve them of specific responsibility for the views I have expressed.

To my co-worker over these years of association with aid policies and programs, Elizabeth Donahue, I am deeply indebted. To the extent that this book avoids being either a tome or a tract, her astringent criticism and balanced judgment are largely responsible. I am also grateful to Houghton Mifflin, and particularly Anne Barrett and Paul Brooks, for their encouragement of this effort to enlarge the understanding of development assistance — and for their own patient and sensitive assistance in developing this effort.

Since my official commission from the President said nothing about the writing of books, I am further mortgaged to my family for their sustained indulgence of this quixotic use of the leisure time I would otherwise have spent with them.

FRANK M. COFFIN

Washington, D.C.

CONTENTS

Foreword　　　　　　　　　　　　　　　　　v

Part I — The Uneasy Partnership

  1 PROFILE OF A DEVELOPMENT DIPLOMAT　　5

  2 THE WORK OF A DIPLOCRACY　　19

  3 THE WEEDS OF INDECISION　　36

  4 THE ANNUAL MINUET　　45

Part II — A Sense of History

  5 THE ROOTS OF POLICY　　63

  6 TIME FOR CONSENSUS　　75

Part III — A Sense of Purpose

  7 THE CATALOGUE OF CONFUSION　　95

  8 THE BLESSINGS OF LIBERTY　　102

Part IV — A Sense of Realism

  9 THE FORCES OF ARROGANCE　　117

  10 THE FORCES OF SELF-DOUBT　　129

  11 THE FORCES OF DESPAIR　　143

  12 AN INVESTMENT PHILOSOPHY　　161

Part V — A Sense of Confidence

13 THE STRIVING WORLD   175
14 ALLIES IN AID   189
15 VIEW FROM THE KREMLIN   201

Part VI — A Climate for Perseverance

16 A NEW PROFESSIONALISM   221
17 CHANGING THE DANCE   235
18 THE NEW DIMENSION OF CITIZENSHIP   247
19 THE NATIONAL INTEREST .   254

Index   269

A NOTE ON SOURCES

Unless otherwise identified, all facts and statistics cited have as their source unclassified material prepared by the Agency for International Development in connection with the presentation of its budget requests to the Congress or for other purposes.

PART I

The Uneasy Partnership

O*ne hundred and thirty years ago a young Frenchman,
Alexis de Tocqueville, came to the United States, traveled
about, observed acutely, and wrote his famed* Democracy in
America.

*While he wrote with admiration of the suitability of a democ-
racy for the conduct of domestic affairs, he made clear his view
that the United States, by location, temperament, organization,
and tradition, should stay out of foreign affairs. "The foreign
policy of the United States," he wrote, "is eminently expectant;
it consists more in abstaining than in acting." This was entirely
proper, because, as he put it, ". . . a democracy can only with
great difficulty regulate the details of an important undertaking, persevere in a fixed design, and work out its execution
in spite of serious obstacles. It cannot combine its measures
with secrecy or await their consequences with patience." [1]*

*This is the pressing issue — even today. The issue is whether
the United States in the latter years of the twentieth century
can prove de Tocqueville wrong. Our ability to "regulate the
details of an important undertaking," to "persevere in a fixed
design," to "work out its execution in spite of serious obstacles"
is nowhere put more to the test than in the field of foreign aid.*

There are three parties in interest — the executive branch,

[1] *Democracy in America.* New York: Vintage Books, 1955 (3rd printing), Vol.
I, p. 243.

*the press and public, and the Congress. This is the triarchy —
the threefold division of power — which governs the concepts
and execution of overseas aid. In a sense, these three, checked
by the Judiciary, determine all our public affairs. But in the
field of aid policies and programs, each has a particularly direct
and immediate influence: the press and public in setting the
mood; the Congress in marrying mood to law; and the executive
in carrying out policy and law.*

*If all three elements of national decision were of substantially
the same view, policy and practice would be joined in happy
wedlock. Mutual accommodation would resolve most issues.
There would be perseverance in a fixed design and the effective
regulation of details in spite of serious obstacles. But this is an
uneasy triarchy. It does not have a common view of the objective or the means of reaching it. The writing, reading, and
talking public lack any steady sense of agreement on means and
ends. The Congress, reflecting this unease, annually seeks to
strike a balance between legislative diplomacy and executive
discretion. Executive branch aid officials, without a domestic
constituency, labor incessantly at the threefold task of responding to changing law and policy, of trying to lay a clearer basis
of understanding, and of improving operations in a complex,
sensitive, and moving world.*

*A point of beginning is to attempt a reconnaissance of aid
from the three points of view — the officials who administer
the aid programs, the public, and the Congress.*

CHAPTER 1

Profile of a Development Diplomat

WHEN John Q. Public lays down his newspaper at night, he has added another tidbit to his knowledge about U.S. foreign aid. The facts he has just absorbed are sorted into shapes and shadows which together form his image of aid. Much of what he reads is a kaleidoscope of unimaginably large and shifting figures — in hundreds of millions and billions of dollars. Sometimes these figures are dutifully reported with obscure labels, such as military assistance, development loans, development grants, and supporting assistance — which mean very little to him. Other shapes are those of things, the big or notorious projects that make the news — a steel mill, a road, a fertilizer plant. These are associated in his mind with waste, faulty planning, corruption, political blackmail, or socialism. Other items from the news-gathering mill are controversial policy issues, arising out of answers to the questions: Who receives aid? Why? What do we get for it? Aid to dictators, military juntas, Communists, double-dealing opportunists, neutralists, socialists, irresponsible or incapable governments — these are unsettling shadows.

Sometimes the picture is pieced out with news of a home-town citizen who returns on home leave from aid work abroad, or news of the awarding of an aid contract to a local firm or university. But even these more intimate glimpses of the aid function show only part of the activities in only one of eighty countries overseas.

Money, projects, policy issues — all three are aspects of aid.

But they fall far short of showing what aid is or how it works. They reveal no more than does a balance sheet about the steel industry, or a price list about the automobile industry. A school textbook would be incomplete without a description of the open hearth furnace and the automobile assembly line. Knowledge of function, process, and action is a necessary underpinning for assessment of policies, results, and requirements. Yet all too few who discuss aid matters with authority pause to question what exactly aid is. What is the activity that gives rise to the issues in the public domain?

Aid in action is best comprehended not in terms of large global figures, remote projects, or abstract policy issues, but in terms of human beings striving, in specific places, to attain limited objectives. Diplomacy comes to life when we view the sensitive balance among words, action, and silence as demonstrated by a skilled diplomat. So also does aid — or development diplomacy — come to life through a close-up view of the development diplomat.

The Mission Director

Although many skilled and talented people share in the work of development diplomacy, the key generalists, through whom all the skills are brought to a focus, are the Mission Directors and Representatives of the Agency for International Development (A.I.D.). They are the little-known top field strategists and tacticians of development assistance. With somewhat lower diplomatic stature and compensation than Ambassadors, and with almost no public visibility in the United States, they are the cutting edge of the aid instrument of foreign policy — an instrument of increasing flexibility and usefulness in a world where economics rivals traditional diplomacy and defense in influencing international relationships.

Behind these men lie the planning and policy-making of Washington headquarters, the President's annual aid message, the Congressional hearings, debates, and votes on money and policies, the public discussions throughout the nation. But when the smoke of debate has cleared, the carrying out of policy and the effective use of resources come finally to depend on the force, imagination, and leadership of these individuals in far-off places.

Two thirds of the Mission Directors are career men drawn from the foreign service, the aid agency, and from other areas of government. The remaining third have temporarily shelved careers in business, uprooted families from comfortable suburbia, and settled down for tours of duty in an alphabetical range of capitals from Accra in Ghana to Vientiane in Laos. Their posts box the compass from Santiago, Chile, in the south; to Ankara, Turkey, in the north; from Mexico City in the west; to Seoul, Korea, in the east. Their "missions" vary in size from a dozen U.S. employees to two or three hundred, depending upon the complexity, size, and range of the program they administer. The average size is about fifty, with most of the personnel being experts in such fields as economics, agriculture, education, and health.

The Mission Director's job is to see to it that a broad range of resources available to him is used in such a manner as to advance the common interest of the United States and the country in which he serves. His task is no less than to be as effective a catalyst as possible in speeding the orderly economic and social development of his host country, within the broad framework of a free society.

His world is bounded by his Ambassador, his own staff, and the country in which he serves.

The Mission Director's first task, upon arriving at his post, is to establish a close and constructive relationship with the Ambassador, who is the chief representative of the United States and the head of the "country team." The team includes not only the Embassy, with its political, economic, commercial, agricultural, and labor experts, but the U.S. Information Service, the A.I.D. Mission, and, in many countries, a Military Assistance Advisory Group. The Ambassador provides the unifying leadership for all these activities.

Formerly it was possible for the Ambassador to deal only with political or diplomatic matters and have very little to do with the Mission Director. Today, aid policy and programs are so vital a part of our working relationship with most countries that a division between diplomacy and economics is no longer possible. In our most successful aid programs overseas, the Mission Director and the Ambassador are the closest of working partners. There are occasions when, if U.S. aid is to exercise an influence toward the improvement and change of governmental policies, the Ambassador himself must be able to talk persuasively to a Prime Minister, or a head of state. There are other times when the Ambassador, counseled by the Mission Director, must face the agonizing decision whether to cable Washington for emergency aid to meet a financial or political crisis or to make it clear to the host government that more is out of the question until taxes are increased, imports are curbed, salaries are cut, or currency is devalued. The former course buys a short-run solution at the expense of public criticism at home. The latter course not only invites personal unpopularity but might risk the fall of a government. But it is in the crucible of such hard decisions that development diplomacy meets its severest tests.

The Mission Director, to be effective, must also extract the utmost loyalty and dedication from his own staff. He may come on the scene and find it demoralized by the latest policy changes airgrammed from Washington, an unbroken series of Congressional and other investigations and visits, consistent criticism in the press, bureaucratic rivalries, endless demands for reports, delays in getting projects approved, troublemaking by malcontents, family problems, sickness, and a host of other grievances.

To gain understanding and support for new aid policies, to redirect and sometimes cut off old programs, to guide the development of new aid strategy, to settle disputes, to begin building morale, to deal fairly with the troublemakers, to eliminate surplus skills and recruit those in short supply — to do all these things and more is a challenge to the highest quality of managementability.

While the Mission Director is getting his own house in order, he must work at his most important objective: earning the confidence of the key officials in the host government. In going about this task, he must be alert to identifying the individuals who constitute the forces of responsible progress.

One experienced Mission Director defined the much mooted phrase "self help" as "working with the modern-minded officials in government." Governments are not monolithic. In all countries there are enlightened, educated or educable politicians, civil servants, and private citizens. They are the precious raw materials of progress. For "self help" is not the imposing of plans manufactured in the United States. It is the selective use of aid to stimulate and make possible new and better ways of doing things, by those who wish to make the effort and who need support for their views.

The successful Mission Director has built the kind of relationship with Cabinet Ministers and senior civil servants which allows them to consult him without embarrassment on a wide range of problems, whether or not they involve aid. In return, it allows him to give constructive suggestions or candid criticisms without fear of rancor.

A Mission Director's Day

No mere cataloguing of functions can portray the range of the Mission Director's tasks, from the petty to the significant, from

dull routine to acute crisis. What follows is a composite day —
a representative rather than an average one — drawn from the
experiences of several Mission Directors.

7.30 — 8.00   During breakfast young student from upcountry
drops in, seeking funds for visit to U.S. Explains requirements and urges him to finish secondary school with high
grades to qualify for university scholarship.

8.00 — 9.00   Gives once-a-week lecture at University School
of Business Administration in "Business Finance."

9.00 — 10.00   At Embassy for Country Team meeting. First
problem — What action, if any, to take on left wing press attack in morning papers that U.S. seeking to overthrow new
government. Concludes that attack is reaction to indelicate
and misleading article in major U.S. publication.

Country's officials have hard time understanding differences between a free press and their own semi-controlled
press. Decide Ambassador should not let this outbreak pass
without discussion and protest with head of government.

Second problem — Since new government's policies in
formative stage, asks Ambassador if, in next talk with head of
government, he would lay groundwork for later talk with
Finance Minister on a tax study recommendation which had
reached the talking stage with the former administration.

10.00 — 12.00   In Mission office. Reads morning cables and
mail from Washington. Groans as he learns that top prospect for post of education adviser was offered promotion by
his university and decided not to leave. Sighs as he reads
priority cable asking for complete report for use in Congressional hearing of all work done under an A.I.D. contract for
past five years. Notes arrival dates of an inspection team, 3
Senators, newspaper feature writer, and a group of businessmen.

Reads reports from staff, including notes for his call later
in day to Minister of Health. Because of disruption in government due to elections, country has not put up its share of
funds for anti-malaria work. If money not available by week-
end, all spraying stops.

Edits carefully biweekly progress report to Washington.

Drafts letter to new Minister of Finance, outlining items to be discussed at hoped for meeting.

Session with Mission's agricultural water resources engineer to discuss draft of report on scheme for irrigating a critical and arid part of the country. Compliments him on thoroughness and imagination. But points out that tone of report, as written, carries implications that U.S. might be preparing to finance the project. Engineer agrees rewriting is needed.

12.00 — 1.00 At Government Building with Minister of Health. Minister not aware anti-malaria work stoppage imminent. Promises to make delinquent payment immediately.

Since this is first discussion with new Minister, discusses current problem posed by government's plan for two new hospitals. Points out that it is more important to increase budget for Public Health Division since 80 percent of hospital cases are direct result of ignorance of simple health precautions. Says U.S. cannot maintain the three public health technicians if no adequate program exists. Closes by saying a public health nurse in every village will do more for nation's health than five new hospitals. Minister points out political appeal and prestige value of hospitals. Asks if A.I.D. would give budgetary help for at least one hospital. Receives flat no. Minister says he will try to persuade cabinet and may need some statistics on experience in other countries.

1.00 — 2.30 Lunch at home for vice-president of large U.S. corporation interested in investing in country. Guests were Principal Secretaries in Ministries of Labor and Finance, Director of Development Bank, and head of Planning Commission. Vice-president very interested in growing, canning, and exporting pineapple. Will send a survey team.

2.30 — 3.00 On way back to office, calls on secretary of the President's committee for education. Has heard that he and others feared U.S. trying to impose its own pattern on curriculum of new Teachers College. Assures him that our only goal is to see the college develop, adapting the best from the developed world to the special needs of the country. Secretary is relieved and will report this to the committee.

3.00 — 6.oo　In office. Sees Administrative Officer. Stenographer, recently arrived from U.S., complains of lizards in her room. Wants to go home. Agriculture Division pressing for more space.

Goes over brochure on aid activities prepared by U.S. Information Officer.

Has session with Deputy Director and Program Officer on preliminary budget submission for next fiscal year.

Desk work: dictates, signs mail and outgoing cables.

6.oo — 7.oo　Reception at Embassy for members of new government.

7.oo — 9.oo　Attends regular monthly evening meeting of American businessmen sponsored by Embassy. Embassy officers summarize political and economic developments. Reports on progress of aid activities. General discussion. Distinct increase in understanding and interest over last six months.

Businessmen optimistic about further investments.

9.30 — 10.oo　Reads local press.

Asks wife how family is doing.

This day contains all the elements of the Mission Director's job — his role in the country team, management of his own staff, public relations, community relations, close and continuing work with the government, serving visitors from the U.S., and constant communication with A.I.D. in Washington. But such a day only suggests the basic tasks of planning, negotiation, and action involved in development diplomacy.

Development Diplomacy

As a manager, the Mission Director's irreducible responsibility is to see that U.S. projects and programs are well planned, that they are economically and technically feasible, and that they are efficiently carried out. The end product of aid is a program for a particular country based on a long-range view of the reasonable possibilities for that country, the extent to which the United States should be involved, and what efforts can reasonably be expected from the country itself, with particular activities addressed to achieving certain priority development objectives.

The act of creation occurs, therefore, in the field, while A.I.D. in Washington sets forth the guidelines and standards, reviews the programs, and allocates the available funds. Planning or programming does not mean an academic blueprint nor does it mean the simple listing of "good" projects. It is no less than trying to adapt what we know about effective government, sound economics, and the good society to the needs, the will, and the capacity of a developing country.

Underlying all the techniques of planning is the role of development diplomacy. This is the broad responsibility of the Mission Director to see that the program as a whole is so used that the host government has been stimulated and enabled to take steps toward economic and social development that it would not otherwise have taken. External aid is far more important for its catalytic action than for the percentage of a nation's resources which it represents. It reaches its optimum potential, therefore, when it helps unleash national productive capacity — through seed capital to build institutions, to develop administrative skills, to devise better laws, to abandon restrictive policies.

The starting point is the broad aid strategy for the country. This must be part of the total U.S. policy thinking about that country. Should there be aid here at all? Indeed if no substantial purpose is served by aid that cannot be served by other means, or if the country is nearing the point of self-sufficiency, the strategy is one of transition aiming at the early termination of assistance. Where aid is seen as necessary, its objective must be defined. Is the major objective to help resist overt aggression? to help combat covert subversion? to help keep a nation from collapsing? to play a modest part in a country's first step toward development? to help it gain momentum in a particular sector of the economy? or to give maximum support to a country with the administrative capacity and determination to carry out a well prepared series of actions — whether these be called a plan or not?

Equally important is the question: What can we reasonably expect from the other country as its part of the contract? Is it tax reform, monetary discipline, agrarian progress, a better allocation of resources for education and development? Or is it simply the will to defend itself and win the allegiance of its citizens to nationhood? The answers to such questions provide the strategic framework for the Mission's planning.

Analysis of the country's resources, plans, capabilities, and needs must then take place to reveal the areas where external assistance can have the greatest effect. Not only the economic effect but also the political and social impact must always be taken into account. The sensitive development strategist realizes that there are times when a proposal strongly backed by the host country or community should be accepted even if the idea sounds bizarre to U.S. ears. In one country, efforts at community development stalled until aid personnel gave support to the desire of town leaders to build a wall around the local cemetery. This project, lacking any inherent economic value, proved to be the springboard for an effective community development program enlisting the cooperation and enthusiasm of all the villagers. The moral: development is not an exact science.

Before even a tentative program is put together, the resources available from other countries, the United Nations specialized agencies, and foreign private business must be estimated. If the country has an office for the coordination or planning of external aid, this task is eased. The U.N. Resident Representative and the aid officials of other industrialized nations are obvious checkpoints.

Only at this stage does it become relevant to look at the resources available from the United States. These are both governmental and private. The activities of U.S. private business, the Export-Import Bank, the Peace Corps, and many voluntary agencies are important parts of the spectrum of development.

The task then is to build a program to meet the aid objectives, using the appropriate combination of aid tools. They include the following: (1) "supporting assistance" — usually commodities — to meet a strategic need arising from the instabilities of the Cold War; (2) development dollar loans for capital projects or for industrial commodities to sustain the momentum of a growing industrial economy; (3) technical assistance — expert training, advice and help in building institutions in such fields as public administration, education, and agriculture; (4) grants or sales of surplus agricultural commodities (under Public Law 480); (5) loans of foreign currencies accumulated from such sales; (6) grants from excess stocks of tools, vehicles, and supplies; (7) sharing in the cost of industrial or commercial feasibility surveys; (8) guaranties of private investment against certain risks such as expropriation and, in some cases, against all nonbusiness risks; (9) the payment of expenses of students and trainees selected to spend a year of study or apprenticeship in the United States or, sometimes, in other countries.

Not all of these tools will be used in a country program but they give wide latitude for a tailored approach to any specific country's problems. When the aid components have been determined, the precise projects and programs must be planned. The field mission must see that feasibility studies are made, that practical plans are drawn up, that there is a satisfactory cost-benefit ratio, that responsible engineers are selected, that quali-

fied individuals or institutions are chosen for technical assistance contracts, that there are plans for turning over training
programs to the host country, that procurement, accounting,
reporting, and legal requirements are understood, and innu-
merable other steps taken.

An example of diplomacy in development is the experience
of one Mission Director who, with the backing of his Ambassador, entered into complicated budgetary discussions with the
officials of his host country. After their study, all agreed that,
if the country was to make progress, the country's development
budget must be increased, while its current operating budget
should be trimmed. It was made clear that new projects would
not be negotiated until this was done. Cutting a budget is not
easy in any country. Some toes must be stepped on. Tension
mounted.

Here is the testimony of one A.I.D. official who was on the
scene:

> "Mind you, we were not getting the world's greatest publicity
> at this stage, but I think most people . . . had confidence in
> our sincere desire to help them. Here again I think we were
> drawing on a tremendous reservoir of good will.
>
> "They knew we were doing it — many of the middle echelon
> civil servants, a proportion of whom have had some training
> in the United States under the A.I.D. program over the last
> decade, figured we were doing this really for the benefit of the
> people . . . that this was not dollar imperialism, as the Com-
> munist press would have it, but in fact, we were trying to get
> their Government off dead center to get it to do something
> positive, to take some meaningful steps." [1]

Despite understandings, the regular budget first appeared
without reduction. The Mission Director conferred again and
held his position. Some weeks went by. Finally a supplementary

[1] Hearings on the Foreign Assistance Act of 1963, Committee on Foreign Affairs, House of Representatives, Part IV, pp. 839, 840.

budget was announced. The regular budget had been reduced and the development budget had been substantially increased.

This is development diplomacy. All depends on the foundation of confidence and trust built by the Ambassador and Mission Director. Without that foundation, their actions would have been resented as arrogant interference. But sensitivity, understanding, and firmness enabled those within the receiving country to do what they themselves knew should be done.

In other cases the "aid bargain" involves changes in monetary policy, better tax collection and new tax laws, agrarian land and credit measures, a stabilization program involving the International Monetary Fund and European creditors. Sometimes reduction in military or civilian government personnel are the agreed upon objective. And in some cases the quid pro quo may be as simple and as fundamental as free elections.

This is aid in action in countries receiving the overwhelming proportion (80 percent) of our development assistance. Aid's most effective use as a fulcrum for self-help occurs in such countries, where the problems of security are secondary and the size of aid is significant.

But even where the aid lever is small, development diplomacy has a role. There are forty-five countries accounting for only 10 percent of our economic aid. In these countries most U.S. aid is directed to the training of selected leaders, to the development of educational systems, and to the building of better public administration and key institutions. Even here it is possible to establish such a basis of confidence that advice is sought and given and a development influence is brought to bear out of all proportion to the amount of the actual assistance given. The A.I.D. Mission in such cases is really treated as an extra resource of experience for a government hard pressed for senior advisers.

In one such country, in Africa, development diplomacy came into play in the following way. Aid was requested in the construction of a road. Before an agreement was entered into, the

Mission Director and Ambassador sought two objectives — the creation by the government of a highway department to assure maintenance of the road and a gasoline tax to assure funds for its maintenance. Both conditions were willingly accepted.

*   *   *

In short, U.S. aid today differs in two important ways from programs of the past. Aid is no longer a series of unrelated but helpful projects in a given country. It is, rather, a "country program" both in the sense that it has been worked out with cooperating host country officials and in the sense that it has one or more priority goals tailored to the country's needs to which all the separate activities must be related. The second major difference is that aid means some degree of intervention. Formerly, "self help" meant merely that on each project the host country would be expected to contribute something — labor, money, or materials. The concept of self-help has now expanded to encompass major policy decisions, legislation, and administrative action.

To be effective in identifying and stimulating such actions, the U.S. Ambassador and the A.I.D. Mission Director must participate in discussions with the country, must ponder what is feasible, and must take and hold positions. The gradations of intervention range from offering information, making suggestions, using incentives, and arguing, to delaying assistance, changing its composition, reducing it, or suspending it.

This is the heart of aid in action. In its demands upon professional competence, common sense, sensitivity to national pride, patience and courage, development diplomacy has few peers among any profession, new or old.

CHAPTER 2

The Work of a Diplocracy

WHILE THE cutting edge of aid is the field mission, the temper of the blade, its size, and style are forged in the Agency for International Development headquarters in Washington. Here are the officials and employees charged with backstopping U.S. aid overseas. Numbering 2700, they are a one thousandth part of the federal bureaucracy, equaling the total employment of the Smithsonian Institution and the Soldiers' Home.

Although part of the bureaucracy, with its own unmistakable set of initials, A.I.D. has a unique role. It is partly a bureaucracy in that it is forced to devise standard operating procedures for a host of functions. But unlike most, if not all, other operations of government, it is concerned not merely with one kind of resource or specialized function but with the whole range of resources, skills, techniques, and concepts encompassed in the effort to help build nations. It is subject to all the sensitivities, intangibles, and vicissitudes of diplomacy. Yet it is but one instrument of diplomacy, confined to the field of economic and social development.

Its officials and employees must be not only good bureaucrats. They must also be sensitive to overall foreign policy, the problems, customs, and personages of other nations. Planners must sense what will work and what will not. Lawyers must know what kind of agreements can be negotiated and what cannot. Even auditors, as they seek to verify invoices from country records, must deal skillfully with foreign sensitivities. To coin a word to describe this mix of duties and qualities, they must be diplocrats. And their agency, A.I.D., is a diplocracy.

Admittedly, this would be just so much word-mongering if aid were simply a huge check-writing operation, with large sums of money being given indiscriminately to bribe, placate, or bail out nations all over the world. If such were the case, missions overseas and staff in Washington would be superfluous. Aid could be almost fully automated.

The silhouette of aid today, however, is completely at odds with this stereotype. Over four fifths of economic aid today is directed at development rather than political or economic crisis. Nearly two thirds of developmental aid is in the form of loans, rather than grants. Four fifths of the loans are concentrated in a half dozen countries. Only rarely is aid in the form of money. Over four fifths of all economic aid today is in goods and services purchased in the United States.

To produce this kind of silhouette — with overwhelming emphasis on development, on loans, on meaningful concentration, on the utilization of U.S. goods and services — in such a way as to serve the overall interests of the United States demands both the specialized skills of bureaucracy and the broad-gauged judgments of diplomacy.

The Xanda Program: A Case Study

No static organization chart or list of functions can convey fully the substance or flavor of this kind of work, its necessity or effectiveness. Realism suggests, therefore, a case study, a cross-section view of what happens to a country aid program after it leaves the field mission and before it becomes reality. The country is "Country X," the mythical nation of Xanda.

The Xanda program is air-pouched to Washington. There the Xanda desk officer, technical experts, and program officers review it for consistency with U.S. objectives and reasonableness of amounts. It is next subjected to further criticism, change, and cutting by the program office for the region (Africa, Latin America, Far East, or Near East and South Asia). It is then submitted to the Agency's central program review staff. Finally it is ready for the Administrator's review.

This review is something like a court of justice. The Xanda program is on trial. The counsel for the defense are the Xanda desk officer and the regional assistant administrator. The judge is the A.I.D. Administrator. Gathered around the long table are the prosecutors — representatives of the Departments of State, Treasury, Agriculture, Defense, Commerce, the Bureau of the Budget, and A.I.D. specialists.

THE ADMINISTRATOR: I guess we're ready to proceed. This morning's country is Xanda. Did all of you receive copies of the program proposed? Did all of you read it? If so, I suggest that we get down to the issues.

DESK OFFICER: I'll try to boil down the facts. As most of you know, Xanda is a fertile, agricultural country. But it is poor and primitive. I have seen farmers plowing with a stick. They live largely on what they grow or barter. There are some markets, but in the rainy season no one can reach them. In the past five years there has been a rising flood of peasants to the two major cities. They are overcrowded and, like so many others, hotbeds of discontent.

Two months ago Xanda elected a new Prime Minister. His campaign was based on what he could do for Xanda. There were some pretty rugged speeches. He was all for disarmament and he wasn't going to be anybody's lackey. He made some anti-Western statements. But you should have heard the opposition. We feel — and State feels — that he is moderate. He is, first, last, and always, a nationalist. He is a politician. His economics leaves something to be desired. But he has assembled a few competent people. His Minister of Economy is quite able, a former senior civil servant when Xanda was a colony.

As to Xanda's importance to the United States, we think it has a chance of making some real progress with its new government. You know that the former government was hopeless. The election campaign was pitched pretty much on development. If Xanda can do well in the next several years, it will have a profound influence on this part of the continent. On the other hand, if it fails, it's likely to be a center of trouble for the entire area.

THE ADMINISTRATOR: Does anyone disagree with this assessment? If not, let's go into the proposed aid program. I take it that in the past we have had a small Teacher Training program, some tsetse fly eradication, and a few students brought here for a year's training in public administration.

DESK OFFICER: Yes. This has averaged about $300,000 a year. There have been some good results. Two of the nine ministers in the present government are former trainees. So is the Director of their budget bureau. But this year the Mission Director and Ambassador have tried something new. They have come up with an aid approach based on the assumption that prompt and forthcoming support, in the early months of this new government, would go far in bolstering the Prime Minister's confidence and avoiding extremism.

THE ADMINISTRATOR: Hasn't Xanda received some Soviet aid already?

DESK OFFICER: Yes. It's precisely because of the experience that this program is recommended. There were seven Soviet projects in the agreement signed two years ago. Only two have started construction. They've been haggling over details most of the time. But what really infuriated the Prime Minister was the involvement of some Russian personnel in the election campaign . . . for his opponent.

THE ADMINISTRATOR: I see. Well, let's get on with the program.

DESK OFFICER: The two key problem areas are rural and urban. The program tries to address both. It would place the project emphasis in the rural sector, helping build a system of farm-to-market roads, connecting a large rural area with centers of demand and opening up new land for cultivation. The program would tackle the urban problem by conditioning the road network on cabinet support of the tax proposal of the Minister of Economy, which would provide revenues for needed urban services, such as education. The road project would be useful in convincing rural taxpayers that they were being fairly treated, while holding out the hope to city taxpayers that more regular and plentiful food meant lower prices.

THE ADMINISTRATOR: I have one question to start with. If we're uncertain about the direction of this new government, shouldn't we stand by, perhaps continue some token technical assistance, but just watch and wait for a while?

THE MAN FROM STATE: If I may, I'd like to back up what the Desk Officer said. We feel very strongly that the rest of the continent is looking at Xanda, to see whether it can pull out of the rut it's been in. Disaffection with Communist efforts is very real. But the Prime Minister has made it clear that he will not go begging to Xanda's former colonial master. This is a case when moderate but timely aid is an excellent investment.

THE ADMINISTRATOR: I understand. But it still seems to me that we don't have to choose between an "all or nothing" approach. For example, is it feasible to break the road network into a series of individual projects, going ahead with comprehensive planning, but making commitments on specific projects as we see effective performance by the government?

DESK OFFICER: Yes, I think that can be done.

THE ADMINISTRATOR: Well, then, let's go ahead on that basis. Our approach will be, so to speak, to keep our commitments on as short a leash as possible, but to aim for a sensible overall program.

THE MAN FROM BUREAU OF THE BUDGET: I note from the Peace Corps program that they plan to send thirty volunteers to Xanda next year. Does anyone know whether they could do the preliminary road surveys?

THE ADMINISTRATOR: That's an excellent suggestion. (*To the Desk Officer*) Will you follow up?

THE MAN FROM DEFENSE: We've been trying in our military assistance program to get the Xanda army interested in civic action projects. This might be a good place to start — if they could do the rough clearing for the roads. We could supply some engineers.

THE ADMINISTRATOR: Fine. I leave it to you to explore that possibility. Yes. Treasury?

THE MAN FROM TREASURY: Do we know how much Xanda is willing to put into these roads? I hope we won't have to finance the local costs of labor and gravel.

DESK OFFICER: I'm afraid it can't put up anything, without printing money and creating inflation. Its budget is fully committed for ordinary operating expenses. But what we thought we'd do was to supply some surplus food and use it as partial payment for wages of the laborers, as we have done in Tunisia.

THE MAN FROM AGRICULTURE: I wanted to ask a question about that. In your "food for work" proposal, you've suggested using rice. We're not sure we'll have enough of a surplus in rice. I think we ought to explore some other commodities. We'll look into it and be in touch with you.

THE A.I.D. HUMAN RESOURCES OFFICER: It's all very well to build roads, but has anyone thought about maintaining them? We've had enough trouble with roads.

THE DESK OFFICER: Yes — we've thought about that. We plan to build into all loans a requirement that part of the money be used to set up a training program for a rural unit of the Department of Transportation. We plan to send over some people from the Bureau of Public Roads to conduct the program.

THE HUMAN RESOURCES OFFICER: I have another question. The feeder roads are fine. But how do we know the farmers will improve their production, just because they have roads? What I'm getting at is that we should do some work in agricultural extension and credit facilities. I've seen too many roads built that accomplished too little. Productivity isn't automatic.

THE A.I.D. OFFICER DEALING WITH INTERNATIONAL ORGANIZATION: I think this is something that the Food and Agriculture Organization of the United Nations would like. They've been looking for extension projects in this part of the continent. On the credit side, I think the best bet is the Common Market Development Fund. If it isn't interested, I think some European country might be. We'll get some cables out to our embassies.

THE MAN FROM AGRICULTURE: These roads are supposed to open up some new land for crops. No one yet has said what's going to be grown.

THE DESK OFFICER: It will be cotton. It's a new crop for Xanda, but your own experts say it's entirely feasible.

THE MAN FROM AGRICULTURE: I was afraid of that. You know, we have a cotton problem in the United States. It isn't exactly in short supply. I don't think Congress would be too enthusiastic about expanding the world supply of cotton.

THE DESK OFFICER: No, no. We've checked this. The staple that can be grown in Xanda is not competitive with U.S. cotton. Besides, the domestic market will absorb all that can conceivably be grown. This is not for export.

THE MAN FROM TREASURY: If this is so, if this won't create foreign exchange earnings, are the road projects really the highest priority?

THE ADMINISTRATOR: Ordinarily I'd agree with you. But I think we have to realize that Xanda's problem is not just that of increasing export earnings. Our basic goal is to help the rural area to prosper, to raise the internal standard of living. It's partly economic, partly social and political.

A.I.D.'s Top Economist: Let's discuss the urban problem for a moment. I seriously question whether a tax proposal, considering the difficulties of getting parliamentary approval, would be as effective as getting a more realistic exchange rate. Part of Xanda's problem is simply an overvalued currency. This encourages imports and discourages exports. If we could reverse the emphasis, export industries would expand, the tax base would broaden and foreign exchange earnings would increase.

The Desk Officer: I agree with you — as a theoretical proposition. I think the answer is simply that the Minister of Economy is ready to back his tax proposal. He shies away from any change in exchange rates at this stage of his government. This may come later, but it's just not negotiable now.

Finally, the Xanda program review comes to a close. The process is later repeated for seventy-five other countries and four territories over a period of five or six weeks. The Bureau of the Budget then conducts a review, paring overall figures to fit national budget requirements. Only then are the programs ready to be presented to Congress. The Xanda program may come in for only a moment's scrutiny. Or it may be the subject of hours and even days of discussion on Capitol Hill.

A year after the Mission Director first bundled his proposals off to Washington, when Congress has at last appropriated money, Xanda's allotment is made.

Then a host of implementing actions must be set in motion. Some preliminary action has already taken place. The Peace Corps survey has been done. A U.S. engineering firm is completing a feasibility study. A loan agreement must now be negotiated. A loan officer, lawyer, and engineer form a team which will stay with the project until completion. Xanda's Minister of Economy has asked the help of a tax expert. A.I.D. calls on the Internal Revenue Service for help. A.I.D. asks the

Bureau of Public Roads for experts to set up a highway maintenance training program.

Orders are placed for future deliveries of surplus food for the road labor. The cost of the project is further reduced when A.I.D.'s excess property office discovers surplus stocks of army shovels in a warehouse in Europe and orders shipment to Xanda. At the same time, A.I.D. is planning for a year's training in the United States of a dozen young Xanda educators and civil servants. It makes arrangements with several departments of government and a half dozen universities.

In this stage of breathing life into what had been only concepts and plans, a wide variety of talent is needed — engineers, lawyers, controllers, procurement and contracting experts, as well as experts throughout government in education, health, agriculture, taxation, aviation, housing, labor, science, and economics.

A.I.D. as a Development Broker

At this stage — that of carrying out programs — A.I.D. acts as a bridge between the infinitely varied resources of the United States and the equally infinite variety of needs in the developing countries. Reaching into the entire fabric of our society, trying to match resources with needs, it is truly a broker of development assistance.

It uses the services of over a dozen departments and agencies of the federal government — for overseas work, for planning, and for training of foreign students and officials.

It programs the distribution of over one and one half billions of dollars of surplus food and fiber a year — almost a third of all U.S. farm exports. This is the equivalent of two 10,000-ton cargo ships leaving the U.S. every weekday in the year.

Its commodity purchases alone involve American industry in over $1 billion of orders and over 600,000 jobs a year. Commodities, material, and services together account for nearly $2 billion a year. A.I.D. has issued over a billion dollars of guaranties to protect U.S. business overseas. It financed, in 1962, 11 percent of all exports — a fifth of all U.S. iron and steel mill products, a third of all fertilizers, a fourth of all locomotives and a tenth of all trucks and buses shipped abroad.

It has over 60 contracts with the 50 Land Grant Colleges, over a hundred contracts with 69 universities of the nation, and over 225 contracts with U.S. firms for services in the United States and abroad.

It brings over 6000 foreign nationals to the United States each year for training in their specialized fields, using hundreds of institutions — colleges and universities, hospitals, business firms, industries, local, state and federal government agencies.

It works closely with 54 private voluntary, charitable, and religious organizations which send and distribute $80 million of food, clothing, tools, seeds, and medicine to some 80 countries. A.I.D.'s only contribution is to pay the freight — $4 million. These voluntary organizations also distribute surplus foods for emergency relief, school lunch and family feeding programs, and such economic development projects as the building of roads, dikes, dams, canals, wells, and houses.

It contracts with such organizations as the National Rural Electric Cooperative Association, the Cooperative League of the USA, the Credit Union National Association, the National Farmers Union, the American Institute for Free Labor Development, savings and loan associations. Such contracts enable A.I.D. to draw upon the diversity of American society and offer experienced help to developing countries in drafting legislation, setting up institutions in both urban and rural areas, organizing training programs, and establishing training centers. Over 500 credit unions are being organized in Latin America alone. The target is a thousand. In 1963 over 100 cooperative

programs were in operation — a threefold increase over 1962.
They are in such fields as housing, trade unions, agricultural
credit, fisheries, water development, farm mechanization, government administration and food distribution. Savings and
loan associations have been successfully introduced in almost
a dozen Latin American countries.

Finally, cities, counties, and states use A.I.D. as a broker to
help establish an "opposite number" relationship. Chile and
California launched the first experiment. Others are in the
offing. City-to-city, county-to-province, state-to-nation, univer-
sity-to-university — these are patterns that are emerging. They
symbolize the deep desire of the people of the United States to
involve its own warp and woof in the fabric of nation building.

As the United States involves itself in assisting other nations,
it comes to the task with the resources of a pluralistic, pragmatic, and individualistic society. The variety of its skills, approaches, and institutions, both within and without government, provides breadth, depth, and flexibility of assistance.
These can never be matched by any monolithic society wedded
to dogmatic theories. In the field of development, strength lies
in diversity.

The Hard Decisions

The planning, refinement, review, and execution of an aid program in a country all involve the meshing of the skills of many
people, both in Washington and in the field, in A.I.D. and
other agencies, inside and outside government. Even though
the unusual and the extraordinary play a part in all these functions, they are part of the routine life of the aid diplocrat.

What remains is the lonely and critical task of making key
decisions to respond to problems, crises, and opportunities.
These are frequently watershed decisions, irreversible, determining for the indefinite future our relations with other coun-

tries, groups of countries, and even the world at large. Time is
often of the essence. The stakes are always high. The alternatives are often limited. If the course taken is successful, the
result is lost in the march of events. If the action fails, the result lives on in memory. There can be no fixed procedure, no
guarantee of comfort in consensus. Proposals, briefing papers,
statements of pros and cons will be prepared by staffs, but the
burden of decision will be lonely. At most it will be shared by
a few officials in A.I.D., the Departments of State and Defense,
and the White House. Sometimes it will rest on one man — the
A.I.D. Administrator, the Secretary of State, or the President.

There are hard decisions to go ahead with aid for a particular
country, knowing that there may be opposition from the public,
the press, and the Congress, and knowing also that all the con-
siderations leading to the decision can not be revealed.

Here are some examples. They are given with trepidation.
For the only certainty about the affairs of nations is that they
are unpredictable. Contemporary history cannot be frozen at
any specific point of time. Decisions which look like successes
may be unraveled, and apparent failures may be salvaged by
subsequent events.

Some of these are dictated by high strategy. The decision to
make military aid available to India in order to meet the threat
of Chinese invasion was an example. The facets of this issue
were many. The precise nature of the threat, both to India and
the entire Asian subcontinent, the extent of Indian will and
capability, the extent of British participation, the reaction of
our ally Pakistan, the possible responses of the Soviet Union,
the effect on India's economic development, the reaction in our
own Congress, press, and public, our available resources and
priorities — all of these had to be taken into account. To help
or not to help; either alternative was difficult. The decision was
made to do the difficult — to help. Not to have helped would
have been to change our view of the strategic importance of the
subcontinent.

Another hard type of decision is presented by country situations which can be called targets of opportunity. These are cases when a decision not to act may not materially worsen our relationships with a country, but where it is possible that a decision to act will improve them.

Such a case was posed by Guinea. Emerging into independence, Guinea broke off relations with France, and sought substantial Communist aid. After considerable exposure to disillusion from political meddling, delay in starting projects, and haggling over costs and quality, Guinea was ready and eager to try a different way. If we were to be responsive, we could be certain of criticism and uncertain of results. Yet to turn a deaf ear, to close the door would be to foreclose an opportunity. Again, the decision was to extend moderate aid. Guinea resumed relationships with France, became interested in private investment, and in numerous ways welcomed closer cooperation.

Another such target of opportunity was Nigeria. A country which had come to independence smoothly, with British help, it possessed a core of skilled civil servants, abundant resources, and a steadily improving development plan. The choice facing the United States was whether to extend token aid in the form of supporting several projects or to back fully an ambitious development effort. Had the first course been chosen, no severe political crisis would have ensued. But an opportunity would have been missed to give a leading nation a chance to stage a breakthrough into rapid and successful development, setting a tone and example for all Africa. The latter course was chosen by pledging substantial and continuing aid under its plan for a period of years. And while the final result cannot be predicted, this was a bold decision which could make a large difference in the kind of development path Africa ultimately chooses to follow.

There is a third kind of decision — where to go ahead is a gamble and to withdraw is certain loss and disadvantage. These are targets of hazard. The objective is not to maximize gain but to forestall chaos. Brazil is a large example. Plagued by inflation, this giant Latin American country sought aid, not for development but to lay the stabilizing foundations of development. A long history of financial irresponsibility dampened any feeling of optimism. The choice faced was to say "no" and await the inevitable debacle or to become involved. We chose to be involved, hedging our bet with precise segments of aid conditioned on precise steps to be taken by the Government of Brazil. Again, there was no certainty of success, but our decision preserved a wide range of options.

Laos is another case of the choice between bad options. On the one hand we could have abandoned this troubled nation of Southeast Asia. The results would have weakened the will for independence throughout this peninsula. On the other hand, we could remain involved, patiently backstopping the tedious struggle to make a nation out of a committee. The decision to remain in the game has already seen an increasing will by the neutralists — our former adversaries — to build a nation. In this case critics charge us with only buying time. But even this is no mean accomplishment, for time is on the side of nationalism.

The casebook on difficult decisions could be written on Vietnam alone. Here the scales always hung in precarious balance. An immediate, continuing, overt and covert thrust to a free nation in a part of the world that would be profoundly affected by the outcome called for our involvement. But internal political, economic, and social policies and attitudes continually raised doubts as to the capacity of national leadership to win and sustain the loyalties of the people. The barometer of progress on these fronts fluctuated violently. As the wearisome struggle progressed, both American funds and lives were spent in this remote battleground. The perpetual question was: Is the effort still worthwhile? The key to all the decisions was the effect of the alternative. Withdrawal would be irre-

versible and final. Such a decision could not responsibly be
made until it became reasonably clear that persistence would
be fruitless. In such a dilemma, there is no course that will
avoid the most violent criticism.

These have been the hard decisions to give aid when the results were uncertain, when the criticism was inevitable, but
when the alternative was to foreclose opportunity for ultimate
success.

There is another type of hard decision almost unrecognized
by a public accustomed to the "giveaway" stereotype. This is
the decision to say "no," to enforce unpleasant requirements,
to risk by action a worse state of affairs than would prevail if
aid were continued on a business-as-usual basis. This kind of
decision, if publicized, could win favor with the Congress and
the public. But it would do incalculable harm abroad. It involves the essence of discreet, sensitive diplomacy. It is one of
the crosses the executive branch of government must bear, for
it incurs the displeasure of other nations while earning no
commendation from its own nation.

There are other unheralded decisions, where projects are
canceled because of fraud or chicanery on the part of some foreign officials or private citizens. In such cases, the friction is
intense because the project may be well advanced, money already spent, and people in high places seriously offended. U.S.
aid officials would appreciate kudos for their "toughness" in
cutting off funds, but the price of public applause would be
expensive in terms of international relations.

Decisions to suspend aid to a country cannot be discreet.
Publicity is inevitable. Ceylon and Haiti are two cases, the
first compelled by a provision of law, the second by executive discretion. These are difficult decisions because the chief
leverage is the threat to suspend. After suspension, the threat
has disappeared as well as the capacity to influence future decision.

Another type of hard decision is to abandon a project, which may be well advanced in its planning, simply because it does not make economic sense. Such a project might be a luxury item; it might violate an understanding with international financial institutions; or its prospects for earnings might not be established. The decision is hard because Cabinet Ministers and U.S. contractors are incensed. Congressional pressure is sometimes applied with force. On these occasions aid officials feel abandoned; they are in disfavor both abroad and at home.

Sometimes the decision is one to turn down aid to a new country. Congress is concerned about the number of countries to which aid is given. It does not know of the requests which have been turned down. Publicity would only aggravate an already sensitive condition.

In other instances the hard decision is to condition aid on new and difficult procedures of administration. In one country further aid depended on the institution of a much tighter system of financial controls. Public knowledge of this requirement would have made compliance politically impossible.

Among the decisions that never come to light are those which discreetly forestall a Prime Minister from pressing for a project which is beyond the bounds of feasibility. Criticism has been levied in full measure on a few projects which appear lush, overdesigned, and exorbitant. There are dozens of others where the most insistent diplomatic pressure has been used to dissuade the proponents from further promotion.

Finally, there is another kind of decision — that to phase out the aid program in a particular country. Aid will be with us for a long time. But aid is not perpetual in any country. As aid proves a successful catalyst, countries will move to the point where they can through saving and normal credits assure their own continued rapid growth. When this point is reached, justice both to other developing countries and to the aiding countries compels a decision to terminate aid. Such a decision may be clearly indicated by the statistics. But it must give some lead time, it must not be abrupt, and, if possible, it must be given and accepted as a badge of pride and success. Even so, it is always hard to decide, hard to announce, and hard for the receiving country to accept.

* * *

The work of A.I.D. lies in programming, implementing, and making critical decisions. All of these functions involve the most sensitive cooperation between the front lines and head-quarters, the use of many skills, the exercise of intuition based on experience. The view that aid is a "giveaway" process, based on short-run political pressures, manned by fuzzy-headed bureaucrats with no concern for the national exchequer is unfounded. The fact is that the diplomacy of aid is one of the most exacting functions of government. On the public understanding of this function, in its depth and complexity, depends the ability of the United States to sustain it successfully.

CHAPTER 3

The Weeds of Indecision

THE PUBLIC VIEW of aid, in the long run, determines the objectives, size, composition, and methods of aid. In government programs the public view is the gyroscope on which a representative democracy must rely for balance, and aid is no exception.

In the case of aid, the public view is more of a centrifuge, constantly whirling and throwing off opinions in all directions. The problem is not apathy or indifference. There exist both a basic instinct as to the importance of aid and a deep concern over all facets of aid policy.

For twenty-two years, aid programs have evolved in concept, in areas assisted, in tools and methods used. These years have seen the United States spend over a hundred billion dollars for all kinds of assistance, military and economic, food, material, money, and men. And, when our professional pulse-takers go to the people, they find almost 60 percent of the people — an increasing majority — being "for" foreign aid.

In January 1963, the Gallup Poll asked the question: "In general, how do you feel about foreign aid — are you for it or against it?" Fifty-eight percent were for, 30 percent were against, with 12 percent having no opinion. Five years earlier, in answer to the same question, 51 percent were for, 33 percent were against, with 16 percent having no opinion.[1]

A poll of 1500 businessmen, taken in the summer of 1963 by the Research Institute of America for the General Electric

[1] Gallup poll, taken in January 1963 and released Feb. 3, 1963.

Forum, reveals an even higher percentage (71 percent) favoring the proposition of major, perhaps increasing, nonmilitary aid to nations where poverty creates a climate receptive to Communist agitation.

This experience reflects two deep intuitions. The first is that the United States is and ought to be constructively concerned with a world on the move. The second intuition is that giving assistance to the nations of such a world is an inextricable part of such a role.

Our problem, therefore, is not that we lack a solid foundation for a steady and coherent set of public attitudes, but that we have not found out how to build on this foundation. Everyone considers himself a master builder. He is not only interested in aid matters; he holds deeply entrenched opinions and is not loath to express them. There is something about aiding other peoples that converts an ordinarily reasonable person, who approaches his own affairs and those of his neighborhood, city, state, and nation with a large measure of tolerance for the opinions of others, into a dogmatic expert on the political, social, and economic problems of over one and a third billion people in eighty countries.

The result is a wide spectrum of conflicting opinions on the why, who, and how of aid. Many believe aid should be used solely as a cold war instrument, deliberately manipulated for immediate and frankly political purposes. Others believe that our objective should be solely humanitarian and that any tinge of political objective would taint our effort. Still others believe that the objective, while political, is the long-range development of nations. Economists, cold war strategists, humanitarians — all wage continuing battle over the objective of aid, and all have their following.

The question, who should be helped, is equally controversial. One school of thought holds the view that we should assist only those nations who have "put their houses in order" and can use aid most effectively. This is countered vigorously by those who say that the interests of the United States range much more broadly, that it is the poorest nations who need help the most and that we cannot ignore the hard-pressed nations on the fringe of the Communist Bloc. Moreover, if "self help" be the only objective, we would find neutrals, dictatorships, and perhaps even Communist countries qualifying as prime candidates for aid.

This leads into another set of issues. A familiar cry is that we should help only "our friends." But this is countered by those who take a dim view of aiding dictators — for we count some authoritarian regimes among our allies. Aid to neutrals is opposed by many, yet most of the developing world is at least nominally "unaligned." And many feel aid should be used to "swing neutrals to our side."

The "how" of aid also spawns a wide divergence of views, because of its complexity and variety. Some say the chief hope for development lies in massive infusions of capital to supplement meager savings. Others argue that the basic need is the development of human skills. Some would have all aid on a loan basis, and on fairly hard terms. Others feel that any kind of aid other than grants is merely deluding both the giver and the receiver. Some feel that effective aid must be given only in exchange for internal reforms. Others warn against interference in the affairs of other countries. Many voice the complaint that there are "too many Americans" overseas; others say that the real bottleneck to development is the lack of trained technicians.

Many charge that aid is too much on a government-to-government basis; others charge that we are trying to superimpose on primitive societies our own form of capitalism. A frequent nostrum urged is that all aid should be administered through international organizations; but just as frequently the complaint is made that we are giving too much support to the United Nations.

One root cause of cultism in any form is that only a partial view of reality is seen. As is often the case, a measure of truth — but only a measure — lies in all of the doctrines.

Aid is an instrument of foreign policy. It cannot be neatly isolated from cold war demands. But, wherever possible, we should aim to produce achievements in economic and social development. We should try to concentrate aid where results are promising, but this cannot mean closing the door entirely to some struggling country where small amounts well used can be of great economic and political significance. While we cannot be humanitarians for all people everywhere, humanitarianism is not only part of our deepest tradition. It is often good policy.

We do right to press for social change but we are unwise to press for too much too soon, or the wrong program at the wrong time in the wrong way. Capital assistance and technical assistance are both needed. The great art is to plan and administer each so that it supports the other and the overall goals of social and economic development. There may be too many U.S. nationals abroad, or there may be too few, but we cannot be sure until we have a better picture of the tasks to be done and the skills needed to do them. The requirements of the past may not be those of the future.

There is much that can be done to take advantage of the resources and skills in the other departments of government, voluntary agencies, universities, and private business while still retaining the advantages of centralized responsibility and coordinated planning involving all resources. There is good reason to give increasing support to international organizations but also good reason to strengthen our own national aid program.

The cults and countercults of opinion about aid range through the entire public domain. They seize those in and out of Congress, isolationists and internationalists, liberals and conservatives, friends and foes of aid, the informed and the ignorant, observers and experts. The result is a constant trench war-

fare between contradictory fixed positions. Public enlighten-
ment and consensus are not advanced. Indeed, whatever basic
public intuition, commitment, and understanding exist tend
to be sapped, eroded, and weakened.

This whirling centrifuge of public opinion has been aided in
creating an atmosphere of general unease by an underlying
feeling of weariness in well-doing. We are all too conscious of
what we have spent in helping others. We look at the world
around us and see open warfare, unremitting subversion, bitter
rivalries between countries, military coups, and continuing unrest. But we seldom stop to reflect on the world as it existed
one or two decades ago and the progress that has since been
made.

We are all too conscious of the aid projects that have hit the
headlines with allegations of waste or corruption. But we have
not read of the thousands of successful projects and activities
that never make news.

We are acutely concerned with our balance-of-payments deficit but we do not pause to consider how little this would be
affected if the aid program were slashed by a third, by one half,
or were abolished.

We are apprehensive of the impact of exports from developing countries on our own economy, but we seldom realize the
stimulus which aid-financed exports give to our industries or
the demand for our exports as countries become modernized.

We look upon the resurgence of the countries of Western
Europe with mixed respect and apprehension and feel that they
should do more to carry their share of the aid burden. But
we overlook the extent of the aid they are already giving.

In short, aid in the public view has been a frail flower,
choked by the weeds of controversy and nagging doubt.

Instead of pulling up the weeds, we have repeatedly pulled
up the flower to see why it wasn't doing better. The administration of aid has undergone no less than seven organizational

phases and as many alphabetical combinations in fifteen years. To some extent these reflected changing responses to new needs, but the very fact of this history of reorganization has added to the sense of impermanence, uncertainty, and indecision.

The revolving-door image has been etched even more deeply by the succession of no fewer than ten top aid administrators in thirteen years, the average tour of duty being a year and a half. In addition, there have been five administrators of the specialized programs of technical assistance and development loans. Their average term was one year.

Building continuity of operating policies, initiating and following through with improvements in management, speaking with authority both within and outside of government, elevating the morale and caliber of aid employees, projecting an image of competence at home and abroad — these require more than ability and dedication. These require time. But time has often been spent without being invested. Continuity has been the missing ingredient. The centrifuge has kept on whirling.

Another index of national indecision about aid is the number of investigations, studies, and reviews of aid organization and program. During the past decade, the Agency for International Development and its short-lived ancestors have been subjected to more critical review, diagnosis, and prescription than any other major function of government.

Congress itself has six committees charged with a standing mandate to oversee aid programs — the House Committee on Foreign Affairs, the Senate Committee on Foreign Relations, and the Appropriations and Government Operations Committees of both houses. Other committees, dealing with specific functions such as housing, education, personnel, small business, and agriculture, also hold hearings and make studies involving aid operations and policies.

Frequently a command performance is required in many Congressional hearing rooms at the same time. For example, during one week in the spring of 1963, the Agency for International Development was involved with no fewer than eleven different committees of Congress, ranging from hearings on its major legislation to inquiries on housing, minerals, drug companies, and fertilizer. Each study or hearing required not only extensive staff work in gathering and organizing material, but the personal attention and time of the top executives of the Agency.

The Comptroller General also allocates part of his investigatory staff on a permanent basis to surveillance of aid activities. Both the Agency for International Development and the Department of State maintain substantial inspection staffs constantly on the move, checking into possible cases of misuse of funds.

As if this apparatus were not enough, aid has been afflicted with what might be diagnosed as the committee syndrome. There has seldom been a year since the end of the Marshall Plan that the President, or the Congress, or the aid agency has not appointed a committee to look over aid programs and make recommendations. One inarticulated major premise has been that those not charged with the responsibilities of either legislation or operation can somehow bring to bear a greater wisdom than those with such responsibilities. Another premise is that by their studies and reports they can do a better job of increasing public understanding and support.

These premises had great validity at the threshold of our Marshall Plan venture. Since massive and sustained economic aid was then largely an idea, not backed by experience, the views of distinguished citizens were often as informed as those within the executive branch. And, since public opinion had to be rallied for a major new initiative, the use of committees in helping launch such an initiative was not only wise but necessary. One of the brilliant aspects of the Marshall Plan strategy lay in the selective use of complementary committees — that headed in 1947 by Secretary of the Interior Julius A. Krug to determine the ability of our resources to meet European needs; that headed in the same year by Chairman Edwin Nourse of the Council of Economic Advisers to estimate the impact of extensive aid on our domestic economy; also in the same year, the President's Committee on Foreign Aid headed by Secretary of Commerce W. Averell Harriman to chart the outlines of an effective program for European recovery; and the Select Committee on Foreign Aid of the House of Representatives chaired by Congressman Christian Herter in 1948.

But, beginning in 1950, the device of the special study was used with almost automatic frequency, averaging over one a year between 1950 and 1963. There have been eight Presidential Committees, four special studies originated by the Congress, and at least three by the executive branch.

The most recent such committee was that headed by General Lucius Clay in 1963. But this was merely the last in a line boasting such names as Gordon Gray, Nelson Rockefeller, Clarence Randall, Benjamin Fairless, the late Eric Johnston, and William Draper.

The committee syndrome is not dead. Each year sees a new proposal in Congress for new citizen committees — to investigate the use of private enterprise, to examine the aid programs in each country, to give overall guidance to the Agency for International Development.

Although the cynic is tempted to say that the strength of the aid program has been proven by its ability to survive this onslaught of committees, these reports have made valuable contributions to the development of aid policies and programs in their formative years. They have also provided the basis — as shall be seen — for a much wider consensus than we realize. But their cumulative effect has been to hang a large question mark over the entire subject of aid. Just as a student reaches the point where parental checking of his homework every night hinders rather than helps, so we have reached a stage where further resort to such committees would serve rather to perpetuate than to allay doubts. To the extent they are used in the future, their mandate ought to be sharply restricted to specialized issues where their professional competence can be looked upon as an added resource for the solution of particular problems.

*   *   *

The fact remains that the American people, despite the history they have written, remain chronically uneasy about aid. It is complex. It is remote. Its failures are apparent. Its triumphs remain obscure. Its effects are not easily measured. The alternatives are never explored. It costs money. There is no clear-cut formula for success.

And so we have reorganized, reviewed, changed administrators, and pushed our pet nostrums, without recognizing that in so doing we have been cultivating the weeds of indecision.

CHAPTER 4

The Annual Minuet

THE UNITED STATES is in a state of chronic anxiety about aid. It can be proud of a broad, continuing, and evolving policy over the years. But it is far from proud. It is uneasy. It worries aid as a dog does a bone, chewing it, burying it, exhuming it. It changes, studies, investigates, reports, and stridently argues. Nowhere is the self-doubt more evident than in the way the executive branch and the Congress come to a decision on aid programs each year.

There is probably no more difficult exercise for a representative democracy than to confront the task of making decisions involving the expenditure of large amounts of public funds for the benefit of remote peoples. The wonder is that so many Congresses have exercised so many collective and difficult judgments sustaining substantial aid programs for a decade and a half. When one considers the complexity of the problems, the violence of opposition, and the lack of a domestic constituency, one is compelled to admiration for these unparalleled efforts. Moreover, Congress is the source of a number of major policy initiatives and procedures which have been proven wise by events. Indeed, the fact that the Congress can claim credit for many of the constructive developments in the U.S. aid programs over the years is proof of its basic resilience and statesmanship. This is a remarkable record in view of the series of customs and procedural forms which have accumulated over the years.

Somehow, the pattern of relations on aid legislation between these two branches has, over the past sixteen years, developed into something so highly stylized, predictable, and irrelevant that it can fairly be called a minuet. Each partner knows not only the steps which the other will take, but the timing as well. Unlike a real minuet, however, neither the music nor the movements are pleasing to the participants. It is painfully tedious, immensely costly in time and effort, with all too few positive results to compensate for the image of indecision we cast abroad. What should be a creative interchange on improving operations and policy in a major field with a substantial and impressive tradition has become a yearly ritual of argumentation that ends by renewing a program without advancing the argument. It is a symptom of a basic unease on the part of the Executive, the Congress, and the people as to both ends and means.

The traditional minuet consists of three steps: a shift from one foot to the other, a high step, and a balance. The aid minuet also has three movements: a shift from last year's program to next year's, the best foot forward in the committee hearings, and a balance finally struck at the end of the Congressional debates.

Preparation of the Program

The process of decision starts each October far away from Washington in the field missions of the Agency for International Development. Here, in some eighty posts around the world, the aid family is faced with two key jobs. At home, the Congress has in its waning hours passed the aid appropriation bill. The fiscal year beginning on July 1 is already one fourth gone. In 1963, half the fiscal year had passed before field missions knew what funds were available. The first task is to trim down the plans for the current year to fit the smaller appropriation pie that Congress finally baked. The second task is to look ahead and make plans for the year that will not even begin until nine more months have passed.

The planning and pruning are completed in January. But, before the program can be presented to the Congress, a publishing venture must take place, remarkable for its detail, its volume, and the selectivity of its audience. Over the years, the inherent uneasiness about aid has created an apparatus of such proportions that information all but smothers communication. From January to mid-March, hundreds of officials in the Pentagon, the Department of State, and the Agency for International Development spend thousands of hours in writing, discussing, and editing a bookshelf of volumes on the proposed military and economic aid programs. The Agency for International Development alone submits six large printed looseleaf books, replete with charts and statistical tables, running well over 2000 pages. Each page must not only be written but also submitted for comment to several other interested agencies. This is the "clearance" process, probably the most complete exercise in developing a group position ever devised by the mind of man.

Finally, in early April, "the books" are bundled off to the printer. When the hearings open, they are trundled daily to the committee room by a military guard where they can be read by about twenty staff members and — if ever there were time — by the eighty-eight members of three committees and one subcommittee. Seldom has so much been written by so many for so few.

The first step in the annual minuet has taken over six months to execute.

The Committee Hearings

The hearings, floor debates, and final Congressional action, take another five to six months. There are two separate pieces of legislation — that which authorizes money ceilings for the various kinds of military and economic assistance, and that which actually appropriates funds within the ceilings. Each piece goes through seven separate stages: House committee action, House floor debate, Senate committee action, Senate floor debate, House-Senate Conference Committee, floor debate, and signature by the President. In terms of time involved, intensity of preparation, controversy of debate, or uncertainty of results, the obstacle course has few, if any, parallels in government.

There are four series of hearings. There is no clear division of labor, for the two authorizing committees (the House Committee on Foreign Affairs and the Senate Committee on Foreign Relations) not only concern themselves with policy but also are involved with estimates of amounts, since they set ceilings for each appropriation category. On the other hand, although figures are the chief business of the appropriation committees, they frequently determine policy through the device of attaching conditions which must be met before funds can be used. The result is that much the same material is presented to all four committees.

The enormity of this task is partly — but only partly — revealed by statistics. In 1961 there were 287 witnesses appearing before the four committees with the published hearings running to 5326 pages. In 1962 there were 289 witnesses and 5659 pages of hearings.

It is safe to say that from April through August or September, one fourth to one third of the time of the senior executives responsible for administering overseas economic and military assistance programs is devoted to the Congressional hearings. The actual days spent in testifying are as the visible part of the iceberg to the submerged bulk. There are lengthy sessions in which the witness's statement is drafted, sent around for comment, redrafted, and polished. There are briefing sessions covering all the points likely to be the subjects of questioning. There are meetings to discuss executive branch policy on particular issues or amendments. There are visits to individual Congressmen and Senators, talks to various state delegations, groups of administrative assistants, preparation of material asked for by committee staffs or members.

But statistics as to the hearings do not tell all. The theory of the hearings must be distinguished from the realities of practice and custom.

The theory of the hearings is that all essential facts are available in the printed volumes; that the testimony highlights policies, problems, and achievements; that the committee members — designated by their committee assignments to be the experts on overseas assistance — have become fully informed and thus are able to speak with authority in this complex field; and that the collective committee judgments result in a deliberate appraisal of the legitimate needs for funds and policy decisions for the future direction of the programs.

The practice is quite different, in large part because of the incredible pressures on the time and energies of Congressmen and Senators. Even the most faithful members of the House of Representatives serving on the Committee on Foreign Affairs, find it impossible to attend all hearings, or read anything more than a fraction of the materials presented. There are geometrically greater pressures on Senators, who have responsibilities in at least half a dozen committees or subcommittees.

In any event, the fact is that the many volumes are largely unread by the committee members, although they are useful to the committee staffs. In the House Committee on Foreign Affairs, where attendance is usually good and interest is high, policy discussion often has difficulty getting off the ground because of the rule, born of necessity, which limits a member's time to five minutes for questions and answers. With 33 members, it is inevitable that, when a major witness appears, such as the Secretary of State or the A.I.D. Administrator, there will be, in a three-hour session, some forty or fifty points touched upon — to the satisfaction of very few. In one session in 1963, when A.I.D. Administrator David Bell was testifying, 23 members asked and received answers to some 74 different questions within two and one half hours. This allowed an average of two minutes for both the question and the answer.

In the Senate Committee on Foreign Relations, with fewer members, there is more opportunity for policy discussion and program appraisal in some depth. But this opportunity seldom is seized because of the multiple demands on Senators' time. Or, to the extent policy is discussed, the focus depends on the interests of the particular Senators who attend.

In the hearings before the Subcommittee on Foreign Operations of the House Appropriations Committee, the focus is not usually on the broad policy issues — indeed this is not intended to be a policy committee — but on the specific projects and programs which have aroused the interest of the subcommittee. Moreover the hearings cannot fail to be influenced by the conviction of the Chairman, Representative Otto E. Passman of Louisiana, who has written, "My contention is that foreign aid is a complete and dismal failure . . ." [1]

The Appropriations Committee of the Senate is again forced to confine itself to the inquiries on issues appearing dominant to the members who can afford to invest time in the hearing.

The imbalance in Congressional committee scrutiny reached a high — or low — point in 1962, when one committee spent 64 percent of its time on a region which accounted for only 13 percent of total regional programs. Most of the questioning related to one of the smaller countries in the region where the aid program was very small, amounting to .02 percent of total regional activities. The committee spent as much time on this .02 percent as it did on an area comprising 40 percent of total programs.

For a variety of reasons, therefore, there is little opportunity for the Congressional experts on economic and military assistance to share in depth either a detailed knowledge of the

[1] "Foreign Aid: Success or Failure?" *National Review*, May 21, 1963.

entire range of activities or a common perspective. The able, interested, and articulate member is more likely to concentrate his efforts on a special phase or problem area. By specializing, he becomes persuasive with his colleagues with the result that the issues he is interested in receive a committee focus, while other issues wither for lack of an advocate. What emerges from committee, unlike the situation enjoyed by other programs of the federal government, is something less than a group of informed legislators, sharing a common conviction as to policy and program, able to move their respective Houses forward to a new level of consensus.

Finally, the judgments of the committees as to the need for funds for aid programs cannot be reached by an analytical process related to the materials, oral and written, presented in their hearings. One Congressman tells of the feeling of shock he experienced when, as a freshman member, after studiously attending most of the hearings and being overwhelmed with facts and figures, he came to the "mark up" sessions, to decide on figures for the authorizing bill. The members immediately began talking about the size of the cuts they should make, and who should propose them. They talked in terms of large, round numbers. A series of cutting proposals ensued, ranging from slices of $200 million to slashes of $1 billion. A bargaining and balancing process then followed, resulting in a final consensus on a reduction of several hundred million dollars. All this was without any apparent attempt at a detailed rationale except the underlying assumptions that there was plenty of "fat" that could be cut out without harm, and that the committee had to make a deep enough slash to retain its leadership in the debates on the floor of the House.

This process is not only repeated but is accentuated at the appropriations stage, where, historically, much deeper cuts are made. Indeed, there is an unwritten code of conduct which has, during the fifties and early sixties, been accepted as a normal

Congressional pattern. The House Committee on Foreign Affairs makes a modest cut in the administration's request (over the past four years this has averaged $200 million); the House itself substantially supports its committee, with full warning of a deeper cut in appropriations;[2] the Senate Foreign Relations Committee votes a cut smaller than the House; the Conference Committee adopts something in between, which is approved by both Houses.

Then at the appropriations stage the House Appropriations Subcommittee makes a massive cut (over the past four years this has averaged $1200 million), knowing that the Senate Appropriations Committee will put the brakes on with far less of a slash, with the Conference Committee voting for something in between, although closer to the House than the Senate figure.

This can well be described as a Congressional roller coaster, with the gentler dips in the authorizing stage and the hair-raising descent coming in the appropriations stage — but jam-packed for thrills all the way.

The Congressional Debates

There are four debates on foreign aid each year. Under the committee system in the House of Representatives, floor debate is generally less exciting or decisive than in the Senate. There are splendid exceptions, when the House comes alive and holds first rate debate which would do honor to any legislative body in its brightest moments. Generally, however, the debate is more pedestrian. The rules, designed to make a workable institution out of a body of 435 members, foreordain this.

Debate is controlled by the committee reporting the bill. A period of "general debate" is set aside during which members

---

[2] This pattern was violated in 1963 when the House, having staved off all cutting amendments on a Thursday, reversed itself and on "Black Friday" passed a catch-all motion to slash the authorization by $585 million.

make prepared speeches which are not generally listened to by many. The period of decisive action takes place when the bill is considered for amendments. At this stage the committee members, with others awaiting their turn, are recognized for five minutes each. If debate on a section of the bill is prolonged and the House is restive, debate will be limited and a member eager to challenge the committee's position may find that his immortal remarks have to be compressed into twenty or thirty seconds.

Under these ground rules, balanced consideration of complex policy issues is difficult. But the basic difficulty is not one of mechanics. It is one of an imbalance of information and commitment. It is easier to be a foe than a friend of foreign aid. The adversary needs only one fact or allegation; the friend needs an arsenal of facts and arguments to counter sharpshooters and guerrilla attacks on whatever front they may occur. What Congressman or Senator stands to profit from such exhaustive labors? The result is that aid objectives, policies, and programs are attacked in detail and defended in generalities. Even aid's stout defenders tire of their role over the years.

So the thrust of all four debates is generally negative, querulous, defensive, and begrudging. Aid is seen from abroad as a narrow, self-serving instrument of U.S. policy. The good done overseas during the year is undermined by the headlines in the foreign newspapers. The specific end results of all debates are votes on specific issues, some of policy, some of funding. Here the key is not usually the decibels of debate but the votes which have been marshaled.

The critical debate is usually that in the House of Representatives on the appropriation bill. Here is where the deepest cuts have been made. Here is one of the most powerful committees of the House, from whom almost every Congressman seeks sympathetic attention for projects in his district. Here is the committee's spokesman, Mr. Passman, armed with facts gleaned from exhaustive hearings. Few, if any members, feel equipped to challenge the facts or the implications. It is understandable, therefore, that more often than not accommodation has been sought with this committee. On only a very few occasions has the instinct of the House been that the committee had gone too far. When that has happened, the committee has been overturned — but usually on aid issues involving the most direct kind of cold war assistance. On the larger questions of development aid, the committee has been allowed to write its own ticket.

This debate usually ends with drastic cuts having made all the headlines. The dog days of summer are spent in trying to convince the harried Senate Appropriations Committee that it should repair as much of the damage as possible.

After that the Senate and House conferees engage in tedious horse-trading sessions during the closing days of Congress. Finally, their report is presented to each House, sometimes on the final night of the Congressional session. And, in an anticlimax of exhaustion, both Houses agree and an appropriation law is sent to the President — who has to explain to the world that a billion dollar cut really does not mean that the United States is wavering in its policy toward the less developed world.

And, this being almost the first of October, our missions abroad set to work revising their plans to fit within what has been appropriated and to begin working on next year's drama.

What has happened is that once again the United States has furnished a substantial proportion of free world assistance for developing countries — but in such a tortuous manner and under such a smog of controversy, confusion, and compromise that the fact has been all but obliterated.

The monotonous minuet is over. The wearied participants stagger home from the ballroom. No one has enjoyed it. Few have learned anything. Congress emerges more anxious than informed. Some new policies have been made, but in the process all policies have been thrown once again into dispute. The people of the United States have been convinced once again that aid is extremely controversial. And the countries of the developing world scratch their heads in amazement at the strange antics of the United States.

The 1963 Marathon

In 1963 the minuet became a nine-month marathon. President Kennedy's aid message was delivered to the Congress on April 2. Final action was not taken until December, when the fiscal year was half over. Apart from this exhausting time span the year's deliberations reached new heights of Congressional criticism, policy making, and frustration.

The fund-cutting roller coaster, breaking recent precedent, gained momentum at the outset — even at the authorizing stage, when cuts have customarily been held to small amounts. The result, a compromise between both houses, was a $900 million reduction, paving the way for a cutback to a three billion dollar final appropriation. This was the largest percentage cut since the beginnings of aid.

Even more unprecedented and disturbing were the policy-making field days on the floors of both houses. Despite extensive amendments made in both authorizing committees, the House of Representatives plodded through 31 separate votes while the Senate registered its opinion no fewer than thirty-eight times. Most of the issues involved more rigid restrictions governing the extending and terminating of aid. So deep had been the impact of the restrictive action that President Johnson, in his first address to Congress, five days after the assassination of President Kennedy, felt impelled to urge ". . . strong, forward-looking action on the pending foreign aid bill, making clear that we are not forfeiting our responsibilities to this hemisphere or to the world, nor erasing executive flexibility in the conduct of foreign affairs . . ."

Two themes of the old minuet, however, were more familiar

— the setting up of new committees to give guidance on aid and new pleas for agonizing reappraisal.

Chairman Fulbright of the Senate Foreign Relations Committee spoke the thoughts of many at both ends of Pennsylvania Avenue when he said, "This last three weeks of debate . . . of all my twenty years' experience, was the most painful that I have ever experienced . . ." [3]

[3] Interview with Howard K. Smith and John Scali, American Broadcasting Company, November 24, 1963.

PART II

A Sense of History

The folkways of thinking and acting on aid call for a "sense of history."

"Sense of history" is admittedly a dangerous phrase. It is a label which can mask many uses and abuses of history. It can be a substitute for hard analysis of current problems. It can be a subtle device for merchandizing a dogma. It can be a crutch for the determinist. A working sense of history, however, gives one a balance between claiming either too much or too little for the uses of the past. It is a way of approaching decision in the present, being sensitive to the traditions, aspirations, and accomplishments of the past, and their relevance to the shape of things to come.

Winston Churchill had such a sense of history, not because he wrote his impressive Life of Marlborough, but because at the crest of one of history's watersheds he brought to bear the uses of the past to shape significantly a future then in doubt. The founding fathers of the United States also possessed this sense. They knew intimately the experience and traditions of the past; they moved to the aspirations of the present; and they were aware of the historic potential that lay ahead.

Arthur M. Schlesinger, Jr., writes ". . . the significant statesman must have a knowledge of history, an instinct for the grand tendencies, a feeling for the direction in which the world is

*moving . . . a sense of history is the indispensable underpin-
ning of statesmanship."* [1]

Such a sense is equally the indispensable underpinning of
statesmanship on the part of people. It can no longer (if, indeed, it ever could) be confined to those with the responsibility
for final action. For we live in an age when the decisions of
leaders are limited by the measure of understanding and support given by the body politic.

The shaping relations between the United States and the
developing nations of Latin America, Africa, and Asia have
reached another watershed, where a sense of history must
dominate and illumine decision — not only by leaders in
government but also by the people themselves. Shadows over
both past and future must be rolled back. For the people of
the United States and their leaders have wrought a tradition
and a policy over two historic decades with only dim awareness
of what they have done and of the age they were helping to
create — the age of development.

This age brings with it new problems and new crises. Each
solution becomes part of the fabric of another problem. The
course of events is far from assured, for development itself is
neutral in mankind's scale of values. It can coexist, at least in
the short run, with tyranny or freedom. The real issue posed
by the age of development is whether it will serve to expand or
compress the freedoms of men and of nations.

The years ahead are both the threshold and the critical years.
They are years of historic decision by the emerging young nations and older, even ancient, nations struggling to break
through the crust of custom. These are also years of critical
decision and commitment for the United States. To rise to this

[1] "The Historian and History," *Foreign Affairs*, Vol. 41, No. 3 (April 1963),
p. 497.

looming test of our time requires, fully as much as did 1776, a deeper pride in the achievements of the past, a more acute awareness of the aspirations of the present, and a more confident will to shape the unfolding future — in short, a working sense of history.

CHAPTER 5

The Roots of Policy

As we strive toward achieving a wise and farsighted relationship with the developing world, we are handicapped by a label. The label, a millstone of imponderable weight, is "foreign aid." It connotes something not only remote but alien. Somehow it sounds better when we say "assistance to other peoples." It is not helping other nations and peoples that is offensive; it is the connotation of foreignness, of being alien, of being un-American. There is something about the phrase that suggests we are being exploited, that this is a strange and unnatural activity.

A more accurate label in a world increasingly engaging in assistance is "U.S. Aid." Ironically, this is how our programs are known overseas. It is only at home that our aid is "foreign." "Foreign affairs" and "foreign trade" have long since lost any alien meaning. It will be a mark of our increased maturity when "foreign aid" is accepted as something wholly within our tradition and serving the deepest interests of our nation. In the meantime, however, within the covers of this book, these words will no longer be joined in uncomfortable wedlock.

Our Own Beginnings

One of the roadblocks to our reaching a sustained commitment to the objective of helping other countries develop in freedom is the haunting question "We did it all by ourselves; why can't they?" The short answer is that we didn't do it "all by ourselves."

To begin with, we waged a successful revolution. But one out of fifteen dollars was loaned to us from abroad. That margin of 7 percent may well have been the critical margin of resources.

When we became a nation, we had the option of building ever so slowly, squeezing consumption out of the hides of our people to make possible new investment, or of getting capital on lenient terms from abroad. We chose the latter course. We began borrowing. After Independence, the debt we owed abroad equaled the value of all our nonagricultural buildings and equipment; it was twice the value of all consumers' durable goods. This debt multiplied one hundred times by the outbreak of World War I.

We quickly became a trading nation — but only because the British gave us cash for exports and extended credit to us for imports. We settled the land and developed communities — aided by credits and community services supplied by foreign land companies. We doubled the territory of the nation through the Louisiana Purchase — by floating a foreign bond issue of some eleven million dollars. We saw the Texas ranges develop the cattle industry — thanks to British money and "technical assistance" in such matters as barbed-wire fences, steel windmills, deep wells, and winter shelters. Our rayon industry started through the efforts of Courtaulds of England, oil development and refineries with the help of Shell, powdermaking and explosives through Du Pont.

The 360-mile Erie Canal opened up the West by cutting transportation costs 90 percent — thanks to $7 million of bonds purchased by the British. States launched ambitious programs of roads, bridges, canals, and banks — by increasing their foreign borrowings over fifteen times between 1820 and 1840. Cities followed suit, with Washington, D.C., floating a bond issue in Amsterdam in 1830, and New York continuing its borrowing abroad until just before World War I. Railroads cut across the new nation, on the basis of foreign capital, lured by the junior position of U.S. loans.

We were not always model debtors. Several states simply repudiated their debt while nine others defaulted on interest during the lean years of 1841 and 1842.

We should not forget this experience as we seek to help others. No new nation, no poor nation can hope for rapid progress without both skills and capital from external sources. The problem faced by so many nations today is compounded. In addition to skills and capital, they also need institutions — banks, markets, tax systems, schools. In our case we had at least the framework of institutions. Moreover, we were the major emerging country to claim the attention of the then industrialized world. Private investment could and did do the job. Today the task can be done only by a combination of both private and governmental assistance from all the industrialized nations and international institutions.

The Beginnings of U.S. Aid

Not only do we tend to forget our beginnings — or that part which we owe to others. We also forget what we ourselves have done. We are fully occupied with today's events and tomorrow's problems. We have little time for the past. In the field of overseas aid, we think, talk, and act as if we were dealing with a new experiment. Each year's debate on aid treats it as a novel venture on which we are being asked to embark.

Certainly, working with other peoples in the task of nation building is and will continue to be charged with both experiment and novelty. But we should look back once in a while and take renewed confidence from the remarkable history which we have written over the past two decades. We could even go back to the era after World War I when our loans to Europe were followed by defaults, moratoria, and cancellation. This was aid, with adjustments to the hard facts of the international economy coming after, rather than before, credits were extended.

Excluding such experiences, however, planned United States assistance to other countries goes back in time at least twenty-two years and has evolved under no fewer than forty pieces of major aid legislation. U.S. aid can trace its history almost as far back as the regulation of securities, the insuring of bank deposits, the underwriting of home mortgages, social security and other governmental functions which have long since become accepted as part of the fabric of national life. It is partly because there is so little awareness of the past that the issues of the present are so cloaked in controversy.

Here, then, is a bird's-eye view of a record distinguished both in motive and in accomplishment. It is one of the noblest, yet least known, chapters of our history as a nation.

It is a proof of our ability to respond under stress that the first technical assistance program was launched in the early days of World War II, with the establishment by Congress in 1942 of the Institute for Inter-American Affairs. A year later, in the depth of the war years, we signed the agreement which was to be the basis for channeling two billions of dollars worth of food and commodities into war-torn countries through the United Nations Relief and Rehabilitation Administration.

Two years later, in 1945, we gave thought to the institutions which would be needed by the postwar world. July saw the broadening of powers of the Export-Import Bank. In December, with our leadership, the International Monetary Fund and the International Bank for Reconstruction and Development (the World Bank) came into being.

In 1947, we realized that our ally in war, the Soviet Union, was not an ally in peace. Both Greece and Turkey were threatened by aggression from without and subversion from within. In February, Great Britain advised us that it could no longer maintain its forces in these countries. In March, President Truman announced his Doctrine — that the United States would not stand idle where nations were so threatened. In

May, Congress responded quickly to President Truman's request for a $400 million program of military and economic assistance. Both nations rallied, secured their borders, achieved internal stability, became staunch members of NATO, and are now deeply committed to their own economic development.

The Marshall Plan

The shining chapter of U.S. aid history is the Marshall Plan. This historic venture is almost beyond controversy. Those preoccupied with the conflict of today's debates yearn for the aura of success, when Titans appeared in league with history.

For "Aid in trouble on Capitol Hill" is one of today's boiler-plate headlines. The vortex of controversy never ceases. The Congressional Record sparkles with such phrases as these:

"It is the road to bankruptcy, and not a very long road at that."

". . . a hodge-podge of gifts of large sums of money to foreign nations, founded upon no principle at all . . ."

". . . in the light of history, in the light of facts, how can any senator rise on this floor and say it will stop communism . . . ?"

"Why should this country . . . pour out money for the aid of a government . . . bent upon going further into the nationalization of industries?"

"Friends cannot be bought, and we do not make allies of nations by interfering in their internal affairs."

We are "unwitting victims of the greatest propaganda machine ever set up in Washington."

There is nothing remarkable about these words except that they are not taken from the debates of the sixties or even the fifties. They are part of the Marshall Plan debates of 1948. But those arguments are the ancestors of the arguments of today: the road to bankruptcy — buying friends — spurring socialism

— international bribery — interference in internal affairs —
no way to stop Communism — victims of propaganda.

Aid — even the Marshall Plan — has always stretched the
statesmanship of lawmakers. Then as now there were often
more linear inches of debate devoted to opposition than support. Aid has always been "in trouble." This is one of the
teachings of history. There is no better way to gain a sense of
history, applicable to our times, than to measure these prophecies against performance.

In 1947 Winston Churchill called Europe a "rubble heap
— a charnel house, a breeding ground of pestilence and hate."
In that spring, a mere six weeks after Congress acted on Greek-
Turkish aid, General Marshall, then Secretary of State, made
a quiet, short speech at Harvard. He pledged the full cooperation of the United States in the recovery of the European economy "so as to permit the emergence of political and social
conditions in which free institutions can exist." He made it
clear that we sought "a cure rather than a mere palliative."

The Soviet Union vetoed concerted action — a historic miscalculation. But within five weeks sixteen nations of Western
Europe had formed the Committee of European Economic
Cooperation. Ten weeks of meetings ended in mid-September
with pledges of self-help action. In the United States, the Congress, the executive branch, and the private community had
mobilized for study, discussion, planning, and legislation. In
March of 1948, debate opened on the European Recovery Program. A month later the bill became law. Three years later
the Marshall Plan ended. The cost was almost seven billion dollars less than the original estimates. Europe went on beyond recovery to new heights of productivity, unity, and strength.

A sense of history cannot rest with evoking the predictions
of failure and the fact of success. It should also refresh our
memory. If today's mood is jaded and weary, there is nothing
more important than to recall what we at our best were capable
of doing.

After General Marshall made his speech, a four-year plan was developed, estimated to cost $20 billion. James Reston of the *New York Times* recalls that when he first wrote a story about it one Sunday morning, he received a call at 10 A.M. from Senator Arthur H. Vandenberg of Michigan, the Republican Chairman of the Foreign Relations Committee, who said: "You must be out of your senses. No administration would dare to come to the Senate with a proposal like that." [1]

Nine months later, on March 1, 1948, later described by the Senate Democratic Leader, Alben Barkley, as a "great day" in the Senate, Senator Vandenberg rose to open debate on the European Recovery Program.

He outlined the purpose — "to sustain and strengthen principles of individual liberty, free institutions and genuine independence" of Europe. He stated "the grim truth" that our self-interest, economy, and security were "inseverably linked" with these objectives.

He addressed the issue of cost by warning of "what we cannot afford not to do." "This peace investment," he said, "might cost one-third as much in four and a half years as we appropriated for war in just one bill that passed the senate in five minutes . . . war has no bargains. I think peace has. I believe I am talking about one now."

Finally came the peroration from the Senator who, nine months earlier, had thought that no administration in its right mind would come to the floor with the bill he had just so ably presented:

> The committee has rewritten the bill to consolidate the wisdom shed upon the problem from many sources. It is the final product of eight months of more intensive study by more devoted minds than I have ever known to concentrate upon any one objective in all my twenty years in Congress. It has its foes — some of whom compliment it by their transparent hatreds. But it has its friends — countless prayerful friends not

[1] *The National Purpose.* New York: Holt, Rinehart and Winston, 1960, p. 114.

only at the hearthstones of America, but under many other flags. It is a plan for peace, stability, and freedom. As such, it involves the clear self-interest in the United States. It can be the turning point in history for one hundred years to come. If it fails, we have done our final best. If it succeeds our children will call us blessed. May God grant His benediction upon the ultimate event.

And then the usually reserved Congressional Record adds: "(Applause on the floor, Senators rising.)"

Senator Vandenberg's speech is good for one's sense of history in rekindling one's faith in the wisdom of a policy proven wise by events.

An Evolving Program

All this by no means exhausted the energies or the vision of the American people. Indeed, the evolution of aid had only just begun. The ten years from 1948 to 1957 were to see United States aid not only fulfill the goals of the Marshall Plan, but also to place increasing emphasis on the problems of developing countries and to complete its assistance workshop.

In December 1948, the United Nations Technical Assistance Program was established. We played a major role. The new year came in, and with it President Truman's inaugural address.

He made a number of points. But one has lived most vividly in history. This was his "Point IV." It consisted of fourteen short paragraphs.

This is the gist of what he said:

> Fourth, we must embark on a bold new program for making the benefits of our scientific advances and industrial progress available for the improvement and growth of underdeveloped areas . . .
>
> I believe that we should make available to peace-loving peoples the benefits of our store of technical knowledge in order to help them realize their aspirations for a better life. And, in

cooperation with other nations, we should foster capital investment in areas needing development.

Our aim should be to help the free peoples of the world,
through their own efforts, to produce more food, more clothing,
more materials for housing, and more mechanical power to
lighten their burdens.

From this sprang the United States Technical Assistance
Program, no longer limited to Latin America, but reaching the
far corners of Asia and Africa.

Like the Marshall Plan, this evoked such Congressional out-
cries as "selling America short . . . [Uncle Sam] has become
the easy prey of foreign and domestic grafters, vampires, and
gold diggers . . . we are now trying to bribe and govern the
world . . . Congress is lost in the dismal swamps of foreign
intrigue." But like the Marshall Plan, Point IV became another splendid chapter in our history.

The next major step came in 1954, with the enactment of
Public Law 480, which made available surplus food and fiber
for developing countries, by sale, loan, or grant. This resulted
in over a billion dollars a year of vital resources for other countries at minimum cost to the United States. This program is
now known under the appropriate name of Food for Peace.

In 1957, the United States added to its development toolshed
the long-term "soft" loan, then repayable in local currencies,
as an instrument of capital assistance which would substitute a
businesslike relationship of borrower-lender for that of grantor-
grantee.

By 1957, building gradually on experience, U.S. aid had left
behind postwar relief and recovery. Its major thrust was directed to the problems of the underdeveloped world. It was
equipped with these instruments to deal with the wide spectrum
of needs in that world:

— military assistance to countries whose independence was
threatened;

— economic grant aid to help sustain these countries;

– technical (Point IV) assistance to develop human skills;
– development loans for capital needs;
– agricultural surpluses for disaster victims and for use in generating local currency for development;
– investment guaranties to attract private capital;
– use of excess stockpile equipment.

Hemisphere Focus

In 1959 U.S. aid policy turned finally, and many would say belatedly, to the very area which saw its beginnings — Latin America. Although this was the locale of our oldest technical assistance program, of many activities by private foundations, and of many ventures by business enterprises, the overall U.S. governmental effort had been small in level of resources, in concept, and in objectives. The Castro revolution in Cuba came soon to be recognized not merely as an isolated political uprising against dictatorial rule, which then became captured by Communist dogma, but as a symptom of a continent-wide demand to break through the economic, social, and political barriers which separated the vast majority of some two hundred million people from a modern world.

The first step was the establishment, on U.S. initiative under President Eisenhower, of the Inter-American Development Bank — an institution which would rely initially on the United States for most of its funds, but which would be jointly administered by representatives of all the free American republics.

In the fall of 1960, the Congress authorized the Social Progress Trust Fund to be administered by the new bank in the form of liberal loans for capital and technical assistance projects in such fields as housing, land resettlement, education, and health.

At the same time, the Act of Bogotá was signed by all members of the Organization of American States except Cuba, setting forth the guidelines "of a cooperative program of economic and social progress," relying on maximum self-help efforts, and stressing the improvement of institutions and practices in taxation, land use, education, health, and housing.

Within one month after the Act of Bogotá was signed, the people of the United States had elected a new President. Before President Kennedy's administration was two months old, on March 13, 1961, he called together at the White House the Latin America diplomatic corps and members of Congress. To them he said:

> Our hemisphere's mission is not yet completed. For our unfulfilled task is to demonstrate to the entire world that man's unsatisfied aspirations for economic progress and social justice can best be achieved by free men working within a framework of democratic institutions . . .
>
> Therefore I have called on all the people of the hemisphere to join in a new Alliance for Progress — Alianza para el Progreso — a vast cooperative effort; unparalleled in magnitude and nobility of purpose, to satisfy the basic needs of the American people for homes, work and land, health and schools — techo, trabajo y tierra, salud y escuela.

The Alianza para el Progreso was formally established in August 1961 by the Charter of Punta del Este. This was a document of development aspirations ranging from the general objectives of social and economic development to precise goals for per capita growth rates, literacy, and life expectancy. It set the stage for one of the most ambitious peacetime international efforts in history.

The Decade of Development

On March 22, 1961 President Kennedy sought new legislation from the Congress. This was not merely an annual request for funds. With the lessons of two decades to draw upon, it proposed a unified organization, with responsibility more clearly defined, equipped to engage in long range assistance based on the principle of self help. These were substantially accepted in the Foreign Assistance Act of 1961 — which remains the basic structure of today's aid program.

Perhaps as important as his specific proposals were his accompanying words:

"For we are launching a Decade of Development on which will depend, substantially, the kind of world in which we and our children shall live."

*   *   *

The roots of U.S. aid go back in time over a generation. Hidden in the welter of reorganizations and changes of name is an impressive chapter of history. It is a history of faith, controversy, courage, and vindication. It is a history of evolution — in areas of service, in techniques, principles, and tools. It has established the United States as a pioneer and leader in the grand enterprise of assisting in the building of free nations. But with ironic perversity, we have all too seldom been either conscious or proud of what history has recorded.

CHAPTER 6

Time for Consensus

THE FINAL PURPOSE of a sense of history, if it is to play a part in the ordering of affairs, is to divine the significance of the present and to heighten perceptions of the needs and opportunities of the times. Franklin Roosevelt had this sense as he wrestled with the crisis of the depression years, gradually equipping this nation to deal with the problems of a new era. He showed it also in his intuition of the darkening shadow of Hitler. He came to the present not with preconception, but with a wholesome sense of its historic potential.

The field of foreign economic assistance policy and programs cries for such a working sense of history. There is, on the one hand, an impressive historic commitment stretching over nearly a quarter of a century. On the other hand, this continuity of policy has always marched under a cloud of uneasiness and self-doubt. The shifts in organization and leadership, the frequent committee reviews and reports, the annual barrage of criticism in the Congressional hearings and debates, the variety of nostrums proposed by experts in government, universities, and the business community — all these have highlighted the basic fact that while the United States has an aid program with a respectable pedigree, it does not have an apparent working consensus backing up the program.

One might think that a citizens' consensus on a subject as complex as aid policy is an impossible objective. Perhaps it is enough that this country continues, however tortuously, to mount a substantial aid program, whatever its ups and downs, its claims and counterclaims. After all, the one certainty for the American taxpayer is the taking of some of his dollars for uses in remote places. What he gets in return is a galaxy of uncertainties. He is not certain that he has added to this country's security. He is not certain that his country has been enabled to "buy" any useful friendships. He is not certain that other human beings have been helped. He is not even certain that his dollars have not added to the evil in the world, whether by aiding dictators, Communists, or ordinary grafters and profiteers. For the list of uncertainties, some would substitute a catalogue of certainties — of injury to the security, the wealth, and the reputation of the United States.

Under the circumstances, the record of continued, if controversial, support in the last two decades would seem to constitute an impressive act of faith, behind which we should not inquire and beyond which we should not ask for anything so difficult and intangible as "consensus." All things considered, the United States has acted with boldness and foresight on the part of its leaders and with considerable understanding and patience on the part of its citizenry. But does the present pattern of annual action cloaked in perennial perturbation serve our best interests?

Among those who have been intimately involved with the aid program, there is the deep conviction that the luxury of excessive turbulence is hideously costly, that our interests demand a consensus in some depth on aid matters, that there already exists more of this consensus than it is fashionable to acknowledge, and that we ought now to set about enlarging and deepening the area of agreement. Our position in the world today, our relations with the developing countries and with the industrialized countries, the problems faced by the Sino and Soviet Blocs — all indicate the pressing need for the United States to substitute attitudes of steadiness, pride, and professionalism for those of uncertainty, self-doubt, and amateurism . . . and at the earliest possible moment.

Consider the effects of our neurosis on aid operations. There is a disproportionate investment of time and energy on the part of all senior officials, both in Washington and in the field, devoted to problems of Congressional presentation, to preparing for committee hearings, to making reports. This leads to a focus not on the problems at hand, but on next year's testimony. To the substantial hazards of prolonged overseas duty and the exacting requirements of development diplomacy, there are added the nagging doubts that further reorganization shall take place, that programs finally and painfully launched shall be cut off because of funding slashes, that new leadership shall make dramatic shifts in direction, and that planning for a solid and rewarding career may once again prove wishful thinking. Recruiting, developing, and retaining gifted people under these conditions become improbable tasks.

As far as Congress and the people are concerned, the hardening of the folkways of doubt and criticism and the institutionalized rituals of hearings and debates tend to perpetuate themselves. Seldom does a citizen or a member of Congress spontaneously rise to evidence a sense of pride in either the aspirations or the accomplishments of aid activities. The fashion for a supporter of aid, even for a Congressional supporter, is to brood in public about all his doubts and then to demonstrate the breadth of this statesmanship by a final defense hedged by hopes for greater efficiency and better administration. In a word, all too few of the observing or legislating public feel "good" about aid. Unlike the other causes hammered out in the halls of Congress, aid lacks a cadre of knowledgeable, respected, and enthusiastic interpreters, able and eager to explain in breadth and in depth the problems, progress, and prospects of aid in action.

But there is a wider audience to our agonizing dramas than Washington or the country at large. There is the developing world, the end and object of aid policy. It is almost impossible to imagine the impact on the capitals and villages of this world of the torrent of headlines flooding their newspapers for six months each year. They read the ringing words of the President as he sends his aid request to the Congress. The words are followed by threats and speculations as to the depth of cuts. As harried spokesmen plead aid's cause, others often see it presented as an instrument, not to help build their own nation, but solely to stave off the threat of Communism.

The mythical country of Xanda offers a typical example. We have earlier seen the thinking underlying the proposed aid program in Xanda. With a new Prime Minister, deemed a nationalist and a moderate, despite some strident anti-Western, anti-imperialist notes in his election campaign, the opportunity presents itself to help launch Xanda on a course of rational development in an area which will be profoundly influenced by its example.

What happens? A Congressman rises to his feet in general debate to make an anti-aid speech, using Xanda as an example, quoting some of the Prime Minister's campaign statements, and calling him a Communist or at any rate a confirmed socialist. He cites his personal observations of the country, its primitive condition, the lack of public services, and its past financial difficulties. He observes that Xanda became independent far too soon, that it is incapable of managing its own affairs. He concludes that continued aid to Xanda would be keeping open one more rathole.

The Committee spokesman rises to the defense. He points out the unique opportunity to help influence the future course of Xanda in a westerly direction. He stresses the fact that any expanded aid will be dependent on Xanda's success in putting its new tax program into effect.

This exchange of debate is a minor one. Actually, very few members are in their seats at the time, for this is the period of general debate. There are far larger and explosive issues to be discussed. Not a ripple is caused in the public press. The debate is not even reported.

But in Xanda? The newspaper headlines scream: "P.M. Called Communist in U.S. Congress," "U.S. labels Xanda Primitive, Incompetent," "Are We a Rathole?" The Prime Minister is asked for comment and there is another round of headlines. Even the stalwart defense, made with utmost goodwill, makes the news: "U.S. Hopes for Change in Xanda Foreign Policy," "U.S. Ties Tax String to New Aid." The editorial mills start grinding. The U.S. Ambassador and the A.I.D. Mission Director are also grinding — their teeth.

When all the smoke has blown away, the appropriations finally approved, the allocations made to their country, is it any wonder that the peoples in the developing countries are confused as to our motives, the steadiness of our policies, or the depth of our commitment to be of help? It is not too unrealistic to say that in our talk for half the year we erode much of the goodwill built up by the actions of the other half year.

We are also observed carefully by our industrialized associates of Western Europe, Canada, Japan, Australia, and New Zealand — all of whom have started considerable aid programs. They watch our parliamentary meanderings with attitudes ranging from bemused sophistication to utter confusion. A year ago, one foreign official, reading the headlines of investigations and budget cuts initiated by the administration, had the distinct impression that the United States had reversed its aid policy and was withdrawing, posthaste, from the field. When a U.S. official pointed out that the President, after all the sound and fury, was still requesting more funds than had been appropriated the previous year, he was astonished. And this was a sophisticated observer. As the other aid-giving countries of the free world attempt to deepen their involvement in development assistance, they cannot fail to be somewhat unnerved and shaken by the violence with which we approach our annual decisions.

Finally, we have an alert audience always interested in our debates, revelling in the shrillness of criticism, exploiting both reasons for supporting and for opposing aid requests. This is the Communist world. Proposals which may seem eminently sensible to us, such as insisting that 50 percent of all aid be used for private purposes, are fodder for the Communist mare. The extreme positions taken in our debate on particular countries, or on their leaders, policies, and capabilities make excellent copy for *Pravda* or its local counterpart.

These reasons all underscore the timeliness of a serious effort to widen our area of agreement, to lower the Hooper rating of the aid question, to strike a tone of confidence and pride rather than one of uncertainty and self-castigation. The maximum effectiveness of aid policies and programs depends almost as much upon the style and manner of our reaching decisions as upon their substance. And a smoother, more mature style depends upon the conscious acknowledgment of consensus.

The March toward Consensus

Part of our trouble is that we are not as much at sixes and sevens as we think we are. We have been acting out the story of The Emperor's New Clothes in reverse. It has long been the custom to deride aid policy and operations as being wholly bereft of the clothing of consensus. In fact, they have gradually become clad with garments whose cut and taste the critical populace approves. But nobody has taken time out from derision to notice.

We have learned much from our two decades of experience. We have attained more of a nucleus of agreement than we realize. Just as it serves our sense of history to be reminded of the chapters of aid innovation and experience which the United States has written in two decades, it should encourage our search for a consensus to reflect on the progress we have made.

The slow but steady growth of consensus can be seen by anyone who takes the trouble to read the yearly reports on aid of the Senate Foreign Relations Committee and the House Committee on Foreign Affairs. It can be seen in the annual messages on aid by Presidents Eisenhower and Kennedy — and now

President Johnson — not to forget the earlier historic address by General Marshall and the Point IV message of President Truman. It can be seen as a thickening thread spun out by all of the presidential citizens' committees which have reviewed and reported on aid policies and programs.

But it has been within the past eight years that the pace of analysis and resolution of key issues has quickened. Before 1956, U.S. aid policy developed as a series of responses to particular threats or opportunities: relief (UNRRA), the survival of Greece and Turkey, the recovery of Europe, reconstruction of occupied enemy areas, rehabilitation of the Philippines, the Korean war, and military assistance to selected nations in the Near East, South Asia, and the Far East. To the standard devices of grants of money, supplies, and military equipment, we added a program of technical assistance (Point IV) in 1949 and the systematic use of agricultural surpluses (Public Law 480) in 1954.

By 1956, the United States began to be introspective about these programs — why they were needed, where they were going, how they should be conducted. In that year the Senate Committee on Foreign Relations commissioned eleven studies and ten on-the-spot surveys on aid, which were eventually to fill a 1600-page volume.

The motive for this significant effort was stated in the preface by the Chairman, Senator Theodore Francis Green:

> The trend of increasing opposition to these (aid) programs would seem to indicate either that their purposes have not been clearly understood or that there is a growing belief that they have in some way failed to serve the national interest. In either event, the trend must be reversed either by clarifying the relationship between the programs and the national interest or by changing the programs so that they may more clearly serve the national interest.[1]

[1] Senate Document No. 52, 85th Congress, 1st Session, "Foreign Aid Program — Compilation of Studies and Surveys," p. iii.

The Senate had started the search for consensus.

The studies spelled out the essential connection between sound overseas assistance programs and the national interest; the vital need for knowledge and skills in developing countries; the unavoidable necessity for capital aid for countries which know how to use it; the need for principal stress on aid as an incentive to self-help efforts by recipient countries; the importance of country development programs; the need for continuity and a long range view, to get away from crisis financing.

In reporting on the studies, in 1957, a Special Senate Committee underscored the basic needs served by aid — defense, economic, political, and humanitarian — and called for clarification of our objectives. It recommended continuance of military and economic assistance to peoples threatened by aggression or subversion; but it looked toward orderly reductions. It reaffirmed the value of technical assistance. Most importantly, it called for enlarged and more systematic capital assistance in the form of loans on liberal terms. Such assistance, in the past, it found, was ". . . a mixture of loans and grants without clear economic criteria for the one or the other." [2] It urged the creation of a development fund. In this recommendation the Senate found a willing and imaginative copartner in the House Committee on Foreign Affairs.

One year later, the Development Loan Fund was established. The arsenal of U.S. aid weaponry was now substantially complete: military equipment and training, technical assistance, grants to support threatened peoples, and capital loans.

But the soul-searching and analysis did not stop.

In 1958 President Eisenhower appointed a citizens' committee under the Chairmanship of William H. Draper, Jr. Although charged with the chief task of reviewing the military assistance program, it devoted one of its reports to economic

[2] Special Committee to Study the Foreign Aid Program, Report No. 300, 85th Congress, 1st Session.

assistance. This Committee, equipped with a staff to make a nine-month study, carried forward significantly the movement toward consensus.

It rephrased the U.S. national interest in development aid: "The strength of our economy and the survival of our free institutions are dependent upon our being a part of a community of nations which is making acceptable economic and political progress." [3]

The report, however, went beyond a description of historical evolution, purposes and programs. It advanced some concepts and principles which this Committee felt should guide the administering of aid. It stressed more selectivity "in choosing those countries and projects which will yield the greatest results in increasing free world strength." It emphasized the principle of self-help: "Our aid should be conditioned on reasonable mutual undertakings, and should be extended only so long as the recipients reasonably carry out their undertakings." It called for "an even more important role" by our western allies and Japan. It urged more emphasis on multilateral assistance and advocated approval of the International Development Association, proposed as a soft loan subsidiary of the World Bank. It underscored the importance of technical assistance and the need to improve its quality by drawing on the universities, foundations, and nongovernmental organizations. It urged a more affirmative attitude toward promotion of private investment. It set forth the objective of reducing grant assistance. It endorsed long range country development planning as the basis for U.S. aid. It called for focusing responsibility "in a single agency for planning, programming and execution of economic assistance within the framework of foreign policy direction by the Department of State."

[3] Third Interim Report, The President's Committee to Study the United States Military Assistance Program — Economic Assistance Programs and Administration, July 13, 1959, p. 2.

Then came a Presidential election year, 1960. If party platforms fairly reflect opinion, the American people had reached a remarkable degree of consensus.

The Democratic Platform read:

History and current experience show that an annual per capita growth rate of at least 2 percent is feasible in these countries. The Democratic administration's assistance program, in concert with the aid forthcoming from our partners in Western Europe, Japan, and the British Commonwealth, will be geared to facilitating this objective.

The Democratic administration will recognize that assistance to these countries is not an emergency or short-term matter. Through the Development Loan Fund and otherwise, we shall seek to assure continuity in our aid programs for periods of at least 5 years, in order to permit more effective allocation on our part and better planning by the governments of the countries receiving aid.

We shall establish priorities for foreign aid which will channel it to those countries abroad which, by their own willingness to help themselves, show themselves most capable of using it effectively.[4]

The Republican Platform said:

We recognize that upon our support of well-conceived programs of economic cooperation among nations rest the best hopes of hundreds of millions of friendly people for a decent future for themselves and their children. Our mutual security program of economic help and technical assistance; the Development Loan Fund, the Inter-American Bank, the International Development Association, and the food for peace program, which create the conditions for progress in less developed countries; our leadership in international efforts to help children, eliminate pestilence and disease, and aid refugees — these are programs

[4] *Platforms of the Democratic Party and the Republican Party,* 1960, U.S. Government Printing Office.

wise in concept and generous in purpose. We mean to continue in support of them.[5]

During the election campaign two forces were at work on rethinking aid policies, programs and organization. Within government, senior civil servants, realizing that the election would bring a new administration, whether Republican or Democratic, began to write memoranda and exchange views looking toward changes in structure and operations. Aid policy and organization also played an important part in Senator Kennedy's extensive research activities.

After the inauguration, George W. Ball, whom President Kennedy had appointed Undersecretary of State for Economic Affairs, carried on informally with a group of newly appointed officials and experienced incumbents to set up the framework of a reorganized aid program to be unveiled in a Presidential Message to Congress. The Message was delivered on March 22 and a week later President Kennedy formally established a Task Force on Economic Assistance to work out the program, legislation, and organization, under the direction of Henry R. Labouisse. The task force was a considerably broadened group which included distinguished private citizens. The legislative group was headed by Theodore Tannenwald, Jr., New York attorney and former Assistant Director for Mutual Security. George Gant of the Ford Foundation headed the group on organization and administration. The group on program development was headed by the author. Professor Max Millikan, Director of the Center for International Studies at the Massachusetts Institute of Technology, directed a panel of private experts on development who were drawn from the academic community.

Five months later Congress approved the new legislation and established the Agency for International Development (A.I.D.).

[5] Ibid.

The new Agency absorbed the International Cooperation Administration and the Development Loan Fund, thus combining U.S. overseas operations — grants, technical assistance, loans and the programming of food. A.I.D. was placed under the direction of an Administrator with the rank of Undersecretary of State, responsible to the Secretary of State.

The new Agency placed major responsibility on four regional administrators having the rank of Assistant Secretaries of State for the operation of programs in their respective areas of the world — Latin America, Africa, Near East and South Asia, and the Far East. The regional bureaus and their overseas missions were to have adequate administrative and program staffs.

The program itself was to be based on a broad view of a developing country's needs, giving, as President Kennedy told Congress, "special attention to those nations most willing and able to mobilize their own resources, make necessary social and economic reforms, engage in long range planning and make the other efforts necessary if they are to reach the stage of self-sustaining growth."

The establishment of the new Agency was evidence of a growing consensus. But the ghosts of self doubt were not yet vanquished. There were delays in acquiring top staff, occasioned in part by delay in determining who was to be the new Administrator. With the appointment of Fowler Hamilton in September of 1961, executive recruitment was aggressively undertaken, both for Washington staff and the overseas missions. There were also the massive difficulties of charting new relationships and lines of authority for nearly 7000 employees, and dozens of organizational units. The new house had to be made out of the bricks of the old houses, without slowing the pace of regular work, involving vital commitments around the globe. There were excessive expectations as to the celerity with which developing countries would or could produce sound plans and carry through difficult reform measures. There were volatile political issues centering about such countries as India, Poland, Yugoslavia, and Brazil. The public unease resumed. The honeymoon enjoyed by the new Agency was almost imperceptible.

When in the late fall of 1962 David E. Bell, the Director of the Bureau of the Budget, was drafted as Administrator, the President convened another citizens' committee to test whether aid programs were "contributing to the optimum security of the United States and the economic and political stability in the free world." This committee was headed by General Lucius Clay of Berlin air-lift fame. It was composed chiefly of citizens who were neither partisans of the Administration nor of aid in general. Their mandate was phrased in the hard, narrow terms of national security.

The findings of such a committee, charged with such a mandate, were far more significant in charting the outer boundaries of consensus than would have been those of a pro-administration, pro-aid committee. When the report was issued, many supporters of aid were dismayed at what they considered a negative tone. This was true. The major criticisms of aid made by many were summarized by the Clay committee in language often pungent. There was little shading of gray between the blacks and the whites.

But the stark fact is that the Clay Report of 1963 was a ringing endorsement of the economic sections of the Draper Report of 1959.

It not only reaffirmed the necessity of "properly conceived and administered" aid programs. It endorsed the validity of the Foreign Assistance Act of 1961 and recognized the improvement that had taken place in personnel, programming, and operations. It was a development-oriented report and concentrated on the conditions of development, laying primary emphasis on self-help and encouragement of private sector activities. It urged deliberate speed in phasing down military and

strategic assistance. But it recognized the necessity for maintaining what it called "the frontier of freedom," even to the
extent of suggesting a reduction in our defense budget rather
than cutting necessary support for the forces of this area.

Some idea of its view of the proper range of aid purposes can
be gained from its conclusions that 91 percent of aid was addressed to the strategic areas on the Sino-Soviet border, the
Alliance for Progress, and our contributions to international
organizations; that, in addition, continued economic growth in
freedom of the Asian subcontinent was of critical importance;
that the United States had a stake "in helping to create a climate
of stability and growth" in Africa; and that increased support
should be given the International Development Association. It
laid stress on involving other industrialized countries in improving their quantities and terms of aid and on hardening our
loan terms as countries increase in their capacity to service debt.

Between 1956 and 1963 United States aid had undergone
intense study by Congress, outside experts, citizens' committees,
and the executive branch itself. We had completed our workshop of development tools with the authority to make capital
loans. We had refined the principles and standards which
should guide development assistance — the concepts of country
planning, self-help, selectivity, planning for termination, coordination with other aid-givers, stimulation of private sector
activities, using the varied resources of the U.S. society, and
minimizing impact on the U.S. economy and balance of payments. Finally, we had built a new and unified assistance organization drawing on the experience of the past.

President Kennedy, who had delayed his aid message of 1963
until he received the Clay Report, underscored in that message
the areas of fundamental agreement and said: "There is, in
short, a national consensus of many years standing on the vital
importance of these programs. The principle and purpose of
United States assistance to less secure and less fortunate nations
are not and cannot be seriously in doubt."

Although the President was right in speaking of the fact of consensus, something was missing. The struggle for funds in 1963 was more intense than it had ever been — even though General Clay, after his committee's hard look, endorsed substantially all of the Administration's request. The debate in Congress, in the newspapers, on radio and television, and on Main Street was just as acrimonious and wide-ranging as ever. The fact of consensus had changed neither the attitudes of the general public nor the duration, uncertainty, and conflict of Congressional decision-making.

What accounts for the gap between the present significant area of agreement and that type of conscious consensus in depth which must exist before this nation can sustain its assistance program with steadiness, sensitivity, and sophistication?

There are four components of what we might call the consensus gap. The first, notwithstanding all the reaffirmations and restatements on the subject, is the continuing confusion as to the basic purpose of aid and its reconciliation with a host of specific objectives. The second component is the set of attitudes which most Americans bring to bear in their consideration of aid matters — attitudes which are so accepted and yet so unrealistic that they are seldom even challenged. So long as they remain unchallenged, no amount of intellectual agreement by opinion leaders will achieve the kind of working consensus which the times require of us. The third ingredient is confidence — confidence stemming from our own experience in aid, from a knowledge of the efforts of other free world countries working with us, and from an insight into the problems of those working against us. The final requirement is a realistic view of what further improvements should take place to enable this nation to deal competently and professionally with this vital problem area in the decades immediately ahead.

PART III

A Sense of Purpose

Aid programs differ from other programs of government. They raise — and require an answer to — the question: Why? In matters of defense, education, health, welfare, conservation, and highways, it would never occur to us to ask why. Our eyes are on the "how" and "how much." This is understandable, for the national interest in aid is not direct, immediate, visible, or even certain.

Thus, much of the controversy about aid, and much of the consensus gap, stem from our insistent search for purpose. This is one field of policy and action which we feel called upon constantly to justify in terms of our objective. There is virtually no speech on aid, in or out of Congress, no book, no article, no testimony, no report or study which does not address itself to an attempted definition of the national purpose of assistance policy.

This self-conscious quest for purpose in aid is part of our quest for purpose as a nation. Walter Lippmann has pointed out that Americans have always been a purposeful nation, that our ancestors crossed an ocean for a purpose, that they then turned to opening up, consolidating, and making secure the continental territory, that under the two Roosevelts and Wilson new improvisations of national purpose in domestic and foreign affairs were demanded and created. Now, he says, ". . . we have reached a point in our internal development and in our *relations with the rest of the world where we have fulfilled and outlived most of what we used to regard as the program of our national purposes."* [1] *He concludes that "We have to be able and willing to pay for what is . . . civilization itself . . . not only to make a better life for ourselves but in order to mobilize the power to avoid a much worse life."*

Much of our quest for purpose as a nation revolves about our quest for purpose in aid, for aid is one of the important external dimensions of the nation. In answering the "Why?" of aid, we will also answer the questions, "What does this nation seek in the world?" and "What kind of nation do we want to be?"

The starting point is recognition that there is much cant, confusion, and nonsense parading in the search for purpose. Not even a simple structure like the Tower of Babel could survive the collective efforts of those who did not understand what each other was saying. This is often the case with aid.

It may be useful first to illustrate the confusion of objectives, and then to attempt to find an illuminating common denominator.

---

[1] *The National Purpose.* New York: Holt, Rinehart, Winston, 1960, p. 126.

CHAPTER 7

The Catalogue of Confusion

IN 1948, the policy behind the Marshall Plan was simply stated: ". . . to sustain and strengthen principles of individual liberty, free institutions, and genuine independence in Europe through assistance to those countries of Europe which participate in a joint recovery program based upon self-help and mutual co-operation."

By 1957, the Senate Foreign Relations Committee was disturbed by the misconception of aid as "an all-powerful device to be aimed at all things, in all nations at the same time." [1] It gave a bill of particulars:

> Foreign aid has been justified at one and the same time as the answer to the prevention of further Communist expansion; as a key to national defense; as a lid to cap explosive political situations like that in the Middle East; as a vehicle for the expression of our friendship and our humanitarianism; as a means of keeping or winning the less developed nations to freedom; as a principal bulwark of world peace; as a stimulator of trade, investment and free enterprise throughout the world; as the answer to the problem of agricultural surpluses and other lesser economic dislocations in this country.

The Committee, as its first recommendation, said, "The objectives of the various foreign aid programs should be separated, refined, and restated, as necessary, by the executive branch and the Congress."

[1] Report of the Special Committee to Study the Foreign Aid Program, No. 300, 85th Cong., 1st Session, p. 11.

Seldom has such a recommendation been so completely ignored. The basic aid legislation, the Foreign Assistance Act of 1961 (as amended), must of necessity contain many detailed provisions of substance and procedure. But its opening "Statement of Policy" ought to be a clear, logical, and persuasive statement explaining why the United States has an aid program and what its objectives are. The statement ought to be both accurate and moving, not only for citizens of the United States but for the entire world — of friend, of foe, and of the uncommitted.

Today, seven years after the Senate Committee's call for clarity, the Statement of Policy is a Sears, Roebuck catalogue of miscellaneous objectives. There are at least twenty-four shelf items, of varying scope and importance, arranged in no apparent order of priority.

This catalogue of confusion presents the reader with the following chronology of purposes: survival of free institutions in a worldwide atmosphere of freedom; better living standards; justice; education; individual dignity and respect; responsible governments; political democracy; economic growth and development of productive capabilities; eliminating barriers to flow of private investment capital; increased economic cooperation and trade; freedom of the press, information, and religion; freedom of navigation in international waterways; right to travel and pursue lawful activities without racial or religious discrimination; eliminating discrimination by foreign nations among American citizens; promotion of adjustment of disputes between countries friendly to the United States; creation by continuity of aid of an environment conducive to constructive purposes; maintenance of freedom in countries threatened by Communism; stimulation of sound plans and self-help efforts; help for countries which share our view of the world crisis and do not engage in military propaganda efforts against us; low interest loans for small farmers, homeowners, and businessmen, for tools and vocational education; strengthening regional organizations; joining with friendly nations in missions to receiving countries to assure better planning and use of aid.

This "Statement of Policy," instead of being a clarion call to the conscience, wisdom, and will of the citizenry, is more like the wheeze from a player piano too often repaired.

This is not all. The Act goes out of its way to tuck in a dozen other specific objectives: atomic energy for peaceful uses; aid for American schools, libraries, and hospitals abroad; transportation assistance for charitable agencies; experimental housing in "rapidly developing" Latin American countries; special attention to agrarian economies with emphasis on community development; encouragement of cooperatives, credit unions, savings and loan associations, free labor unions; discouragement of monopolistic practices; the equitable participation by small business; the avoidance of adverse impact on the U.S. economy and price undercutting of U.S. commodities; avoidance of discrimination against marine insurance companies authorized to do business in any state; protection of U.S. drug patents; special authority for use of funds in West Berlin; planning for a dependable supply of fuels.

All of these objectives and "special attentions" bespeak a pluralistic society with many interests and purposes, which has not yet sorted out on paper which ones are major and which are secondary. The result is confusion to the citizen, to Congress and the executive branch whose lawyers are kept busy trying to assess the relative emphasis to be given all of these provisions. The Act itself is like a stalactite, lengthening and thickening with the accretions of time. What began as a program coming to a point has become a shapeless bulbous protrusion.

In quite a different category are the seven major negative objectives of the legislation. These are spelled out in sections which prohibit assistance or compel the stopping of assistance under the following conditions: if a country ships to Cuba; if a country is dominated or controlled by the international Communist movement; if a country refuses to pay a debt owed a U.S. citizen or business; if an enterprise to be assisted will compete with U.S. business, unless export to the U.S. is limited to 20 percent; if a government has expropriated the property of a U.S. firm or citizen without taking appropriate steps to pay fair and speedy compensation; if aid assists a foreign aid project of Communist countries; if the General Accounting Office or a committee of Congress having jurisdiction requests documents from the head of the aid agency which have not been turned over within thirty-five days, unless the President certifies his reason for refusing.

The important point about a specific, negative prohibition, frozen into the law, is that it takes precedence over all other foreign policy objectives. For example, a country, with whom friendly relations are of strategic and overriding importance, might renounce a debt to a U.S. firm incurred under suspicious circumstances by a prior and discredited administration of the country. The United States, through diplomatic efforts, may have tried hard to secure payment. These efforts may have failed because of the political odor which surrounded the original transaction. Under these circumstances, the U.S. is, by law, compelled to suspend all aid — an act today which rivals that of breaking off diplomatic relations. In such a case, the overall foreign policy objectives of the U.S. are subordinated to the objective of debt collection. The point is not that we should not encourage the payment of bills, but that we should not allow ourselves to be placed in a position where we are forced to cut off our nose to spite our face.

The same point can be made about the requirement to suspend aid if a government expropriates property without making fair compensation. No U.S. citizen would deny the validity of the objective. But such an ironclad rule, which cannot be waived at all by the President, places us in a straightjacket. For example, the expropriation might be the act of Communist officials heading a state or province of the country, who are deliberately trying to create a crisis between the two countries. In such a case, we would have no alternative but to stop our aid. By our own law, we would have handed over control of our foreign policy to a few strategically placed Communists in a city or state of another country. We would have declared the principle of fair compensation for private property to be more important than the security of the United States.

Most, not all, of these negative provisions give the President a limited flexibility to make exceptions. But to the extent they impose upon him one of these negative mandates, they are declaring in advance that a specific, secondary purpose of the United States shall take precedence over our more basic, general, and primary purposes.

Justice Holmes, speaking about judge-made law, said, "The life of the law has not been logic; it has been experience." In the case of the legislation governing aid policy and programs, the law also reflects experience — the experience of committee drafting sessions and debates in Congress stretching over two decades. Not all of the experience, however, merits the cloak of immortality.

The deliberations of Congress are entitled to great respect. The genius of Congress lies in its various processes by which representatives of widely divergent views and constituencies come to agreement on policies for the nation. But Members of Congress themselves would be the first to admit that not all their efforts deserve enshrinement in perpetuity. Many amendments are written in the heat of a particular issue which time has cooled. Some amendments are the result of the zeal of a committee member who may have felt more strongly about a point when he insisted on it than he will ever feel again.

When legislators are weary, tempers are frayed, and time is

running out, an invaluable engine of accommodation comes into play. It is the attitude that unless a particular amendment is very bad, the committee will "go along" with the particular member rather than court his bad humor and lack of support in the forthcoming floor fight. Sometimes a member who has sat through hearings for days feels that his time will have been wasted unless he can put a few trademarks in the language of the law. Sometimes he wishes to advance the cause of an interest group — an important industry, labor, or farm organization. On other occasions, particularly in the waning hours of deliberations, an amendment will be proposed that sounds reasonable and to which nobody readily thinks of an objection.

Finally, some members, like others of the human race, feel that they can say something in a more compelling way than have their more prosaic predecessors; and so for hours the committee will wrestle with resounding phrases. The result is a few more clauses, repetitive of existing thoughts, but designed to strike a more responsive chord in the minds and hearts of men.

When the legislation reaches the crucible of floor debate, it sometimes happens that the mood of the House or Senate is such that amendments which strike a sensitive nerve are likely to pass in almost any form. And although the two-house system usually eliminates extremism, there are exceptions. Communism and private property are two such sensitive nerves. On these subjects amendments are often both unpredictable and uncontrollable.

The great majority of accretions to the law have served a useful purpose, by rectifying an imbalance, by giving a Congressional push to a neglected emphasis, by serving notice to the world of Congressional concern about an issue, by tightening administrative standards, or by gaining the support of a significant body of U.S. citizens. But this body of lore and law, in its present form, is not sacred and, indeed, could well stand reappraisal, restructuring, and reemphasis.

The Senate Committee on Foreign Relations, which had called for such a reappraisal in 1957, showed its continuing dissatisfaction in 1963. In one of its meetings on the current aid legislation, it struck out the entire "Statement of Policy." Later, not wishing to break a lance on this particular windmill, it reluctantly restored the section. But the restiveness remains.

To sum up, our law today is an anarchy of purposes. It includes not only a multiplicity of objectives, without judgments as to their relative importance, but many concepts which falsely masquerade under the label of objectives. Some are proper purposes for the United States government but are not feasible purposes for the instrument of aid. Some are valid aid purposes but are so specific that to crystallize them into law is to distort their importance. Some "purposes" are really standards which should govern the administration of aid; others are really procedures. Some are frankly improper and undignified under any category. Some are inconsistent with the major historic objectives.

The law ought to be more than a legal basis for and a limit upon action. It ought also to advance the sense of national purposes. Today, while fulfilling the first function, it cannot be said to fulfill the second. It is more like a hall of mirrors, confusing the wayfarer as he searches for purpose.

CHAPTER 8

The Blessings of Liberty

WHAT IS THE purpose of a sense of purpose? It ought to provide more than an intellectual framework for aid policies; it should convince us that we must carry out policies and instill a sense of commitment. It is a disservice if purpose is phrased in utopian global goals, however desirable they may be. It is a disservice if purpose is phrased too narrowly or negatively. If it is stated too simply, our complex interests in a complex world are distorted. If purpose appears as a lengthy catalogue of specific interests, the confusion of objectives will still remain.

The search for purpose begins in simplicity and ends in complexity. The tap root is the Constitution. Here can be found our earliest aspiration. The Constitution states a fundamental proposition in simple terms. In so doing, it is the key to the search for purpose.

It is the Preamble, drafted by men only dimly aware of Asia, Africa, and Latin America, which provides the rationale for overseas assistance. In declaring the purposes of the Constitution, the founding fathers listed a more perfect Union, domestic Tranquility, the common defense, and the general Welfare. Then followed the words, ". . . secure the Blessings of Liberty to ourselves and our Posterity . . ."

They capitalized "Posterity" but not "ourselves." They cast their eyes not merely to the future but to the ultimate generation. In so doing, they established a policy benchmark of far-reaching significance. When this generation is taxed to assist other peoples in building their nations in an orderly manner, in enjoying greater prosperity, in having free institutions and in learning increasingly to live and trade in an interdependent world community, it is doing what it can to "secure the Blessings of Liberty to . . . our Posterity . . ."

Were we to think only of ourselves, or no farther than our children, our options would be immeasurably greater because our sights would be infinitely narrower. We could be indifferent to the fate of South Korea, Vietnam, Laos, Thailand, Indonesia, and Burma; we could look upon Pakistan and India as holding operations, and view Africa with a bland complacency, selecting for assistance only a very few immediately strategic countries where we had bases or other facilities. We might wish to moderate passions in the Middle East to stretch out the availability of oil. We would want to help a few major Latin American countries where trade could be brisk, but would not be deeply disturbed if some of the nations became satellites of the Communist system.

We could view the encroaching tide of frustration, disorder, subversion, and Communism with equanimity, because for a time, we would continue to enjoy security, liberty, and luxury. But what of the future?

"Après moi, le déluge" reflects an attitude that is implicit in some of the opposition to aid policy. It is phrased in violently pro-American language — "Let's solve our own problems first. What about our own depressed areas?" But, if we accept the standard of the Preamble of our Constitution, we would have to say that what appears pro-American is really pro-American for the time being. But the Preamble contains no such comfortable limitation as the time being. "Posterity" is a long, long word.

The founding fathers were not only concerned with their own posterity. They labored in the tradition of another document, drawn up only eleven years earlier — the Declaration of Independence. This document, in its first substantive sentence, said, "We hold these truths to be self-evident, that all men are created equal, that they are endowed by their Creator with certain unalienable Rights, that among these are Life, Liberty, and the pursuit of Happiness."

Should any doubt remain that the Declaration was intended for Americans only, it was removed by Lincoln, when he said, in Independence Hall, Philadelphia:

> I have often inquired of myself, what great principle or idea it was that kept this Confederacy so long together. It was not the mere matter of the separation of the colonies from the mother land; but something in that Declaration giving liberty, not alone to the people of this country, but hope to the world for all future time. It was that which gave promise that in due time the weights should be lifted from the shoulders of all men, and that all should have an equal chance. This is the sentiment embodied in that Declaration of Independence . . . I would rather be assassinated on this spot than to surrender it.[1]

Today, lifting of weights from the shoulders of all men and moving toward an equal chance for all mean something in addition to both national independence and the assurance of equal civil rights. They also mean lifting the weights of poverty and giving a far better opportunity to live a better life. It is this merging of interests which lies at the heart of aid policy — a policy appealing at once to long range self-interest, to our posterity, and to those we seek to help.

In recent years, as we have struggled for clarity and simplicity in communicating the purpose of U.S. aid, the theme of security has been dominant. The Clay Committee had as its formal name "The Committee to Strengthen the Security of the Free World." This stemmed from the widespread opinion that statements of aid purposes had been too diffused and that the irreducible hard-core objective of security furnished the most understandable and acceptable basis for national agreement. Secu-

---

[1] *Collected Works of Abraham Lincoln*, ed. Roy P. Basler. New Brunswick: Rutgers University Press, 1959, IV, p. 240.

rity, the cold war, the threat of international Communist aggression and subversion — these have been the principal notes in the melody.

To be sure, security has been defined in terms of our broadest and most far-reaching interest in a world community of free nations with free institutions. As it has been so defined, there is nothing narrow or shortsighted about security. It is consistent with the aspirations and interests of the countries we seek to assist.

But it is an inadequate statement of our deepest purpose. It is a static word. Its tone is that of holding the line, of repulsing attack, of defending. Great causes are not long sustained and won under its aegis. It invites one to think in terms of permissible stages of retreat rather than possible lines of advance.

For the United States, security has not been a prime mover in its thrust westward, in building a modern society, or in winning two World Wars against tyranny. Security is for us a statutory, not a constitutional, word. In the Declaration of Independence the word is used as a verb — "to secure." To secure what? The rights of "Life, Liberty and the pursuit of Happiness." In the Constitution only the verb is found, ". . . secure the Blessings of Liberty to ourselves and our Posterity." Only in the Fourth Amendment is the word used other than in conjunction with liberty, and this in relation to the right of people to be secure against unreasonable searches and seizures.

Security today connotes military defense, the strength of allies, protecting bases, sources of strategic supplies, vital waterways, and, above all, containing Communism. All of these are necessary objectives. But they do not do full justice to the basic character and motivations of a people who began national life by seeking liberty.

For the developing nations, the theme of U.S. security — however broadly defined — is something less than a rallying ground for partnership in a great joint enterprise.

To accept the concept of liberty as the basic purpose of aid places today's aid programs in a more accurate perspective. When we assist any nation in its struggle against the aggressor, we are striving to make that country secure. But secure for what purpose? Secure to develop as a free nation. Our efforts are not only military, but also in the direction of helping create institutions and better living conditions among dwellers in the countryside. The military effort is that of nation saving; the economic effort is that of nation building. The objective is not merely a military victory and the temporary security of an armed camp, but a nation which has earned the right and developed the capability to remain free by enlisting the loyalties and energies of its citizens in working for a better life.

This is our objective, because only this kind of nation has a chance to control its destiny. This is not a static objective. To the extent any nation succeeds, it reinforces the determination of other nations. The frontier of this kind of freedom has only one way to move — forward — not in terms of conquest, but in terms of example and emulation.

In such cases security and liberty are really the opposite sides of the same coin. There can be no real security without enlarging the political, social, and economic liberty of citizens. And there can be no real increase in these liberties without a nation secure from aggression or subversion.

When we consider aid to countries whose security is not immediately threatened, the need for a positive goal becomes even more compelling. When we make large development loans to Latin American countries, or Nigeria, Tunisia, Greece, Turkey, India or Pakistan, a rationale based expressly on security does us a disservice. Admittedly, a chaotic, hostile, and expansionist Nigeria would wreak havoc in West Africa — or, in the case of Tunisia, in North Africa — with immediate repercussions on the United States. A weakening of will in all the border countries from Greece to India would have profound implications for the world balance of power.

But more is at stake for these countries and for ourselves than that they maintain themselves in a precarious condition of political stability with just enough economic progress to avoid internal subversion. We want them to succeed gloriously — to reach the position where they are not only free from reliance on external aid, able to trade with other nations on favorable terms, able to help less advanced nations, but by their very success become convinced apostles of economic, social, and political freedom. The best assurance of the blessings of liberty to our posterity lies in increasing the numbers of nations who convince themselves that an open society and free economic and social institutions are the best construction materials for building a durable nation.

The development of advocates of liberty does more than serve our long-range security interest; it enlarges for us as well as for them the blessings of liberty in a world increasingly enriched by the interchange of ideas, cultural contributions, people, and commerce. Apart from the obvious political implications of the cold war, whenever a nation chooses the controlled social, political, and economic approaches of a totalitarian government of the left or right, the liberties of all other nations are compressed. Cultural exchange becomes narrowly contrived. The traffic in ideas — scientific, governmental, technological, artistic — shrivels. Commerce ceases to flow naturally; trade becomes a matter of political subsidy, dumping, barter, and bilateral deals. There exist no reliable bases on which to build or diversify industry other than uncertain political arrangements.

This is why the rationale for aid should encompass the broad and more dynamic purpose of liberty rather than just the narrower and more static one of security. It is more accurate.

It is also a more compelling purpose.

A sense of purpose should embody not merely rationale but conviction and motivation. The free and developed nations of the world stand at the threshold of an era which they will immensely influence — by their action or their inaction. If the enlargement of the liberties of all, the developed and developing world alike, is seen as the fundamental goal, there is far greater likelihood that this era will prove to be a benevolent one than if security is seen as the solitary touchstone.

Europe, a participant in more wars than it cares to remember, and now the apprehensive buffer between two great powers, is not likely to look on assistance to Latin America, Asia, or even Africa as a very significant key to its own security. But it understands liberty. It has sired the prophets of liberty — political, social, and economic. It knows that, with limited population and natural resources, it can best enjoy the blessings of liberty in a world of free nations, living, trading, and communicating with a minimum of national barriers. This proposition holds equal relevance for such other nations as Canada, Japan, Australia, and New Zealand.

All of these nations together face the opportunity, wholly apart from any threats of communism, to shape relations for decades to come between themselves and the developing world. Together they, and the international institutions which their contributions so largely support, have the material and human resources to accelerate measurably and in an orderly way the realization of the liberties so valued by the developing peoples and so long enjoyed by themselves — freedom from desperate want, from preventable and curable disease, from ignorance, from political oppression.

On timely, forthcoming, generous and sustained assistance in these threshold years will depend the atmosphere, the political stability, and the economic well being of the world for long years to come. This statement has little to do with gratitude — a transient and ephemeral attitude which plays a miniscule role in the relations among nations. It is rather based on some of the more predictable realities of international life.

For if countries use their limited resources unwisely, if education is not broadly shared, if economies become artificially distorted, if internal frustration is relieved in expansionist adventures, if embittered blocs and groupings proliferate, the blessings of liberty will have been eroded for all.

To approach assistance as a vehicle for liberty rather than security can make a dramatic difference in the quality, quantity, and steadiness of response by the free and developed nations to those nations trying to shape their attitudes toward themselves and the rest of the world.

As far as the developing countries are concerned, there is no doubt that the commonalty of interests can be much more convincingly and enthusiastically described in terms of liberty than of security. To them the dimensions of liberty are often more social and economic than political, apart from the primal raw political liberty in the form of national independence. Indeed, national independence once gained has often appeared as a cruel hoax when they face the difficult tasks of establishing a government, building institutions, making laws, and finding competent officials. In seeking independence, they often included among their heroes Washington, Jefferson, and Lincoln. Our own Declaration of Independence formed part of their inspiration. As they now move into these formative decades of independence, should we not continue to build our relationships on the firm rock of liberty?

All of this has been said without reference to the threat of Communism. This approach is based on the view that the primary fact of international life is the widespread condition of poverty, and that the existence of the Communist conspiracy is a vitally important fact, but a secondary one. The threats posed by the Communist dogma of world conquest, whether it be Moscow's peaceful coexistence or Peking's intransigent militancy, reinforce the wisdom of a liberty-oriented rather than a security-oriented purpose.

Our basic posture, therefore, should be that of action, not reaction. So long as security dominates our action, it takes on the coloration of reacting. No matter how sophisticated we are in our definitions, the leaders of the new and poorer nations must not be blamed if occasionally they are tempted to experiment with Communist aid, not merely to obtain needed resources, but to use it as leverage for greater free world aid. The cause of security has too often been the anvil on which has beaten the hammer of Communism. The cause of liberty, a perennial questing by man, is by its very nature a hammer. Aid, so conceived, can be the thrusting, moving force of freedom throughout the world. The United States and the other free industrialized nations working together can sustain an initiative in the name of liberty, one which can mark this new era with distinction for all time.

There is an important qualification to this concept. Neither the United States nor its partners in aid can guarantee political, economic, or social progress for other nations, any more than we can guarantee to individual citizens education, property, or happiness. The individual must decide how he will use his life, whether to be really free, and how to pursue happiness. In a liberty-based aid relationship we should strive to achieve two major objectives.

We can and should offer military and economic assistance to nations needing help to remove the obstacles to freedom imposed by aggression or subversion. Nations have to survive and be politically stable in order to have an opportunity to harvest the fruits of liberty. It is part of our purpose to strive to see that no nation is denied this opportunity.

Beyond this, we can and should extend assistance in economic, social, and political development to nations willing to work toward increasing freedoms for their peoples. We cannot be arbitrary or impatient in what is at best a long and difficult process. But neither can we lose sight of the basic objective of increased freedom from the great enslavers of mankind — want, disease, ignorance, and oppression. Our objective is not merely to be partners in nation building; it is to help build the kind of nations which in the long run will help secure the blessings of liberty.

PART IV

A Sense of Realism

A deeper sense of history and a clearer sense of purpose can give both momentum and direction to the pursuit of the grand design of assisting other peoples. But they cannot, by themselves, long sustain it. They must be linked with and supported by a sense of realism.

A sense of realism must embody a set of attitudes compounded from intellectual, emotional, and moral discipline. These attitudes stem from our view of the uses and limits of power, both of men and of nations. They determine our thinking about the nature of the development task, our role in it, and above all, our expectations. They are the unseen yardsticks we use to measure success and failure in the present and past, the binoculars we use to scan the prospects of the future.

In most of the thinking, talking, and writing about aid, these attitudes have escaped attention. Seldom have we asked the questions: Are we being realistic about our assistance relationship with the developing world? Do our attitudes help or hinder the fulfillment of our historic purpose? It is as if, in the struggle for consensus on aid, the regular, visible troops — the arguments marshaled from the selected facts — were reinforced and replenished after every encounter of fact and logic by a vast and camouflaged army of guerrillas — the attitudes we widely share. Lurking behind the cover of consciousness, and seldom being exposed to the fire of critical analysis, they are invulnerable.

There are two regiments of these guerrilla attitudes. Their regimental colors contrast violently with each other. But each accomplishes the same mission — to erode our effectiveness and our will.

The first reaches its objectives indirectly through creating a set of excessive expectations which can lead only to irritation, frustration, and disillusion. Its banner is arrogance. The second marches directly to the objective by sapping our own self-confidence while at the same time portraying the insuperable obstacles to lasting achievement. Its banner is self-doubt rampant on a field of despair.

Reinhold Niebuhr has sharply defined the targets of these two regiments: "Nations, as individuals, may be assailed by contradictory temptations. They may be tempted to flee the responsibilities of their power or refuse to develop their potentialities. But they may also refuse to recognize the limits of their possibilities and seek greater power than is given to mortals." [1]

Until these attitudes and temptations are exposed and engaged, therefore, we cannot hope for any sustained national consensus and commitment.

[1] *The Irony of History.* New York: Charles Scribner's Sons, 1952, p. 130.

CHAPTER 9

The Forces of Arrogance

VOICE OF THE CITIZEN: *The trouble with our aid policy is that we have no standards. I'm not against aid as such. I know we have an obligation. And I would support a sensible aid program. But it should have clear criteria, and if they weren't met, no aid.*

For example, if one country is making trouble for a neighbor, if it refuses to settle its border disputes, if it insists on having too big an army, or if it makes too big a nuisance of itself with its propaganda, I'd cut off aid. What sense does it make to help two nations who are at each other's throats?

I would also have a political test. If nations want our aid, they ought to be friendly. I can't see why we send our good tax dollars to so called neutrals, who are ungrateful, who criticize us in public, and even vote against us in the United Nations. They are either with us or against us. Neither can I see why we give aid to kings, dictators, or military cliques. We ought to have a clear requirement that nations we help should have a democratic government with free elections — and a bill of rights.

On the economic side, I would insist that nations we help be required to put their house in order. This means private enterprise, a capable civil service, honest officials, sound budgeting and planning. Otherwise, our money is wasted.

In the social field, I want to be sure our aid reaches the people. I don't want to help make the rich richer. I wouldn't stand for any foot dragging on land reform. And I would insist on an end to racial and religious discrimination.

Now, with that kind of an aid program, people would understand it and support it.

This is the voice of arrogance. Its strength lies in its surface reasonableness. Are not all of the objectives both desirable and reasonable? Yet it is time to face the unpleasant truth that here, in much of the supposedly sophisticated thinking about aid, is the last-ditch stand of American arrogance.

Arrogance is a strong word. It has, happily, become increasingly obsolete as a label which can justly be applied to us. Historically a confident people, we have had seizures of arrogance. As we subdued a continent, pushed back a frontier, developed our rich resources, built a dynamic economy, and realized a society ever broadening in equality of opportunity, we marked ourselves as doers and achievers. Few things were impossible.

The accumulating problems of industrialization began to temper our overweening confidence. The depression years gave us a rude and lasting shock. We began to learn the lesson of humility, that there are problems which defy ready solution. Today's problems of racial fairness, educational opportunity, equitable taxation, dignity for the aged, juvenile delinquency, urban congestion, agricultural surpluses, and automation command all our ingenuity, will, and endurance. We have come to accept the spasmodic and often crabwise pace of progress.

Even in the stranger realm of foreign affairs we have come to accept the limitations on our power to work our will. Gone are the days when problems could be solved by the landing of Marines. Reluctantly we have developed a patient steadfastness in our attitudes toward Berlin, the Soviet Union, disarmament negotiations, the infinite debating of complex issues in the United Nations. We fully comprehend that this is not an age of neat solutions or decisive victories. It is an age where tedium and talk may themselves be the watermarks of successful diplomacy.

But the tempering or maturing process has left untouched our attitudes toward aiding other nations. It is not willful. It is not conscious. It is a compound of attitudes, unarticulated, and not patently unreasonable. But they add up to an arrogance which destroys through the frustrations it creates.

The "sensible" aid criteria, accepted by so many, involve unintentional arrogance in five respects. They assume an omnipotence which the United States does not possess. They overestimate the power of aid as a lever. They assume our omniscience about the process of development. They are based upon unrealistic and excessive expectations of the capacity of the developing world to change. And they give undue weight to the will-o'-the-wisp, international gratitude.

The Power of the United States

The United States is the most powerful nation on earth. But its usable power to exert influence on most problems most of the time is limited. This is not a novel proposition. What is not well understood, however, is the feasible range of usable power, consistent with the interests of a nation that must deal actively with many other nations every day on a host of serious issues. Every day sees a third of a million words of cable traffic between the Department of State and over three hundred diplomatic posts around the world. All of them deal with problems, many with crises. They all demand a judgment as to the quantity, variety, and timing of U.S. influence and action which should be brought to bear on a specific issue.

In the face of global responsibilities, the political credit of the United States is a commodity to be carefully husbanded. Its wise expenditure is the chief business of the President and the Secretary of State. We cannot meet every issue with special trade arrangements, massive aid, an embargo, an agreement among allies, a Presidential visit, a commitment of a fleet or a squadron of aircraft.

Even if the reserve of usable power suffered no such limitations, it would still be confined to a narrow range of feasible acts. Each country, no matter how small, faces its own battery of problems, limitations, and aspirations. Among these are its new-found sovereignty, its relations with its neighbors and with its former colonial master, domestic political problems, the harsh realities of international trade, traditional modes of thought. When we speak expansively of the power of the United States we should remind ourselves of the difficulties in asserting federal power in an attempt to influence the social and economic policies of our own states.

The conclusion to be drawn from a realistic view of the uses of power in international affairs is not that we should cease trying to pursue a wide range of objectives. It is our obligation and opportunity to use our considerable power in all possible combinations skillfully, sensitively, persistently and resiliently to help create conditions looking toward the easing of social, political and economic tensions, to prevent problems from erupting into crises, and to strengthen the chances for orderly problem-solving. In the long run the steadiness and patience resulting from such a view of the boundaries of power will serve us better than the harvest of frustration resulting from excessive expectations.

There is one dimension of U.S. power which has been until recently underestimated. This is our power to make progress in solving our problems at home. To the extent that we make measurable progress in realizing racial equality, full employment, steady economic growth, greater educational opportunity, and our other key domestic objectives, we shall dramatically contribute to our reservoir of usable credit abroad. Continued rapid progress in dissolving racial barriers will do more to advance U.S. influence abroad than reams of painfully negotiated protocols.

The Leverage of Aid

The corollary of the attitude which assumes the omnipotence of U.S. influence overseas is that the extension of aid is an all-powerful lever for all purposes we seek to achieve. We see the flowering of this attitude in the catalogue of objectives in the aid legislation and in the aid debates.

Aid is expected — wholly apart from contributing to the survival and development of independent nations — to assist expropriated companies to obtain fair compensation, help collect debts owed to private firms, abolish racial discrimination, secure support for our positions in the United Nations, implant private enterprise, discourage monopolistic practices, maintain the free use of international waterways, and bring forth settlements between India and Pakistan, Ethiopia and Somalia, Ecuador and Peru, Afghanistan and Pakistan, Cambodia and Thailand . . .

Aid is thought to be Paul Bunyan's axe, Merlin's wand, Arthur's Excalibur. The underlying assumption is that the giving or lending of resources to another nation is so sacrificial and benevolent on our part, and so vitally needed on the part of the receiving nation, that it is reasonable to make aid do all the work we would like to see done.

Such an attitude assumes that the social and economic development of an open and independent society is an inadequate objective, that the basic aid bargain of resources in exchange for this kind of development is one-sided, and that other tangential quid pro quos can always be reasonably expected. It does us the great disservice of leveling all our objectives to a linear dimension, equating the solid and orderly development of a free country with other, lesser objectives.

It also vastly exaggerates the value of aid, as seen through the eyes of the receiving country. The developing countries earn some thirty-three billion dollars a year from their exports.[1] The total official aid flow from the U.S. in 1962 was $3.6 billion, or one ninth of their receipts from trade. Moreover, the prices

[1] *International Financial Statistics,* International Monetary Fund, August 1963 (1962 figures).

of the commodities produced by the developing countries have tended to fall in recent years while the prices of manufactured goods have steadily increased, with the net adverse movement of the "terms of trade" being such as to offset part of the aid which they received. We ought, therefore, at least to understand, if not wholly agree with, the developing countries when they talk of aid as merely compensatory financing for export losses.

Few realize the extent to which aid is only a marginal resource for all but a very few countries. Even in India, the largest recipient, our aid of about half a billion dollars a year accounted, in 1961, for about 2.2 percent of its gross national product. Yet, with this lever of 2.2 percent, we expect India to settle all its foreign and domestic problems overnight — border disputes, domestic unrest, population growth, the development of an adequate private sector. All of these objectives are, we think, desirable in India's own self-interest. We shall continue to work toward them in many ways. But to condition the continued extension of our aid on any one of these is to lose sight of the large goal of India's orderly economic progress while preserving and strengthening its free society.

The percentages of U.S. aid to gross national product are of the same order of magnitude in other major aid-receiving countries: 1.3 percent in Greece, 1.6 percent in Iran, 3.5 percent in Turkey, 5.4 percent in Pakistan, 1.6 percent in the Philippines, 4.6 percent in Taiwan, 1.5 percent in Brazil, 1 percent in Argentina, 1.7 percent in Colombia, .5 percent in Nigeria. When we think of using aid as a lever, we should keep in mind the size of the lever.

The Exportability of Experience

Another fountainhead of arrogance is the unquestioned assumption that we know what is best, that we have the answers for those who have the good judgment to heed our advice. Even for otherwise sensible people, the temptation to play God appears to be irresistible. In pretending omniscience we sacrifice one of the priceless qualities we can and should export — pluralism, the concept that there are many avenues to progress.

The United States is pluralism incarnate. Cities are governed by Boards of Aldermen, Commissions, and City Managers. States have large and small legislatures, one being unicameral. They are financed by sales taxes, income taxes or a combination. Most states recognize the necessity of financing through borrowing; some do not. The variety of powers enjoyed by county government is almost infinite. Indeed, one of the basic values ascribed to the states is their utility as "laboratories" for pluralistic approaches to problems.

To abandon this tolerance for diversity in our efforts to help the developing countries of the world is to abandon one of the mainstreams of our own development. If our individual dogmatism about what makes progress could be confined to individual views, no harm would be done. But we write some of our preconceptions into law.

We write into our law mandates supposedly insuring special support for the private sector, for the rural sector, for housing, for savings and loan institutions. As long as the mandate is expressed as an objective to keep in mind and work toward, there is no harm done except to the clarity of our basic purpose. But when Congress fixes a dollar or percentage figure for the support of particular kinds of economic or social programs, it often imposes a rigidity which can only be self-defeating.

For example, a 1963 amendment requires that 50 percent of developmental loans be channeled into private business activities. On the surface, this is reasonable and accords with our view of a well-balanced economy. Actually it could well have, if narrowly applied, the unintended effect of slowing down a nation's development of the power, roads, ports, communications, public administration, health, police, and education systems which are required as a base for successful private ventures. It is wise to urge the kind of laws, taxes, and monetary responsibility that will attract the needed human and material resources of private investment. But it is folly to set arbitrary requirements and prejudge the pace of progress.

The truth is that a developing country must take action on all fronts — the education and training of its people, the building of institutions and a capable governmental bureaucracy, the creation of the capital base for a more modern economy, the improvement of agriculture, the stimulation of private investment. There is no one royal road to development, no magic formula. Helping in the building of eighty nations is the essence of complexity. Humility, patience, and pragmatism are better attitudes for the task than arrogance, impatience, and dogmatism.

The Capacity to Change

After years of striving for a rationale for aid administration, we have finally achieved one — self-help. To be sure, it was explicitly stated in General Marshall's speech and in the Marshall Plan legislation. But, as we broadened our sights to include the emerging, developing world, we all but lost sight of the concept. Then, with the array of studies culminating in the new aid legislation, and particularly in the Alliance for Progress, self-help has been established as the rudder of rationality in aid relationships. This appeals to our Puritan ethic; our assistance is to be extended to stimulate the doing of those things which others ought to do to help themselves.

The trap we may have laid for ourselves is not the concept of self-help, which is both valid and essential. The trap could be our unrealistic views of the time span within which basic economic, social, and political changes can be made. The classic setting of the trap can be found in the debates on the first Congressional appropriation for the Alliance in the spring of 1961. Here funds were defended on the ground that they would not be made available to Latin American countries until they had "put their houses in order" and "pulled up their socks." Consequently, even though it is now clear that the best we can hope for is a process where funds are extended at the same time that efforts are made to make changes, in a parallel phasing, or a step-by-step process, there is still widespread criticism of the slow pace of change.

This attitude bespeaks a curious myopia on our part. It ignores our own history, past and present. It ignores the incomparably greater problems faced by the tradition-bound societies, limited not only by custom and social attitudes but by lack of skilled human and capital resources, by class divisions, by increasing populations, by disease, illiteracy, and hunger.

As a young nation, we might have had difficulty in qualifying for aid from a self-help standard. Our early fiscal and financial practices were far from model. Our early state and federal governments were often more disorderly than orderly. Favoritism, corruption, the defaulting of debts, monopoly, and the settlement of disputes by violence were far from unknown. The Civil War itself makes the Congo look lackluster. It took us well over a century to adopt the income tax, a century and a half to regulate securities. The fight to end racial discrimination has entered its second post–Civil War century.

For decades we have labored painstakingly in social welfare work, criminology, drug addiction, juvenile delinquency — spending large sums in the knowledge that there would be many false starts and that much effort would be in vain. But we sensed also that persistent work over time was the hallmark of a society with a conscience and that in the long run such expenditures were a smaller outlay than the social cost of doing nothing. Even in enterprises where the human factor might be expected to play a minor role, such as the construction of roads and public buildings, we have recognized that we do not always proceed with rationality and economy.

We despair of the administrative ability of some of the developing countries to make prompt and effective use of aid funds. Roads have been a frequent magnet for criticism, in Cambodia, Burma, Thailand, Peru, and elsewhere. We have a right to be concerned, but not to indulge in a righteous indignation that ignores our own performance at home, where many a highway investigation has revealed lack of planning, excessive payments for rights of way, failure to make field tests, unqualified appraisers, payoffs to inspectors and appraisers, and contractor influence on officials.

Finally, as we survey our own difficulties in making modest changes in tax laws today or in providing adequately for public education or for health care for the aged, we should be realistic in applying the doctrine of self-help in our aid program.

The time span for significant changes which can endure will be much longer than we have dared to think. Change will be difficult enough without shackling ourselves with excessive expectations and those we help with excessive demands.

The Desire for Appreciation

Part of our problem is that we personalize relations between nations. Even the criticism of aid that "You can't buy friends" implies that friendship is our final objective. Because we expect the amenities shown by one friend to another, we cannot understand why a nation we have helped with large amounts of aid persists on being a neutral, why it may vote in opposition to us in the United Nations, why its Prime Minister makes embarrassing or hostile statements, or why it refuses to settle a border dispute with a neighbor who is equally a friend of ours.

Admittedly, a perennial posture of hostility in statements, votes, and actions by a nation receiving large and consistent amounts of U.S. aid raises the relevant question: Do we hold the same basic objectives in common? This is the test among nations, not the slender and short-lived reed of friendship but a mutuality of self-interest. Here our objectives and policies have a firm foundation, for our long-run self-interest lies in the building of progressing and responsible nations — the same goal held by all serious national leaders. This is why Secretary of State Rusk has said that nationalism is our ally.

Once we accept this proposition, we can begin to realize that our aid is not conferring such favors on other countries that we can expect gratitude. We shall often receive it but the kind to be valued is that which develops over years of constructive activity, not the temporary gratification of transient cabinet ministers or even heads of state.

There is a better short-run by-product of aid than gratitude or affection. It is respect. Respect is wholly consistent with goals held in common. It is consistent with differences in views and national sovereignty. It can flourish only if developing nations understand more clearly our objective, if they know that it does not conflict with theirs, if they appreciate the means we intend to use and if they recognize that we are realistic and serious in our expectations.

In short, our goal is a society of free nations standing on their own feet. Our means is the development of discipline within developing countries, which is necessary for nations who must telescope the accumulating experience of the past into years, half decades, and decades of rapid growth. There comes a point when failure as to means implies failure as to ends, when serious lack of discipline casts grave doubt on the ultimate capacity of a nation to be a nation in any long-run, popularly supported, progressive sense. To maintain with sensitivity but with firmness the relationship between means and ends is the key to enduring respect.

*   *   *

To build a relationship based on respect, therefore, requires us to be realistic in our expectations. We must be highly selective in using the credit of the United States. We must not generally expect aid to carry burdens beyond its capacity. We must not assume that our knowledge, experience, and institutions are automatically exportable. We must remember our own past and present as we seek to work out reasonable goals of self-help. And we must be prepared on occasion not to be liked, without wavering in the pursuit of our ultimate goal.

Finally, we must rediscover patience. As the distinguished British economist, Barbara Ward, points out, "If the men of 1776 had attempted the opening up of America with the testy impatience of so many politicians today, they would barely have crossed the Adirondacks." [2]

[2] Address, "Prelude to Independence." Williamsburg, Virginia: Washington *Post*, June 2, 1963, p. A.8.

CHAPTER 10

The Forces of Self-Doubt

VOICE OF THE CITIZEN: *I have always supported U.S. aid. I think the Marshall Plan was a great success. But we're up against something entirely different in trying to help everybody all over the world.*

Look at all the waste and corruption in aid projects. I just don't think we're very good at this business. Also, we're not a nation of unlimited resources. Since World War II, we've spent over $100 billion. Perhaps we could afford it then, but times have changed. This constant drain will bankrupt us.

I'm worried not just about the dollars but about the gold drain. We just can't go on with a continuing deficit in our balance of payments. It's more important to the free world that we maintain a sound dollar. So I'm for cutting way down on aid and stopping the gold drain.

I'm also worried where we as a nation are going, helping put other nations in a position where they will be competing with us — with low cost labor.

This is the voice of self-doubt. Its strength lies in its "realistic" appraisal of our capacity. It is the very opposite of arrogance. It enables one to argue for withdrawal from aid activity without being accused of isolationism.

Arrogance we may deplore. But we can understand it. It is a human trespass beyond our tradition of confident striving. While it stems from exaggerated notions of our ability to shape events, it at least implies that we care, that we want to be involved, and that we desperately want ourselves and others to achieve.

But attitudes alien to all our traditions have begun to mark us in recent years — attitudes of weariness over the burden we have borne, of criticism of our past efforts, of doubt as to our ability to help others.

These attitudes take a variety of forms, some of which are rapidly becoming a new generation of clichés. Their very statement often closes the door to further thought. The three principal ones relate to our ability to be effective, the burden we bear, and the feasibility of withdrawal.

The Ugly American Complex

We, who subdued a wilderness, built a nation, helped win two World Wars, orbited the earth — we doubt our ability to be effective in helping other peoples. We not only doubt our ability; we are pretty sure that the next fellow is apt to be better at this than we are.

Perhaps our self-confidence began to wane because of our attitude toward waste. We became aware of roads that led nowhere, windfall profits to importers, industrial plants which would not function, gifts for short-run political purposes. Our impression has been that aid projects and programs were honeycombed with poor planning, sloppy administration, and even corruption.

There is only one thing that succeeds like success and that is failure. For the publicized miscarriages of aid have created an impression of ineptitude far in excess of reality. A balanced view, however, is of crucial importance now. For what is at stake is not the reputation of some anonymous government official or a particular appropriation request in Congress. What is at stake is our pride in our efforts. No other country — ever — has helped in more good works for more people than has the United States, or for more constructive reasons. We should take as much pride in our peacetime assistance as in our military victories. But we do not. We are ashamed because we do not think we have done well.

We have sold ourselves short — very short. We have accepted every tale told, whether founded in fact or not. In a decade and a half there have been several score of "horribles" paraded before us. They have been almost equally divided into three kinds: those absolutely true, those absolutely false, and those where the facts are accurately stated but the conclusion to be drawn is one about which reasonable men can differ.

When the admittedly bad mistakes are winnowed from issues of judgment or complete misinterpretations, the record is not one for sackcloth and ashes. The record should be judged against an eighteen-year outlay of $104 billion, and literally thousands of individual projects, in over a hundred countries which have at some time received aid. Viewed against this horizon, the instances of waste dwindle down to size, a size no greater than that in domestic programs.

Indeed, the incidence of waste in aid programs should be considerably greater, for in domestic programs people share the same culture, are subject to the same sanctions and the same motives. Vastly different customs, levels of education, incentives, and values will inevitably influence, divert, and distort some of the best-laid plans.

The old stories, whatever their validity, never die. Whether the charge be financing wife-buying in Kenya, an inoperable fertilizer plant, a luxury yacht, bathhouses for camel drivers, defective highways, jet planes, two rifles per soldier, nine stalls per bull in a stock-breeding farm, their memory lingers on. Most of such stories are either without foundation or have been distorted beyond recognition. Some were admitted bloopers. But, whatever may be the category, they still make the headlines.

We are ready to believe the worst of all Americans who serve overseas. In the book, *The Ugly American*,[1] the hero had competence, imagination, dedication, and empathy to the nth degree. But the title may have helped crystallize a cult of self-criticism.

The new sophistication allows us in the name of international sensitivity to call for drastic reduction of United States citizens abroad. We can argue for withdrawal of assistance efforts under the camouflage of insistence on quality personnel — personnel who by definition are extremely rare.

We have carried our inferiority complex so far as to assert that Communist field personnel are superior to ours. This is one of the fashionable non-facts about aid. There is gathering evidence that Communist technicians are not generally trained in the local language, that they insulate themselves in compounds, that they are looked upon as overpaid by receiving countries, that their planning frequently has been faulty with the result that projects have not moved ahead, that they have had their share of embarrassing or scandalous incidents. Countries which once welcomed them have asked that they leave.

The point is not that all personnel from Communist countries are bumbling, insensitive, and mechanistic, but that U.S. personnel in the field have a far better record for quality work, for flexibility, for endurance under difficult living conditions, for sacrifice, and for good relations with the host country officials and people than we care to acknowledge.

Our perverse insistence on demeaning our personnel in the field is allied to a fear of numbers. U.S. aid personnel overseas total under 5000. There are about 9000 foreign nationals employed. Some Congressmen, Senators, and private citizens go into a state of shock on hearing such figures. They profess to believe that "a better job can be done with half the people"

[1] *The Ugly American*, William J. Lederer and Eugene Burdick. New York: W. W. Norton & Company, Inc., 1958.

and that "we cannot possibly find that many qualified people."
This is, at rock bottom, a scathing indictment, not of aid
but of the human resources of the United States.

Here are some facts to put this particular numbers game in
perspective:

   – Although we have aid programs in over twice the number of countries and territories as the Communist countries,
they have over twice as many aid personnel abroad as we
have. Last year they fielded at least 11,000 personnel in thirty
countries, almost a 50 percent increase over the past several
years.

   – Britain has about 17,000 employees in the field, working
with developing countries, over three times the number of
U.S. personnel.

   – France has seven times as many, 28,000 to 30,000.

   – Tiny Belgium fields 2000 overseas employees.

   – The United Nations has 5000.

   – There are at least a score of U.S. firms whose overseas
operations involve personnel in excess of 20,000. The Ford
Motor Company, General Motors Corporation, and the International Telephone and Telegraph Company each have over
eight times the overseas personnel of the Agency for International Development, including U.S. and foreign nationals.
International Business Machines, Singer Sewing Machines,
Socony Mobil have over twice as many.

All of these firms, and more, have mounted and sustained
impressive operations abroad in extracting, manufacturing, and
distributing. Their fields include automobiles, air travel, oil,
cosmetics, cash registers, sewing machines, communications
equipment, aluminum, rubber, farm machinery, elevators, and
soap. And yet we are afraid that 4000 U.S. citizens abroad are
too many to do a job that for complexity, sensitivity, and importance far exceeds that of any of these great companies. Here,
truly, self-doubt becomes a psychic hazard of major proportions.

A ratio of one technician to a third of a million people is hardly excessive for the role we ought to play. This is not to say that the quality and training of our personnel cannot be improved, that some missions may not be overstaffed, or that we do not have a surplus of some skills and a deficiency in others. But we can say that building institutions, working with other peoples long enough so that skills and practices will endure, developing cadres of trained administrators, educators, and entrepreneurs in depth take both time and people. The transfer and telescoping of experience have not yet been reduced to automation.

The Burden in Perspective

Another doubt gnawing at us is whether we can continue to afford aid. After over a decade and a half of helping other nations, we doubt our ability to carry on. We talk of whittling down our level of aid at the threshold of an era which should see steady increases from all industrialized countries.

This feeling is understandable. We are weary from well-doing. After sixteen monotonous annual agonies of aid argument, with few spectacular or permanent victories to point to, with many frustrations abroad and nagging problems at home, we would like to forget the whole business. And so we take the easy way out, the way which places us in the best possible light. We like to consider the inviting prospect of withdrawal, while not offending our internationalist conscience.

Our first escape hatch is another numbers game. Just as the number of employees in aid programs is used to prove we are doing too much, so we point to the magic figure of over $100 billion we have spent on aid since 1945, to prove that we have spent too much. Here again, we play the part of Pavlov's dog and react without analysis. We yield to the luxury of despair and say, "If our $100 billion accomplished so little, why continue?"

The fact is that only about one fourteenth of this amount has been planned and spent for the primary purposes of economic and social development of developing countries. Yet it is this program which is on trial today. This is the leading edge of our aid policy, backed up by an important but diminishing amount of military assistance. In eighteen years we have devoted approximately seven billion dollars to the kind of development grants and loans, which are the heart of our programs today. The remaining amount was spent for a dozen or more vital purposes — but not for the primary purpose of development, which did not receive substantial sums until 1958.

Moreover, the total funds spent for all these purposes during the past eighteen years have amounted to 1½ per cent of our total gross national product during this period.

We cannot fairly say, therefore, either that we have given excessive systematic development assistance to developing countries or that the amounts we have loaned or granted to other nations were beyond our means. We can, however, say that these funds worked well for us.

Leaving aside an invocation of gross sums spent over most of two decades, the annual controversy over aid assumes that this has been an increasingly burdensome program. The reverse is true. The burden has declined — both relatively and absolutely.

At the start of the Marshall Plan, economic aid expenditures amounted to 1.7 percent of our gross national product and 11.5 percent of our total federal expenditures. Today they amount to only .37 percent of gross national product and about 2.2 percent of our total federal expenditures. Today's economic aid expenditures are about one twenty-fifth of current defense expenditures.

In terms of dollars per capita, the burden of economic aid has been halved. Between 1948 and 1951, the days of the Marshall Plan, our burden per person was $35 a year. Today it is $16.

Between 1948 and 1954 the Congress appropriated on the average of $5.3 billion a year for military and economic assistance. During these years our gross national product averaged about $300 billion a year. For the fiscal years 1960 through 1963, the Congress has appropriated on the average of $3.8 billion a year for these purposes. And, for fiscal year 1964, the appropriation was substantially below even this figure. During these years our gross national product has climbed from $503 billion in 1960 to over $600 billion in 1963.

To place cost in perspective is always difficult. Often the mere repetition of large lump sum figures distorts perspective. Probably very few realize that we spend more each year on cosmetics than we do on economic aid, twice as much on tobacco, over three times as much on liquor, and about nine times as much on tourism. Something would be wrong with our scale of values if we felt we could not also afford to assist other nations.

The persistent deficit in our balance of payments has provided the basis for a new argument against aid. Even though imports, military expenditures, investment abroad, and tourism also contribute to the deficit, aid has magnetized public attention. The argument is cloaked in the garments of international finance, with an urgent appeal to preserve the soundness of the dollar. It is a misleading and dangerous argument. It is vital that there be accurate understanding of this issue.

The argument is the essence of simplicity. It is in the form of a syllogism: our total deficit is $2.3 billion; economic aid accounts for $3.5 billion of debits; therefore, cut out economic aid and we shall be back in balance, with a net credit of $1.2 billion.

This argument is dangerous because it could lead a well-intentioned but apprehensive Congress and public down the garden path of international withdrawal.

It is misleading both in its analysis and in its prescription of remedy. Six facts are necessary to place this issue in proper prospective.

Fact No. 1. The net current dollar outflow from economic aid is not $3.5 billion. It is $1.1 billion, with the remaining expenditures for U.S. merchandise exports and services having no effect on dollar outflow.

Fact No. 2. The adverse effect of aid on the deficit has shown a distinct drop and will, from policies already in operation, continue to show a downward trend. In 1960 only one third of aid expenditures were in the form of U.S. goods and services. In 1960, 1961, and 1962 procurement became increasingly tied to U.S. exports. Today over four fifths of A.I.D. funds are committed to the export of U.S. goods, not dollars. The overwhelming part of the balance will be spent in less developed countries — not in the developed countries whose surpluses give rise to our deficit. This means that the $1.1 billion figure is now under $700 million and will soon be down to $500 million. This result is not wishful thinking; it has been built into procurement decisions already made.

Fact No. 3. A slash in aid funds, accordingly, will slash U.S. exports over 80 percent with a balance of payments savings of less than 20 percent. This means that a cut of $1 billion will cut exports by over $800 million and will net a balance of payments saving of something under $200 million. To put it concretely, if all aid loans to India and all of Latin America were stopped, we would have reduced our balance-of-payments deficit by under 8 percent.

Fact No. 4. Both in the short run and in the long run, there are further gains in the balance-of-payments picture not shown by present official statistics. In the short run, much of our "untied" aid funds will ultimately be spent in the United States. Much of our contributions to the United Nations, around 40 percent of the funds made available to developing countries generally, and 55 percent of the foreign exchange of

Latin America are finally spent for U.S. goods and services.[2]

In the long run, countries buy more as they prosper. Our exports to Western Europe more than doubled between 1953 and 1962; our exports to Japan tripled between 1950 and 1962. Even in countries currently receiving our aid, commercial exports thrive. A recent study of thirty-two countries outside of Latin America, receiving about 80 percent of all U.S. aid and surplus food assistance between 1957 and 1962, revealed that total imports from the United States rose about four and a half times as fast as economic aid.

Fact No. 5. Our total assets abroad have increased at a faster pace than the balance-of-payments deficit. President Kennedy, in his Special Message on the Balance of Payments, July 18, 1963, reported that at the end of 1962 U.S. assets, private and public, exceeded total liabilities to foreigners by $27 billion. Between 1946 and 1961, the net increase in U.S. total assets over sales of gold and foreign investment in the U.S. was over $20 billion.[3] This represents both long-term strength and a continuing increase in annual income from these assets.

Fact No. 6. The balance-of-payments deficit, stemming from a number of sources, is and should be attacked from many directions. Its solution will be a result of increased productivity and competitiveness of U.S. industry and labor, expanded export promotion, aggressive U.S. travel programs, tying of military as well as aid expenditures, the wise use of interest rate and tax policy, the promotion of foreign investment in the United States, and, as President Kennedy noted in his Special Message, strengthening the defenses of the international monetary system against raids on any major currency.

[2] The United States Balance of Payments in 1968, Waltar S. Salant and others. Washington, D.C.: The Brookings Institution, 1963, pp. 189, 190. The study prepared for the Joint Economic Committee of Congress, concludes that aid programs presently foreseeable will have "a nearly negligible net adverse effect" on the balance of payments.

[3] Balance of Payments Division, Dept. of Commerce.

Such a many-pronged approach is the only kind that will effectively solve this problem. Aid will make its contribution. To follow any other course would be a sign of bankruptcy in economic, fiscal, monetary, and political leadership.

As we have become more burden conscious than obligation or opportunity conscious, we have yielded to fears for our own continued economic strength. This fear stems from the assumption that in helping other nations diversify their agriculture and move toward industrialization, we shall be equipping them to compete with us on the world market — and at far lower labor costs.

For one who harbors this fear, it does not suffice to point out that over 600,000 U.S. workers are employed directly or indirectly because of the demand for goods financed by aid. He worries over long-range economics. But when we take inventory of our advantages by way of access to capital, research, technology, managerial skill, trained labor, and large domestic markets, fears for our overall economy ought to be quieted.

There is a more specific basis for confidence. It lies in the gradual increase in purchasing power on the part of the developing countries, which will create markets as well as competition. Indeed, the seeds of future markets are being sown wherever the equipment of an industrialized country is being used on a project. The mathematics of potential consumption are exciting. The free and developing world contains 1.4 billion people. Their average per capita income is $138 a year. If they were to reach a minimum growth rate per capita of 4 percent a year, five years would see an increase of $29.90 in that income. Total annual purchasing power would have increased by $41.9 billion. A computation of the import statistics for seventy-six free and developing countries shows an average import level for calendar year 1961 of 23.6 percent of GNP. This would mean that at the end of five years the annual demand for imports would have increased by $10 billion. The United States, as the world's largest trading nation, having almost one fifth (17 percent) share in world export trade would have increased its own exports to developing countries by $1.7 billion a year.

The key ingredients for the future of the U.S. economy are those which lifted us to the level of prosperity we now occupy — imagination, energy, productivity. We should not fear the kind of peaceful, interdependent, trading world we are trying to help create.

The False Option of Withdrawal

Undergirding all our self-doubts about the burden we carry and our ability to administer our programs effectively is the unspoken assumption that we have a reasonable alternative, that of complete or partial withdrawal from our assistance programs.

The extent to which frustrations, disillusion, and self-doubt have seized us is shown by the fact that the basic questions about aid are phrased in terms of continuing at the level of prior years or of phasing down. One would think that, with our resources increasing, with our experience and techniques maturing, and with the developing countries accelerating in their ability to use aid effectively, there would be voices in the land urging that we prepare to meet the enlarging requirements and opportunities, if we are to continue our privileged role of leadership in the age of development.

But no. The alternative is phrased in terms of cutting down on the number of countries, the amount of funds, the number of people abroad. Our basic attitude is that we can economize by phasing down. Seldom in the Congressional debates of 1963 or for that matter, in prior years, has the cost of withdrawal been faced.

Our frustrated desire to see European countries carry more of the burden has not been accompanied by any analysis of the hazard to our own objectives if we retrench out of pique. We are apparently willing to say to them, "You see? Our boat is sinking because you didn't plug the leak when we gave up."

Our weariness over our deep involvement in the Far East is never linked with a picture of a Peking hegemony stretching from Burma to Australia, if we were to cease being involved.

Our irritation over the long-standing Kashmir dispute does not leave room for contemplating the results of chaos and despair in India and Pakistan if we were to withdraw.

Our apprehensions over Pan-Arabism in the Middle East do not allow us to visualize that area where we would have no calling card except to tiny, isolated Israel.

Our desire to "let Europe have Africa" fails to raise, not to mention answer, the question of the impact on us of unilateral withdrawal from a strategic continent containing almost a third of the members of the United Nations.

Our impatience to see quick and dramatic social and economic change in Latin America leads us to a "do this or else" attitude that never stops to analyze the "else." The "else" could very well mean an incalculable and interminable expenditure of funds and energy to wholly defensive and containing purposes, to minimizing our loss rather than maximizing mutual gain.

Withdrawal or involvement are the options of small powers. There is no such thing as withdrawal for the United States, for it would be succeeded by forced involvement on terms not of our choosing . . . or the declining liberty and security of a leader who refused to lead.

*   *   *

Weak nations are those which can afford the luxury of noncommitment. The United States has long ago crossed the threshold of responsibility and leadership. It has done well — much better than it has cared to acknowledge. It has both learned and suffered through hard experience. It has profited by that experience. It has developed a dedicated and talented corps of key workers, effective organization and procedures. It need not be ashamed of the quality of its work abroad. But it is constantly striving to improve that quality.

It has borne its great burden of the past without undue sacrifice. Its sinews for peaceful international assistance are stronger today than ever before. Its prosperity has already reaped the fruit of past efforts.

The possibility of withdrawal is a mirage, lacking in substance. As Senator Vandenberg pointed out in that distant debate in 1948 on the Marshall Plan, "The greatest nation on earth either justifies or surrenders its leadership." That this spirit still lives was evident when President Kennedy, in his 1963 aid message, said:

> The United States — the richest and most powerful of all peoples, a nation committed to the independence of nations and to a better life for all peoples — can no more stand aside in this climactic age of decision than we can withdraw from the community of free nations.

CHAPTER 11

The Forces of Despair

VOICE OF THE CITIZEN: *It's time we stopped deluding ourselves. We can't hope to help all of the developing world. We're talking about almost one and a half billion people. The gap between their standard of living and ours is bound to increase, not decrease.*

Neither we nor our European allies have the resources to do the job. It is a bottomless pit. No matter how much aid we give, it doesn't even make up for the foreign exchange losses they suffer from trade. We take one step ahead and two steps backward.

If we think that these countries are going to develop in an orderly way, our eyes are going to be opened. The strains, tensions, and frustrations that these people will experience will result in nothing but chaos, tyranny, totalitarianism. The idea of democratic evolution is fine, but it just isn't going to happen.

To cap it all, there's the population explosion. How in the world can we expect a rising standard of living, when the underdeveloped world is hell-bent on doubling itself in the next couple of decades?

This is the voice of despair. It is a sophisticated voice, based on a candid, intellectual appraisal of the problems that lie ahead. It slices through much of the overoptimistic thinking that we once enjoyed about aid. It recognizes that we are not dealing with specific, time-limited goals. It is a new sophistication, one which deserves the most painstaking appraisal. For in its approach to realistic thinking, it sows the seeds of despair. It poses the three big questions for the age of development, which, indeed, it might label the age of frustration. They are these: Are there enough resources to make a difference? In an era of cataclysmic change, can we hold out any hope for the open society? Can there be any real progress in the face of the population explosion? Resources, process, people — must they give rise to despair?

The Widening Gap

The case for despair rests on simple arithmetic. In 1961 the free industrialized countries accounted for approximately 20 percent of the world's population, and 60 percent of its gross national product ($963 billion). The free and underdeveloped countries accounted for 46 percent of the population, and 12 percent of the gross national product ($189 billion). The average per capita GNP for the peoples of the developing countries was $138. That for the people of the United States was $2823; for Europe, $1079.[1]

Even assuming a steady and substantial increase in rate of growth and a static population, the inescapable fact is that the gap between the rich and poor nations will widen for the foreseeable future. After all, 2 percent of $2823 is $56.46 while 2 percent of $138 is only $2.76. At the same rate of growth, a year's per capita increase in U.S. gross national product would be twenty times that in the developing countries. Even if the United States were to creep forward at a 1 percent rate, with

[1] These figures represent the dollar equivalents of national currencies using official exchange rates in most cases and, in some cases, effective rates. They do not take into account the variations in the purchasing power of the dollar among the countries. Figures are based on AID Statistics and Reports Division, "Estimates of Gross National Product, Calendar Year 1961, in Current Market Prices (Dollar Equivalents)," April 30, 1963.

the developing countries racing ahead at a 5 percent rate, the per capita increase in the United States would be four times that in the developing countries. To a lesser extent the same dynamics of disparity would apply between Western Europe and the developing countries.

This arithmetic should have the effect of reinforcing our determination to increase both the quality and the quantity of our assistance. To despair of making progress in the face of the widening gap is to miss several crucial points.

First, our objective, and that of other industrialized countries, for the foreseeable future, cannot be to eliminate the differences in standards of living. Our objective is a much more modest and realizable one — to help other countries reach the point where they can generate continued satisfactory growth from their own resources, from trade, from private investment, and from loans based on their creditworthiness. This is the stage of self-sustaining growth, where external aid is no longer necessary to insure continued rapid development. Japan is a dramatic case in point. And yet its official gross national product per capita is only $502, half the level of Western Europe and one fifth that of the United States.

The prophets of despair also overlook the effect of progress and motion. Their analysis tends to rest on static facts, to be wholly materialistic. For example, they will measure progress by so many more bicycles or theater seats per hundred people. By this yardstick, progress will be agonizingly slow. But what they overlook is the resurgence of confidence and hope as people begin to see schools, roads, irrigation ditches, dams, laws, organized markets. And so another realistic objective is to bring about and sustain this sense of forward motion, even in countries which have a long road to travel before they can be called self-sustaining.

Another antidote to despair is a look at what has been taking place — at a time when development was only beginning to emerge as an objective of policy, when resources were scattered and uncertain, where knowledge and techniques were haphazard, and when skilled personnel were few and far between. The fact is that many different kinds of countries have developed impressively even in the gray dawn of the age of development.

It is true that Europe possessed abundant human resources and institutions. Yet the Marshall Plan achievements defied the plausible prophecies of the skeptics and constituted an unparalleled feat of rebuilding nations at forced draft. So did Japan, a classic case not only of recovery but of rapid revitalization. In a sense, these experiences unlocked the door to realizable aspiration and taught that large thoughts were sometimes the most practical ones.

Taiwan and Israel are harder to discount. True, massive external resources were made available to determined and skilled populations. But in both cases the physical resources were so meager as to cast a dense cloud of uncertainty over the future. Who, a decade ago, would have predicted that the 1960's would see both nations throbbing with dynamism, nearing the point of self-sufficiency? Yet Taiwan and Israel have, for a decade, maintained an annual per capita GNP growth rate of 4.2 percent and 7.4 percent respectively.[2]

Greece, in danger of its independent political life only a decade and a half ago, has shown a capacity for growth, largely from its own resources, that brings it within reach of economic independence. Malaya, with British help for both survival and growth, responded dramatically and is today a sound economy, the keystone of a Malaysia devoted to its own independence.

A partial roll call of nations which have managed to sustain a per capita GNP growth rate of over 1.5 percent a year for at least five years includes the following countries:

[2] These and following growth rate figures are based on A.I.D. testimony before the Subcommittee on Foreign Operations, Committee on Appropriations, House of Representatives. *Hearings,* 1963, p. 5358.

5 to 8% – Greece, Yugoslavia, Israel

4 to 5% – Republic of China (Taiwan), Jordan, Venezuela, Ethiopia

3 to 4% – Jamaica, Liberia, Spain

2 to 3% – Burma, Philippines, Thailand, Iran, Turkey, Brazil, Nicaragua, Panama

1.5 to 2% – India, Bolivia, Colombia, Costa Rica, Ecuador, Guatemala, Mexico, and, within the past several years, Pakistan

Here, in short, are twenty-six countries, accounting for 65 percent of the developing world — almost a billion people — which have sustained measurable progress for a substantial period of time. This is not merely national progress. This is progress on a per capita basis, taking into account the growth in population.

All of these nations have started their forward movement. Some are at or beyond midstream in moving toward their own economic independence. Some are very close to being self-sustaining. We and other industrialized nations do not start from scratch in helping these countries. They have plans, administrative ability, and a determination strengthened by the progress they have already seen. Our task is to help sustain and accelerate the momentum.

There are other countries only now emerging from tribal economics. Still others require internal financial discipline before real progress can take place. The spectrum of development is a broad one. But this fact is clear: the task is a practicable one. It is longer for some than for others, but it is not endless. The catalogue of countries is not one of despair but of realistic hope.

As we survey the long list of developing countries, their increasing populations, the point from which they commence their development efforts, we fall prey to despair over the magnitude of the task. As we peer into the developing world, we tend to see it as a bottomless pit.

In fact, however, the gap between the need and the supply of capital aid is not a discouraging one. In attempting to measure the size of this gap, one proceeds at his peril. Indeed, much more analytical work needs to be done on the long-term capital needs of developing countries. But such projections as have been made indicate that the need is well within the capacity of free world nations to respond.

Professor Rosenstein-Rodan, in a 1961 study, estimated the need for capital aid for three five-year periods beginning in 1961, if realistic rates of growth were to be realized.[3] His estimate for the first five-year period, 1961–1966, was an annual figure of $4.3 billion, which excluded technical assistance, food, and strategically motivated kinds of aid. Under this limited definition, the United States is already at a level in excess of $2 billion a year, with her other partners approaching this figure. While it is already apparent that even Rosenstein-Rodan's estimates have been outrun by increasing needs, the conclusion is still valid that the industrialized West has the resources to meet the needs of those countries equipped through planning and economic discipline to put them to good use.

In 1962, Paul Hoffman, Managing Director of the United Nations Special Fund, made this computation of the capital needs for all developing countries, for the decade of the sixties, based on an average 5 percent increase of gross national product per year, and a 3 percent average increase in GNP per capita:[4]

Total imports	$440 billion
Total earnings	378
Excess of imports over earnings	62

[3] *The Emerging Nations,* ed. Max F. Millikan and Donald L. M. Blackmer. Boston: Little, Brown & Co., 1961.
[4] *World Without Want.* New York: Harper & Row, 1962, pp. 100–131.

Add: debt service and transportation	8
Total capital need	70
Aid already received, 1960–1962	14
Balance needed 1963–1969	56
Aid at current rate, 1963–1969	35
Balance to be met through further aid and private investment	21
Private investment expected	7
Balance to be met through additional aid for 7 year period	14

In other words, the "resource gap" to be filled by all the developed world would be only $2 billion a year. Others estimate a much larger need, particularly toward the end of the decade when the capacity to use capital productivity will have substantially increased. Even more ambitious estimates, however, are not beyond the reach of the developing capacity of the industrialized nations of the free world.

The free world's gross national product was almost $1000 billion in 1961. By 1963 it probably approached $1200 billion. For several years a wide, although unofficial view has been held that the nations of Western Europe, Canada, Japan, and the United States should aim for a goal of 1 percent of their GNP to be allocated to economic aid. This would be $12 billion a year, or twice as much as the current levels. Even an average of three-fourths of 1 percent would yield $9 billion, a 50 percent increase in free world aid. These same countries have, in the Organization for Economic Cooperation and Development, to which they belong, pledged themselves to work toward a goal of a 50 percent increase in GNP in the decade of the sixties. Should they achieve this goal, their combined GNP would approach $1500 billion. A 1 percent aid contribution would then be $15 billion a year, or two and one half times the present levels.

Clearly, there is no cause for despair because of lack of material resources.

There is a final footnote that should be added to this discussion of the resources that will be realistically required. It concerns the terms of trade, the relationship of prices or goods exported by the developing countries to the prices of goods exported by the developed countries. The blanket assertion is frequently made — by critics of aid and by spokesmen of the developing countries — that the balance is so adverse to the developing countries, which chiefly produce primary products, that all the benefits of aid have been wiped out.

Since the time of the Korean War, when the supply of primary commodities was such as to keep prices relatively high, the terms of trade have indeed deteriorated for the developing countries. In the late 1950's, prices of their products on the world markets decreased, while the prices of manufactured goods increased. The twofold result was that developed countries paid less for their imports from developing countries while the latter paid more for manufactured goods.

In a particular country, or group of countries, a decline in the world price of a specific commodity can go far to offset or even exceed the amount of external aid. For example, a drop in the price of coffee of one cent a pound can cost fifteen Latin American countries $50 million in foreign exchange.

But it is not true to say that adverse movement in the terms of trade has "wiped out" aid. If we choose a recent year, 1958, when raw material prices were neither at boom or bust levels, and assume that the price relationship of that year applied to

1961, we can approximate the magnitude of the net disadvantage. The industrialized countries would have paid, roughly, almost $1 billion more for their imports from developing countries and would have received some $200 million less for their exports to them. This means that the "gains" of the developed countries through the dual movement of the terms of trade were about $1.2 billion.[5]

In that same year, the official flow of aid to developing countries from Western Europe, the United States, Canada, and Japan amounted to almost $6 billion.[6] The effect of the terms of trade, therefore, was to diminish by one fifth the net transfer of resources accomplished by aid. In 1960, the gains to the developed countries, computed on the same basis, were about $600 million, while total official free world aid was $4.9 billion. In that year, the terms of trade offset the flow of aid by one eighth.

Terms of trade adverse to developing countries, therefore, while an impediment to development, are not by any means an equal and counterbalancing force.

The future ought to see a steady and substantial increase in free world aid resources, perhaps doubling the present level within this decade. On the other hand, it is not unrealistic to assume that the effect of adverse terms of trade will be minimized through the greater diversification of production and exports which development should bring.

This issue, therefore, is real and serious. But, like all the others in the age of development, it is not one which is completely insoluble. It is not a cause for despair.

[5] This approximation is based on an analysis by the Office of International Resources, Bureau of Economic Affairs, Department of State, March 22, 1963, using available data from the United Nations.

[6] *Development Assistance Efforts and Policies in 1961*, Report by the Chairman of the Development Assistance Committee on the Annual Review, Organization for Economic Cooperation and Development, September 1962, Table 1, p. 17.

The Chaos of Development

Another overshadowing cloud in the age of development is the prospect of such cultural shock, uprooting of tradition, and frustration at the slow pace of visible progress that anything approaching political democracy will be wishful thinking. The cascading impatience of the poor, the overcrowding of cities, the lack of employment for the newly educated, the dearth of administrative skills may well see resort to autocracy in many forms.

Realism requires that we face the fact that, as new, under-manned, inexperienced nations strain to live up to the demands of their peoples, many experiments will be made. Some will resemble sailboats at the start of a race, tacking to starboard or port, before gauging the wind and settling down to a steady course. We have already seen this happen in Africa. If only the West wind blows steadily, we need have no fear as to the long-run course which will be chosen.

Essential to an attitude of steadiness, however, is the realiza-tion that what is important is substance, not form. We can hardly expect that some eighty nations will pliantly accept at the outset all of our bill of rights, our system of checks and balances, popular representation, multiple political parties, free-dom of speech and assembly, the paramount rule of law, trial by jury, and religious tolerance. We must expect twistings and turnings. What we should steadily seek to encourage is a movement toward the freedoms of an open society, where con-test of ideas, of people, of parties becomes increasingly possi-ble.

While recognizing the volatility of political conditions in any developing country, the record to date is reassuring rather than depressing. A.I.D. Administrator Bell, in testifying before the House Committee on Foreign Affairs[7] made a perceptive and significant statement. He selected for discussion the performance of the 40 countries which had received the largest amounts of U.S. aid for development purposes since 1945. Of these countries, 14 were no longer dependent on external assistance and 10 had shown both satisfactory growth and progress in limiting or reducing their dependence on aid.

"In virtually all of the twenty-four countries . . ." he said, "democratic institutions have been strengthened or less democratic regimes liberalized." Of all forty countries, he said, "Although the possibility of economic progress leading to political backsliding cannot be ruled out, there is no clear case of this phenomenon among the countries to which we have extended substantial amounts of development assistance. The relationship is overwhelmingly in the other direction." He was careful to add, "There are a great many countries in which conditions remain unsatisfactory or in which conditions could worsen in the future."

But of one conclusion he was sure. It was ". . . that while there is no guarantee that improved political institutions will follow in any automatic way, it seems clear that without economic progress the chances for strengthening democratic processes in the less developed countries would be greatly diminished."

In some of the lands where tradition has governed for centuries, new forces are at work. The Shah of Iran stakes his leadership on land reform. President Ayub Khan of Pakistan presides over the creation of a new and more liberal constitution. King Mohammad Zahir of Afghanistan works for constitutional and electoral law changes to widen public participation in government. India holds the largest free election the world has ever seen.

[7] Foreign Assistance Act of 1963, *Hearings* before the Committee on Foreign Affairs, House of Representatives, 88th Congress, First Session on H.R. 5490, April 23, 1963, pp. 188, 193.

This is not the whole picture. Coerciveness remains in many places. African leaders are on the whole insecure in their position and in their ability to meet their problems effectively, but a surprisingly large number of them give promise of constructive, imaginative, and tolerant leadership.

The Population Problem

One of the darkest clouds overhanging the age of development is politely referred to as the population problem, or, more stridently, the population explosion. Historian Arnold Toynbee minces no words in saying that "we have been rabbit-like in our unplanned breeding of ourselves." [8] At the presently probable rates, the world's population of 3 billion will more than double by the year 2000, reaching about 7 billion. At the present rate of increase of 2 percent, the world's population will be 150 billion within two centuries. In the next fifteen years another billion people will be added — the same figure which it took the world all the millennia until 1830 to reach. During the second half of this century the developing countries alone will increase in population more than the increase of all mankind throughout all time — up to the present. [9]

A graph of world population projections portrays one of the simplest and most ominous of trajectories. After two millennia of nearly horizontal motion, it now, in the closing years of the twentieth century, points skyward like the great intercontinental missile which it really is. For population growth is a worldwide phenomenon. At present rates the United States will contain a billion people in one more century. Even if we halve our present rate, we shall be a nation of 416 million in another century. [10]

---

[8] Speech to World Food Congress, June 5, 1963.
[9] *The Population Dilemma*, ed. Philip M. Hauser, The American Assembly, Columbia University. Englewood Cliffs, N.J.: Prentice-Hall, Inc., 1963, p. 3.
[10] Ibid., p. 4.

As to the developing areas, the haunting question is: What is the point of striving to increase aid from all advanced countries to a figure of $10 or $15 billion by the end of the decade if shortly after that there are an added 500 million people? This question understandably paralyzes action. The danger is that in sounding the alarm, tensions and burdens of overpopulation are so portrayed as to throw doubt on the wisdom of any aid so long as the problem is not solved.

To strike a balance of sober and determined realism in the face of this problem — avoiding both Pollyanna optimism and enervating defeatism — is perhaps the most difficult task confronting the developed world in this century.

Realism compels a recognition that continued increase in developing populations is inevitable for years and decades to come. But it also requires a clear understanding that there is still time to take action to avoid regression in the living levels of the population of the world. What is done, or what is not done, in the next quarter century will be of crucial importance in answering the question: Has mankind the ability to prevent itself from being its own worst enemy?

The fact that there is time to act should itself galvanize action. The dynamics of development is today temporarily outpacing the dynamics of demography in most of the populous places on earth. As for the adequacy of natural resources, raw materials, and food, Joseph L. Fisher and Neal Potter look ahead to the year 2000 and conclude that living levels in most developing countries will increase despite population gains and that the chances for "take-off" in a number of countries will not be prevented by resource shortages.[11]

But this note of reassurance is only to say there is time in which to work — to perfect research, communicate knowledge, induce motivation, and launch effective programs. The long-run effect of continued birth rates at existing levels on the prospects of development has been pointed up by comparing

[11] Ibid., ch. 6 ("Resources in the United States and the World"), pp. 120, 121.

per capita income in a country where such rates continued for the next fifty years with that in a country which achieved a 50 percent reduction in fertility within twenty-five years. In addition to the short-run gains from reduction of child dependency, higher levels of investment, and more productive uses of investment, the latter country would enjoy a 40 percent additional gain in per capita income in thirty years, 100 percent in sixty years, and 500 percent in one hundred fifty years. Even postponing reduction by thirty years would add 64 percent to the ultimate population.[12]

Such a goal — 50 percent reduction in twenty-five years — is not beyond aspiration. Even though governmental programs promoting fertility control have not existed long enough to produce reliable data, there have been successful experiments. In Singur, India, relatively untrained personnel, using simple means, reduced the birthrate in the experimental area 15 percent in four years. In Ceylon, a Swedish effort, a more concentrated one involving a more literate population, reduced the birthrate in experimental villages by one third. The National Academy of Sciences reports results of 5 to 10 percent reduction in other tested communities.[13]

That a climate of concern has been building up is indicated by activities on many fronts. There are the governmental efforts of such countries as Japan, Korea, India, Pakistan, the United Arab Republic, Turkey, and Tunisia. There are other countries in which pilot projects are under way — Free China, Jamaica, Ceylon, and the United States, particularly Puerto Rico.

The United Nations took a significant step on December 18, 1962, with a 69-nation vote in the General Assembly for a resolution recognizing the relation between population growth and economic development, and requesting that the U.N. take

[12] Ibid., ch. 4 ("Population and Economic Development"), Ansley J. Coale, p. 68.
[13] *The Growth of World Population*. Washington, D.C.: Publication 1091, National Academy of Sciences — National Research Council, 1963, p. 13.

steps to provide assistance on population problems. Other
U.N. initiatives are the Asian Population Conference in 1963
and the second World Population Conference in 1965.

United States policy became more explicit during the Seven-
teenth Session (1962–63) of the U.N. General Assembly with
the statement that the United States will help other countries,
on request, "to find potential sources of information and assistance on ways and means of dealing with population problems."
On April 24, 1963, President Kennedy stated that the United
States "certainly could support" increased research in fertility
and human reproduction and make the results "available to the
world so that everyone can make their own judgment." Subse-
quently the United States announced a grant of $500,000 to
the World Health Organization for such research. Already,
however, as shown by a report of the National Institutes of
Health, the federal government was financing over half of the
known research on fertility control by U.S. public and private
agencies.

As for the Roman Catholic Church, long dedicated to almost
total condemnation of birth control, it is in the throes of what
New York Times reporter George Barratt described as "a profound ferment," with increased debate and a wide divergence
of views and attitudes on philosophy, research, methods, and
community approaches.[14] Professor Frank Lorimer comments
on the fact that the emphasis placed by the Catholic Church
on periodic continence stemmed from scientific discoveries made
less than forty years ago. After considering the possibility that
other discoveries might offer a basis for the development of
principles facilitating "the rational regulation of births," he
concludes that it would be "rash to assume that this will happen." But, he adds, while Catholic doctrine may well remain
unchanged, "there can, however, and quite probably will be,

[14] "Catholics and Birth Control," a series of four articles by George Barratt in
the *New York Times*: August 5, 1963, pp. 1, 12; August 6, 1963, pp. 1, 16;
August 7, 1963, pp. 1, 18; August 8, 1963, pp. 1, 12.

significant changes in *emphasis* and in *political action* in this field." [15]

While this climate of concern is becoming steadily more distinct and pervasive, optimism is being expressed over the possibilities of discovering reliable, suitable, and inexpensive methods of fertility regulation. The National Academy of Sciences cites four methods "of great promise." [16] Top officials of the Population Council write that ". . . the prospects are excellent for obtaining much more suitable methods than were formerly available." [17]

But there is some danger that more aggressive action will be suspended until social consensus and scientific knowledge have made further advances. What is not recognized is that much work, vital to any substantial success in the next quarter century, can be done outside the field of sensitivity or controversy.

Research, already on the increase, must be accelerated. As Professor Lorimer aptly puts it, research in population problems is just as strategically important as atomic research in military affairs. Field tests in a wider variety of country situations must be conducted. Development planning must no longer blandly ignore programs aiming at a reduction in the rate of population growth.

Finally — and most important because of the size, complexity, and lead time implicit in the task — is the urgency of developing the organizational structure which will be necessary to carry out any program, utilizing any method, profiting from the experience of any research and field experiment. As Messrs. Notestein, Kirk, and Segal observe:

> Before any of the underdeveloped countries can effectively spread the practice of family limitation, they must have reason-

[15] *The Population Dilemma,* ch. 8 ("Issues of Population Policy"), p. 157. (Italics are author's.)

[16] *The Growth of World Population.*

[17] *The Population Dilemma,* ch. 7 ("The Problem of Population Control"), Frank W. Notestein, Dudley Kirk, and Sheldon Segal, p. 142.

ably well-developed services in maternal and child health, health education, and community development. Work in these areas is not sensitive but does require a great deal of organization, training, and equipment. Once such work is established it will be much easier for the governments involved to introduce their own services in the field of birth control.[18]

Today, increasing numbers of nations are coming to see the crucial relation between their population increases and their chances in the long run for achieving a better life for their people. Economic and social development are in themselves conditioners of population trends.

Increased hope, wider opportunity for compensated work, better education, more varied and active community activity, and increased urbanization tend to slow down the rate of population growth. As the need diminishes for children to serve as day laborers to supplement the subsistence of the family, and as the prospects for fruitful lives increase, much of the rationale for large families disappears. Evidence of this cause-effect relationship exists in the history of the industrialized countries of Western Europe and Japan. It also exists within some of the more prospering areas in developing countries. The National Academy of Sciences states[19] ". . . every country that has changed from a predominantly rural agrarian society to a predominantly industrial urban society and has extended public education to near-universality, at least at the primary school level, has had a major reduction in birth and death rates . . ."

But nations now realize that they cannot wait for this kind of population adjustment. They know that if they wait, their chances of attaining sustained development are dimmed. And so they seek guidance for more positive action.

To sum up, the threat of unbridled increase in population becomes less of a threat to the extent that there is awareness

[18] Ibid., ch. 7 ("The Problem of Population Control"), p. 140.
[19] *The Growth of World Population*. Washington, D.C.: Publication 1091, National Academy of Sciences, National Research Council, 1963, p. 13.

of its existence. The past few years have seen the beginning of this awareness. The constructive response to this threat is to realize that development efforts cannot wait upon demographic solutions and that fertility restraint cannot await the full tide of development. Both are part of the modernization process and progress in both areas must proceed together. To despair of meeting the threat effectively is no more rational than to cease trying for reasonable arms controls because of the knowledge that other powers also possess the supreme weapon. But time is exceedingly precious. Each day and each year of delay compound the burdens all must some day carry.

*　　*　　*

The problems of the age of development are not small ones. They have often been underestimated and glossed over. But this is a far cry from saying that we should despair — should be without hope.

What is important is movement, sufficient movement toward a better life to give courage and hope to each generation that those following will have a substantially better life. Resources are not the bottleneck. The critical factor is the ability to use resources wisely.

There will be drastic upheavals as old ways are abandoned for new. The path of progress will not be routine or predictable. But even now there has been enough experience to give confidence that human values will not long suffer in the march toward dignity.

The critical question, looming over the entire scene, is whether the peoples of the world will take timely action to restrain the ominous trend in population growth. But here again, the present ferment of thought, research, experiment, and opinion gives promise of mankind's ability to forestall the statistician's projections. The remedy is action, not despair.

CHAPTER 12

An Investment Philosophy

WHAT IS THE basic transaction? This question is seldom asked. We concern ourselves at great length with the purpose of aid, its principles, methods, and tactics. We clothe our thinking with a set of conflicting attitudes ranging from excessive optimism to abject defeatism. But we have not paused long enough to think through what kind of an activity aid really is. We have not developed a way of looking at aid that at once makes sense, is realistic, and serves our basic purposes.

Much frustration and discontent stem from the tacit assumption that aid is either a gift or a purchase. If it is a gift, we expect gratitude. If it is a purchase, we want to see what we have bought. When we see neither gracious acknowledgment of our generosity nor an inventory of results purchased, our faith, will, and self-respect are deeply wounded.

In many governmental activities, the basic transaction is one of purchase. We are buying something we can see and use, whether it be so many troops, aircraft, or missiles; miles of highways, numbers of dams, breakwaters, and irrigation projects; numbers of school rooms, hospital beds; or money for underwriting farm and home mortgages. We are buying subsidy payments for farmers, maintenance of parks, and all kinds of services — customs, tax collection, law enforcement, social work, postal services and regulation of major economic activities. We are buying payments to veterans and their families, grants in aid to states, and interest payments on the national debt.

Sometimes what we buy with our tax dollars is not so tangible. When we appropriate monies for education, we are buying visible facilities — but our act is partially one of faith that more widely spread and better education will produce better citizens. We know that not all the young people produced at the far end of the educational pipeline will be good and useful citizens, but the effort is clearly worthwhile.

The same act of faith is made when we commit billions of dollars to all kinds of research. We know when we make these commitments that missiles will misfire, that new drugs will prove unusable, that diseases will continue to resist cure. But we have the conviction that enough valuable results will flow from research to justify the expenditure. And we reject out of hand the alternative of abandoning it and drawing on our intellectual capital until it is exhausted.

In such vital areas we are accustomed to act not so much as purchasers buying a commodity that we can immediately see, feel, test, and use. We act like investors who are willing to risk funds in the hope of future good. We deliberately choose to sacrifice current consumption for future welfare. We take a measured look at the alternatives open to us, weighing the certainties of nonaction against the uncertainties of acting. And we elect to take the risk.

This trait comes close to the heart of our tradition. Those intrepid souls who settled the shores of the North American continent weighed their alternatives: comfort, predictability, and oppressions, against hardship, hazard, and freedoms. As their descendants pushed westward across the Alleghenies, they were staking all on an uncertain future. Then followed generations who built communities, industries, and the great institutions of the land — all the product of measuring present certainty against future possibilities, all the product of a risk-taking, investment-minded people.

This nation was built not by those who would purchase what

the present offered but by those who invested in what the future could yield.

Aid is like this. It is far more of an investment, risk-taking venture than a simple purchase transaction. The distinction is vital to both its understanding and its success. So long as aid is judged in terms of purchase, it shall be doomed to distorted justifications, excessive expectations, and the frustrations of apparent failure. This is true whether the purchase is seen as buying friends, buying votes, buying popularity, or even buying instant democracy and instant development.

The investment nature of the aid-giving process is the committing of limited resources, where knowledge is less than perfect, with limited power to influence events, and where the results are not wholly predictable. This is the classic condition in which any investor finds himself. To the extent that the future is predictable, the transaction becomes less of an investment and more of a purchase. Just as the investment spectrum runs from low interest government bonds where payment is predictable to highly speculative, highly uncertain stocks, so does the aid investment encompass a wide variety of risks. Some countries have demonstrated a solid record of political, social, and economic growth. Others have almost no record at all as a basis for predicting. Still others have a record of violence, disorder, and economic stagnation. But in all the risk component is high, at least in the short run.

The portfolio of risks embraced by aid operations resembles a mutual fund or an investment trust, composed of securities of varying nature. There is the investment in a country's military and economic strength devoted to resisting external aggression or internal subversion. There is the investment in strategic facilities, this being more of an immediate purchase of privileges than an investment. Sometimes there is simply the buying of time, which, despite criticism, can be a most precious commodity and sometimes a vital solvent. Often there is the long term investment in economic and social progress. Finally, when we contribute to the United Nations and its programs we are investing in an institution devoted to preserving peace, protecting sovereign nations, and advancing social and economic growth. Unlike an investor with a highly specialized interest or with a narrow purpose, we cannot pick and choose from only one kind of security. The interest of the United States encompasses all. We realize that investing in the long run development of Nigeria might well prove fruitless if West Africa were in flames, that a few islands of development in Latin America would not long exist in a sea of economic chaos and political upheaval.

The investor approach to aid is not only to be distinguished from that of a purchaser. It is also to be separated in our thinking from that of a speculator. A speculator picks some sensational risks and, when he has made all the profit or has sustained all the losses he dares, liquidates his investment and looks elsewhere. An investor, particularly an investor interested in a widely varied portfolio of growth stocks, remains involved. He is not overly disturbed by fluctuations in the market of some of his securities. He knows that not all will consistently maintain an upward trend. He does not panic. He has invested for a long term.

This psychology is essential in assisting many nations at various stages of development. New nations will be unstable and uncertain. They will have economic reverses and political changes of course. There will be instances of waste, poor planning, and misuse of funds. These phenomena are not always confined to the politically mature and economically advanced nations. To act like a speculator, fingering his ticker tape, determining our aid relationship on the basis of the trends of the moment is to sell short both ourselves and the developing countries.

This means that we should not react in haste or panic, by

terminating aid if a country engages in a flirtation with Communist aid or trade, if its ministers make anti-western statements, if they cast a rash vote in the U.N. We, as a long range investor in development in freedom, should be deliberate and measured in our judgments. When one of our stocks has gone sour, we should not abandon our whole portfolio. A growth investor has time on his side.

All of this does not mean that we should persist blindly and stubbornly in maintaining investments in all of the countries we seek to help. The purpose of the investment is long range development. Should some countries indicate by consistent performance that they are not equally dedicated to this objective, we should be prepared to withdraw — not over an event, a statement, or a passing mood, but over a sustained absence of commitment. We should stand for, and be seen to stand for, development. If our investment proves to be profitless, to us and to the receiving country, we owe it to our general objectives to divert our resources elsewhere.

The steady view of a long-range, growth stock investor is peculiarly appropriate to the entire field of foreign policy and its large subdivision, aid. In this field, victories and defeats are both transient and ephemeral. There is no possibility of closing the covers of the book of our relations with a country and saying "This is finished. This is a success story." New problems, new strains and crises constantly come to the fore. If a victory has been won in foreign affairs, talking about it erodes its effect. The silent victories are often the most enduring. In matters of aid, accomplishments in economic development can be undermined by the same kind of crises to which we ourselves are subject. The political weathervane is even more subject to the winds of opinion. If we can view, therefore, the accomplishments and setbacks in our efforts to help other nations as a steady investor views good and bad days in the market, we shall greatly have advanced our ability to succeed in our policy.

So far the thought has been advanced that aid is an invest-ment, not a simple purchase or an in-and-out speculation. The key elements are a wide variety of risks held steadily, but not inflexibly, over a long period of time. The question remains: Is the investment a reasonable one?

This question raises the bed-rock issues faced by every in-vestor. He must first settle the fundamental issue which divides him and other men. This is whether it is better to forego some current use of resources in favor of a future return, even though that return is subject to some risks. He must then settle the secondary issue — what is the best course to follow?

Both issues raise the question of alternatives. At this point investment in aid takes on a different coloration from the choices posed to an ordinary investor. For the ordinary investor always has the choice, as did the cautious steward in the Parable of the Talents, of not using his money lest any be wasted.

That is not the choice confronting the United States. Our major choices are:

1. We can carry on a broad-based assistance program on the principle that we are interested in the security and develop-ment efforts of all nations firmly committed to their own in-dependence.

2. We can confine our efforts to countries around the Sino-Soviet fringe struggling to retain their political independence.

3. We can confine our efforts to a few significant and promis-ing leaders in development efforts.

4. We can make our aid frankly a short-term political instru-ment to exact concessions, actions, and votes which would be currently desirable.

5. We can confine our aid to Latin America.

6. We can adopt any combination of 2, 3, 4, and 5.

7. We can channel all our aid through the United Nations.

8. We can withdraw totally from all forms of aid.

The first possibility is the present basis of U.S. aid policy.

Even though it is the broadest in scope and the most ambitious in its objective, the amount being invested — a relevant fact for any investor — is about .7 of 1 percent of our gross national product. In other words, the current postponement of consumption is not excessively sacrificial. As the other possible courses of action are considered, involving smaller amounts, the key question is whether the current savings are worth the ultimate sacrifice.

Confining aid to the most harassed area of the Cold War would "save" perhaps a fourth of our cost, while taking us effectively out of Latin America, Africa, and the Middle East. We would still be spending at a substantial rate, but only for the crises of today. Tomorrow's would be left to ripen on the vine.

If we were highly "selective" and picked only a few leaders in development, the Far East, most of Africa, Latin America, and the Middle East would be left to shift for themselves. We would "save" perhaps one fifth of our aid budget, at the expense of depriving ourselves of influence in the very nations where little aid goes a long way.

If our aid were placed on a short-term power politics basis, everything we did would be suspect; the price of favors would rise; a body blow would have been dealt those who are pledged to development; and our total aid cost might very well not fall. We would have institutionalized international blackmail. Our basis of assistance would be what helps us in the short run, not what helps all in the long run. In the interest of being "political," we would have made a naive and disastrous political miscalculation.

Were we to confine aid only to Latin America, the Far East would be a tantalizing vacuum for Red China. India, Pakistan, and all of South Asia would have no alternative to vastly increased dependence on Communist sources of assistance. The Middle East would follow suit, and Africa would divide its relations between Europe and the Communist world. In such a world not even Latin America, no matter how highly favored, would remain as a junior partner of a nation which deliberately withdrew its leadership to an isolated hemisphere.

To the extent specific purposes are combined, the possibility of dramatic savings is curtailed. Indeed, the combination of aid to countries struggling for existence, the most promising developing countries, Latin America, and some aid for "political" objectives is almost a description of the coverage of the present program. What is left out is a minor amount of very useful assistance distributed among some forty-five countries.

As for channeling all aid through the United Nations, this is not a realistic alternative. About 3 percent of our present aid budget goes to the United Nations, where our contribution to the Special Fund and Technical Assistance Program is 40 percent of the total. It is inconceivable that the other nations would, in effect, multiply their contributions forty times so that all of our present economic aid ($3 billion) would not exceed 40 percent of the total, or that the United States could conscientiously become the 97 percent underwriter of U.N. economic activities.

Finally, the alternative of complete abandonment of aid is not a real one, unless we are willing to abandon the world, lock our gate, and let posterity take care of itself.

With this view of the alternatives, the United States faces an easier decision than most investors. It is as if an individual whose income was $20,000 a year, and rising, were asked to contribute $140 (.07 percent — the ratio of aid to GNP) to help make his community a safe, decent, progressive place for his children. The difference is that even without his contribution the community would probably get along — or the children could go elsewhere. But the chances of the world developing in free patterns without the United States are nil . . . and there is nowhere else to go.

The gain from the prudent investment of modest amounts is so significant over the next two decades, and the loss from inadequate response so incalculable and irreparable, that the investment analogy breaks down. There is only one rational decision. But, having made that decision, the attitudes of investment are ones that can sustain us — taking risks, accepting unpredictability, persevering in the face of temporary reverses, and enduring through time to the ultimate objective, with confidence that there are no acceptable alternatives.

*   *   *

Each day the New York and American Stock Exchanges report a trading of five to six million shares of stock, a billion and a quarter shares a year. Almost 200 Mutual Funds are regularly traded over the counter. The economic health of the United States rests in large part on the taking of risks — by individuals, companies, and institutions. We have led the world in the variety of forms for taking risks. Ours is the largest risk-taking population in the world. In our scale of values we esteem a healthy gambling on the future far more than excessive prudence in preserving the accumulations of the past. The recluse with cash in his socks or in the vault is a pitiable eccentric. It is this willingness to take risks and to bet on the uncontrollable, unknowable, but exciting future that we need to transfer to our thinking about aid.

If we can bring this heritage to our relations with the developing peoples of the world, we shall have attained realism in our attitudes. And we shall have laid the foundation for the most fruitful investment of our time.

PART V

A Sense of Confidence

So far, we have looked inward. We have dealt with what has happened in the United States as it has carried out aid programs over the years and with the broad, intellectual, and subjective areas of national purpose and attitudes. For the most part, what has happened elsewhere in the world has been a muted background theme, even though as persistent and controlling as the four dramatic notes of Beethoven's Fifth Symphony.

It is now time for this theme to be dominant. For it is not enough to look on the present as a critical opportunity to exercise a creative sense of history, to gain a clearer vision of our purpose, or to accept new attitudes. We are only part of a quadratic equation. The developing countries themselves — their resources, competence, leadership, and will — are the dominant factor. In addition, there are two forces which we in our insularity often overlook: the assistance efforts of the Communist world and those of the industrialized countries of the free world.

All three areas are relevant to what we do and how we look at what we do. All three have a bearing on our confidence. Confidence is undermined so long as we assume that developing countries are making no real progress, that Communist aid efforts are infinitely superior to ours, or that our free world partners are shirking their responsibilities.

A look at the world in perspective — at the efforts of developing countries, at the increasing commitment of our industrialized partners, and at the problems faced by Communist aid efforts — should lead to a sense of confidence.

CHAPTER 13

The Striving World

HOW CAN PROGRESS in building nations be measured? Aid officials, the Congress, and the public hunger for assurance of achievements. This hunger has gone unappeased partly because of a seemingly chronic inability to tell effectively what aid has accomplished. But the larger reason lies in the difficulty in measuring the infinitely complex process of national development in an ever-changing world.

How, after all, would one measure "progress" in the United States over a decade? If there were some omniscient international referee charged with the duty of grading our progress, he would have all kinds of income, investment, employment, and consumption data. But in the realm of social progress, how would he rate us? What weight would he give to race discrimination, urban slums, juvenile delinquency, educational inequality? As he viewed our state legislatures, our city party machines, the quality of our political campaigning, our reluctance to reorganize voting districts, our resistance to rules reform in Congress, what rank would we receive for "political development"?

It is not easy to measure progress in nation building at any stage. The difficulties of measurement are compounded when we seek to establish yardsticks for fourscore nations differing in starting points, human skills, raw materials, cultural backgrounds, problems and opportunities.

One approach is to collect "success stories" — the saving of millions from starvation; winning mankind's war against smallpox, yellow fever, and malaria; improving the productivity of tens of millions of acres of land; multiplying the numbers of schools and teachers; establishing banks, savings and loan associations, credit unions, cooperatives; training leaders for development work in thousands of villages; harnessing the power of great rivers.

More of this is needed. The achievements of thousands of skilled field workers in thousands of projects over two decades constitute an unprecedented and monumental contribution to the welfare of other peoples.

But this is not enough. A compilation of good works would have been an adequate response in the earlier days of our evolving aid programs, when we sought through Point IV "to help the free peoples of the world, through their own efforts to produce more food, more clothing, more materials for housing, and more mechanical power to lighten their burdens." These specific aims were capable of specific measurement. Now, however, we aim to achieve these goals, not as ends in themselves, but as the inevitable by-products of nations which can use their resources wisely and fairly.

The root cause of our unsatisfied quest for proof of accomplishment, therefore, lies in the scope of our goal. It is not just to help people. It is not just to achieve impressive growth rates. It is to help build good citizen-nations. How does one measure progress toward such a goal?

Until better gauges of progress are available, the best measurement of achievement is not quantitative, but qualitative. It looks not alone to the houses built, the jobs created, the teachers trained with aid funds. It looks also to the condition of striving by the developing countries themselves. For if aid at best is marginal, if the real prospect for development lies in the will and intelligence of the nations being helped, the basis for confidence in the future is the evidence of national energy and determination. The key to development is self-help. The key to self-help is the hard decision that costs a government popularity, that invokes opposition, that demands skill and courage.

This is a limited but revealing standard. But it has meaning for us who know the difficulties and delays of passing legislation which imposes or shifts burdens. Measured against this standard of striving, what is the record of the developing world?

The spectrum of striving is a broad one. Some countries have only just begun; some are in midstream, with gathering momentum; others, after a brave start, have had reverses; still others have broken through the most formidable barriers, have compiled a record of sustained success, and are within sight of their goal. The course of development for any nation, particularly in the short run, defies confident prediction. Nation building does not follow mathematical projections. A military coup, a balance of payments crisis, a runaway inflation, a series of provocative adventures by political leaders, a popular uprising can, in a day or a month, set back what had been the most promising efforts. At any given time there are enough such crises around the globe to cast a pall over the prospects of all.

What is important, therefore, is the perspective of time. Even though the age of development is still in its morning years, there is impressive evidence of successful striving in the areas where external assistance had had time to come to fruition — in the Middle East, South Asia, and the Far East.

India and Pakistan together contain almost 600 million people. Here are concentrated dual efforts of development in freedom unprecedented in history.

In its first decade of development, India's national income rose 42 percent; despite a population increase of 21 percent, its per capital income rose 16 percent, industrial production rose 94 percent and agricultural production 41 percent. Its percentage of young people in schools increased 85 percent. Faced by the twin demands of defence and development, it called on its people last year for over half a billion dollars in increased taxes and other levies. Although India began with a per capita income among the lowest in the world, its goal is to be independent of external assistance by the end of its fifth five-year plan in 1975.

For U.S. aid, this is a most dramatic "bargain." Until 1956 it amounted to only $75 million a year or less than twenty cents a person. Even now with a level of roughly $500 million a year, our aid is but a little over $1 per person. It is only 2.2 percent of India's gross national product, and only 10 percent of its gross investment. But its critical importance is shown by the fact that it is approximately half of India's inflow of foreign capital. Contributions in food from the United States have amounted to about half of our assistance, while accounting for 90 percent of India's supply of grain. It is not too fanciful to say that without the wheat farmer of the U.S. midwest, the Asian sub-continent would not have had the peace, freedom, or energy to develop.

Today over half of the free world's external aid for India's development comes from other countries and international financial institutions.

Pakistan presents a similar pattern of determination and progress. During the first half of its second Five-Year Plan Period (1960–1965), agricultural output increased by 7 percent and industrial production by 13 percent. Foreign exchange earnings rose by 16 percent. From 1959 to 1961 per capita GNP rose from $69 to $75, an increase of almost 9 percent. It too has increased its taxes by over $100 million and restricted nonessential imports.

In the Middle East, Greece, by 1961, had managed to achieve a level of investment of 24 percent of its gross national product. Turkey, now giving overdue attention to fiscal and other reforms, is the object of a multi-nation joint effort.

Lebanon, now a prospering nation, no longer receives U.S. aid. Israel, benefited by U.S. aid, private donations, and reparations, has so wisely used these resources that it has maintained a per capita growth rate of 7.4 percent for a decade, a total GNP growth rate of 10 percent a year, exceeding that of Japan and West Germany. This nation will soon be able to finance its further development from its own resources and normal world capital markets.

In the Far East, progress has been sustained the most in the island nations which have not had to cope with the instability of bleeding borders. Japan is now a developed country, with its own expanding aid programs. The Philippines, having achieved internal political stability, is on the verge of such prospects for development that it is attracting increasing amounts of private investment. It could, with the benefit of steady leadership and sound policies, become self-sustaining within a relatively short period of time.

The Republic of China on Formosa is one of the outstanding case histories of success. Scarcely a decade ago, it was the barren refuge for the Chinese people who had fled to freedom; today it is a thriving and dynamic economy with bright prospects for the future. It has adopted liberal investment laws, a unitary exchange rate, and established a stock market. Its gross national product per person has increased 13 percent in three years. Its growth rate is now a bustling 7.5 percent, with agriculture growing at 4 percent and industry at 10 to 12 percent a year. Its investment is at the high rate of 22 percent of gross national product. Despite an authoritarian rule, social benefits are real; literacy is 90 percent, while 85 percent of its farmers own their land.

These countries are the leaders in development efforts. There are others where the record of accomplishment and the prospects for the future are far less bright. But their experience, covering a significant proportion of the developing world, provides a solid and encouraging core of achievement. Africa and Latin America are continents new to sustained development efforts and sizeable amounts of external aid. In assessing these efforts, we are denied the perspective of time. It is perhaps too early to speak of the permanent accomplishments of specific nations. But it is not too early to point to a record of serious striving that augurs well for the future.

The continent of the newest nations, Africa, has already, in the infancy of independence, begun to write its record of striving.

Algeria has increased taxes and cut the salaries of government employees. Ethiopia, with a new tax law, doubled its revenues in four years. Ghana has adopted an austerity budget and increased taxes. Liberia now has a minimum wage law. Nigeria, with a vastly improved development plan, has cut government salaries, reduced subsidies, broadened its tax base, and restricted non-essential imports. Tunisia has restricted such imports and achieved a balanced operations budget.

The record of some eighteen countries in Tropical Africa analyzed by the Agency for International Development reveals twelve countries which have adopted development plans, twelve which have created new credit facilities since 1960, eleven with new investment codes, nine which have effected budget reforms and eleven which have realized tax reforms.

In the drama that is Africa today, the leadership potential ought not to be underestimated. The caliber of African leadership and the depth of genuine nationalism have been the rocks on which Communist aid efforts have foundered. The deep commitment of African peoples and their leaders to the task of building their own nations is the best assurance for the staying power of free world assistance.

Africa faces many travails, many experiments, many forms of repression as well as increasing freedoms, many regressions as well as advances, frustrations as well as successes. Anti-colonialism still has cause to be a rallying cry. Communist China is already stepping up aid, trade, and cultural activities. Trade

terms will be a major cause for united demands. But resources are rich; the markets and the major effective sources
of aid are in the free world; leadership is not lacking; and the
springs of freedom are deep. With steadfastness and sensitivity,
we have every reason to attack with confidence the task of helping brighten this continent.

Finally, we come to this hemisphere and Latin America.
Here judgment is made difficult because nations are old, well
established, with many of the attributes of modern industrialized society. We tend instinctively to feel that such nations,
so endowed, ought easily to make rapid and steady progress. It
has been difficult for us to grasp the magnitude of the problems
of making basic institutional changes, responding to broad social needs, imposing administrative, fiscal and monetary discipline, and adhering to constitutional processes in societies
where other values and other ways have been ingrained for
centuries. Such problems, in their way, are as difficult as those
facing more primitive nations whose tasks are largely to create
rather than to change.

The Alliance for Progress is not yet three years old. This is
only another way of saying that organized efforts in pursuit of
a comprehensive set of objectives are new in Latin America.
Because there is so much to do, it is easy to believe that nothing
has been done. Because this volatile continent, in the throes of
underlying social, economic, and political change, constantly
exhibits one or more nations in crisis, it is easy to lose sight of
the record of constructive striving which has already been written.

For all its twistings and turnings, its coups and its conflicts,
Latin America, within an incredibly short period of time, has
become a continent set in purposive motion.

The Charter of Punta del Este did more than pledge an Alliance for Progress. It did more than establish a partnership
among the American Republics. It polarized the abundant

energies of Latin America, working with the United States, toward "accelerated economic progress and broader social justice within the framework of personal dignity and political liberty." Its three keystones are economic and social development, economic integration, and increase in export revenues. Planning and action in all three areas are intertwined. Development planning now aims not only for economic productivity and social benefits but the wider goals of regional integration and the diversification of products for exports.

Much of this is still concept and aspiration. And yet this channeling of energies is one of the real, if intangible, achievements in Latin America. There are also harder, if narrower, facts. The crisp, dry figures mask concrete acts of discipline, sacrifice, and risk, which reveal the underlying commitment of the overwhelming majority of the countries of Latin America. These, therefore, are a measure of performance, not promise. It is a record of difficult decisions that rivals that of many a developed country in a similar period.

We begin with the countries which have already made dramatic progress in development. Mexico, having put into effect a series of tax reforms, saw its tax receipts increase by 12 percent between 1961 and 1962 and distributed 8.5 million acres of land to small farmers. Venezuela increased its receipts from income taxes by 30 percent in 1962, cut the salaries of top civil service employees by 10 percent, and, by the end of 1962, had distributed land to over 56,000 settlers, and enlarged its incentives for private investors. The newly independent countries of Jamaica and Trinidad-Tobago, not yet signatories to the Alliance for Progress, have both made significant progress in planning, tax reform, and in expanding incentives for private investment.

Colombia and Chile, while facing monetary and balance-of-payments problems, have the resources, the administrative potential, and the professional planning to enlist the active assistance efforts not only of the United States but of the World Bank and of Europe. They are prime developmental targets. Colombia, starting with a progressive tax system, increased its income tax declarations in 1961 and 1962 by nearly 20 percent, devalued its currency, and gained approval by leaders of both political parties for a tax bill which would increase its revenues by $80 million a year. Chile, in addition to reforms in public administration, created a tax institute, rewrote its tax laws, increased its revenues from tax reforms by $42 million in 1963, passed an Agrarian Reform Law and accepted the fiscal and monetary restraints contained in a stand-by agreement with the International Monetary Fund.

El Salvador, with a 7 percent growth rate, and many significant pieces of social legislation to its credit, has overcome its balance of payments crisis and increased its income tax revenues 40 percent. Costa Rica has increased its revenues 12 percent, passed agrarian legislation, and realized an elevenfold increase in investment after new incentives became law. Ecuador has made a start on a career civil service system, enacted a new fiscal code, strengthened its reserve position, and extended incentives to new industry. Panama — favorably situated, and enjoying a high (8 percent) growth rate — has increased its income tax collections 40 percent and created an Agrarian Reform Commission to prepare resettlement projects. Uruguay — with per capita gross national product of $450 — increased its revenues by 20 percent, distributed land to over 15,000 persons, and has extended incentives to new industry. These are all countries where a basis for optimism exists.

Two highly significant countries, with great potential, are Brazil and Argentina. They alone contain almost half of the people in Latin America. Brazil itself, the India of the continent, with one third of its people, is still an agonizing question mark. Although its growth rate has been consistently high, it is plagued with inflation. It has moved to broaden its tax base, increase tax levies, and raise shipping and railroad rates, but the major task of stabilization still lies ahead. Argentina, through increased taxes and tightened enforcement, expects to increase its revenues 15 percent, and has reduced federal employment by almost 25 percent.

Nicaragua, with a new administration on record in favor of Alliance reforms, passed an Agrarian Reform Law which includes power to tax idle land, to designate land for redistribution, to finance housing, schools, and cooperatives, and to administer agricultural credit. Bolivia, plagued by Communist obstructionism, has nevertheless maintained a good growth rate (2.5 percent GNP per capita in 1961 and 1962), has initiated a government reorganization, is adopting a consolidated budget, has increased its tax and customs collections, the latter by 35 percent, and passed incentive legislation for private investment. In Paraguay, for the first time in many years, an opposition party participated in a national election, and with 7 percent of the vote, occupied the one third of the seats in Congress reserved for the opposition. Income tax receipts increased by 30 percent in 1962 and title to almost half a million acres was turned over to 8600 squatters.

Tax reform, tightened administration, land distribution, reduction in governmental salaries and employment, incentives for private investment, currency devaluation — these are not paper measures. Every one of these issues was hard fought. Every one was hard to propose, hard to vote for, hard to accept. But each is proof of dedication to the idea of development.

Political upheaval, social unrest, Communist subversion, coups and military juntas are still all too much a part of Latin America. As we strive to induce a deeper respect for constitutional processes, we see that the ancient pattern of violent overthrow and authoritarian rule has been forced to yield to change. The past decade has seen a withering away of the old style one-man regime bent on self perpetuation. Juntas are no longer respectable means for accomplishing political change. They are a sign of abnormality, not business as usual. They are forced to move toward re-establishment of constitutional government. In Argentina and Peru, the military takeovers in 1962 were in fact succeeded by duly elected presidents. And in Venezuela, where constitutionality faced one of its most critical tests, 95 percent of the people braved massive terrorist opposition to cast their ballots. The record leaves much to be desired. But, viewing the sweep of history from the vantage point of a decade or more, one can be cautiously optimistic. The tide of progress, even political progress, is a rising one; like all tides, it comes in with individual waves that sometimes advance and sometimes recede.

There is another way to look at Latin America. It is to review the forces at work, all of them being catalyzed by our aid relationship but being outside of it. Here in a sense is the profile of progress in Latin America today.

The most strategically placed are the official leaders. While not all are dedicated to the Alliance, a growing number are. This is evident in the sober attention being given to serious planning, with seven countries having submitted their development plans for Alliance scrutiny, and nearly all working on such programs. It is impressively demonstrated by the fact that no fewer than eleven countries have launched major tax reforms and at least ten countries have started programs of agrarian reform. Finally there is a growing determination of Latin American leaders, sparked by former Presidents Kubitschek of Brazil and Lleras Camargo of Colombia, to play an increasing role in the direction of the Alliance. Meeting in São Paulo in the fall of 1963, representatives of the American republics agreed to form the Inter-American Committee for the Alliance for Progress to supply this direction. In every country there are younger leaders, businessmen, professors, economists, labor leaders, who are economically, socially and politically aware, concerned, and determined.

A second significant force in Latin America is the Catholic

Church. Most of the hierarchy has supported the Alliance for Progress. In thousands of villages the Church is lending its prestige to the building of roads, schools, clinics, often using its own resources, often administering, as do other organizations, large scale distribution of U.S. agricultural commodities. From the pulpit comes the social gospel; from the parish study, counsels for orderly but quickening progress. An example was the statement by the National Council of the Bishops of Brazil, on May 1, 1963, which spoke in some detail of the need for broad based education and orderly agrarian, business, tax, administrative, and electoral reforms. Another example was a similar pastoral letter issued by the Catholic clergy in Chile.

A third group is private investors — local, United States, European, and Japanese. The current legend has it that capital goes only one way — out. "Capital flight" has become one of the features of a psychology of defeatism. Few stop to question so accepted a wisdom. It is true that any capital flight drains an economy of strength and that there is still too much of an outflow for the job that has to be done. But the basis for growing confidence exists in such facts as these:

– In 1962, if we exclude the repatriation of earnings from the oil companies of Venezuela, there was a net capital inflow of $159 million, with net inflows being registered in eight of twelve major countries.[1]

– The new inflow is largely concentrated in manufacturing, rather than traditional extractive industries. Growth in U.S. manufacturing production in Latin America in 1961 reached a sensational 18 percent.[2]

– U.S. investment, generated from past earnings in Latin America, is at a higher level than usually recognized. Including net capital flow to Latin America, reinvested earn-

[1] Department of Commerce, Office of Business Economics, data from reports as of April 1, 1963.

[2] This and the following material is taken from *Latin America: A Positive View*, VISION, Inc., May 1963.

ings, expenditures for depletion, depreciation, amortization and other plant retirement, the total U.S. business contribution in 1961 was $1 billion, a sum equal to all assistance loans and grants from the United States in that year.

– New U.S. investment, despite "flight" psychology, has quietly made progress. Ford in Brazil and Venezuela, Bethlehem Steel in Chile, Caterpillar in Brazil, J. I. Case (tractors) in Argentina, Phelps Dodge, Sears, and Westinghouse in Central America are some of the new starts or expansions. U.S. Banks have recently expanded in several countries.

– Other investors have not been idle. Germany's Latin American investments have doubled in three years, are five times its investments in Africa, and seven times those in Asia. In 1962 they increased 27 percent, mostly in Brazil and Argentina. Steel works, copper refining, and Volkswagen are prominent. Japan's investments, about $400 million, are growing by almost 25 percent a year.

These are not the winds of oratory; they are the fruits of decision based on confidence despite all the uncertainties.

Another tangible basis for confidence is the regional institutions that are already in existence in Latin America. Five nations — Costa Rica, El Salvador, Guatemala, Honduras, and Nicaragua — comprising twelve million people, have established the Central America Free Trade Area. Intercountry trade barriers have been eliminated on 95 percent of the items in the tariff lists. Obliged to establish a common external tariff by June of 1966, the member nations have completed the tariff schedule on 90 percent of the items. Even by 1962 trade within the area increased by 35 percent. A Central American Bank for Economic Integration is already in existence. Our aid has helped, together with a $2 million capital contribution from each member country. A Central American Clearing House is handling 60 percent of all intercountry financial transactions. Common fiscal and monetary policies are contemplated as well as an overall plan for regional development to be financed by a regional tax. The five national universities are working toward a regional system, fostering specialization without duplication.

A more ambitious Latin America Free Trade Association comprises Mexico and eight South American countries with 80 percent of the continent's population and product. In 1962 its intraregional trade increased 20 percent, with Mexico's exports jumping 112 percent, Argentina's 39 percent, and Peru's 60 percent. Shipping between Mexico and Brazil increased eighteen times in one year.

One cannot yet talk in terms of permanent "accomplishments" in any Latin American country. But one can talk of the process of accomplishing in almost all of the countries.

Perhaps the best basis for long-range confidence in Latin America lies in reflecting that more effective force has been brought to bear on social, economic, and even political development in 1000 days than in 500 years.

*   *   *

This is a record of striving. It is not a complete record. It is not a final record. Reverses will occur. But it is a record of hard decisions. It is good, measurable evidence of the willingness of the developing countries to impose discipline on themselves. There are many gaps and the problems are immense. But a basis for confidence exists in every region of the world, in terms of past experience, present efforts, and future potential. We do ourselves a grave disservice if we deny ourselves this sense of confidence.

CHAPTER 14

Allies in Aid

ONE OF THE sources of corrosion of confidence is our picture of the United States as a tiring Atlas, alone shouldering the burdens of an immense globe. Our reservoir of goodwill is drained by the suspicion that we, who have done so much for so many, are being exploited. Why don't others share the burden?

In our quest for the springs which can refresh both confidence and determination, we do not have far to travel — if we but look at that part of the world we have helped make strong. As the age of development unfolds, other nations which are both free and advanced possess a potential of critical significance.

A look at the global balance sheet is revealing. In 1961 the gross product of the Communist world was roughly $418 billion, or one fourth of the world's total. That of the free and advanced countries of Western Europe, Oceania, Canada, and Japan was roughly $430 billion, or over one fourth of the world's total.[1] The United States alone, in 1961, reached a gross national product of $519 billion or one third of the world's total. Today it is approaching $600 billion. Together, the United States and other free industrialized nations account for an annual product of almost a trillion dollars and 60 percent of the world's total — almost two and one half times the material wealth of the Communist world.

[1] Source of Bloc figures; Bureau of Intelligence and Research, Department of State; source of free world figures, Statistics and Reports Division, Agency for International Development.

The resurgence of Western Europe and Japan, and their continuing high rates of growth are miracles of the post-War world.
They have become familiar facts to every citizen. Within the
past several years the maneuverings centering about the Common Market have become common talk in the remotest
county seat in the United States. Amazement at post-war recovery and growth have yielded to apprehension over competition, the issues posed by trade and tariff policies, and differences in defense strategy. Although we have become increasingly Europe-conscious in such matters, we have been largely
oblivious to what other free nations have done and are doing in
the aid field.

In our concern over our own assistance programs and problems, our view of the rest of the free and industrialized world
has been at best fragmentary. It has been hard for us to imagine
nations in dire need of help little more than a decade ago doing
anything worth noting in the assistance field. In our preoccupation we have overlooked one of the historic developments of
the past few years: the emergence of a substantial and serious
free world assistance movement.

The word "movement" is appropriate. It describes not a
haphazard series of assistance gestures to a few former colonies,
but a growing consensus that assistance to developing countries
is an essential instrument of modern foreign policy.

It is ironic that at the very time when consensus is threatened
at home, it is on the rise in the community of free nations.

The evidence lies in the widening fraternity of aid officials
in all developed countries, in the diversity of international institutions of aid, in the increasing size of aid from outside the
United States, in the improving quality of aid, in the numbers
of workers abroad, in more effective coordination, and in the
range of assistance from private sources.

Plus ça change . . . A source of continuing amazement to
the U.S. aid official, Senator, or Congressman, as he visits the

capitals of Western Europe, Japan, Canada, and even Australia and New Zealand, is the recurrence of a familiar pattern. Everywhere he sees bureaus, boards, offices, corporations, services, even cabinet ministries, and Agencies for International Development administering aid programs. He talks with officials who specialize in capital loans, in technical assistance, in investment guaranties, and even in equity financing.

He reads, with nostalgia, accounts of parliamentary hearings, inquiries, and debates on aid. If he is a U.S. aid official, he nurses a grudging envy of the parliamentary system which allowed one major country, in 1962, to confine its total annual aid debate to a mere two hours — during the dinner period. He reads of aid financing a gold bed for an African dignitary, and is relieved to know that, for once, U.S. aid was not the culprit. He sees the same unbroken succession of heads of state and finance ministers from developing countries bent on winding up their visit with a communiqué announcing "frank and full discussion on problems of mutual concern" . . . and an aid commitment.

National Aid Organizations

During 1962 alone, at least five countries established new organizational entities for administering assistance. Norway has created its own Agency for International Development and has levied a separate development assistance tax. Denmark has mounted a national fund-raising campaign for technical assistance, with the government matching the funds raised. The United Kingdom, France, Belgium, and the Netherlands, long accustomed to overseas colonial assistance, have radically adapted their policies and procedures to the era of independence. Germany, Italy, Japan, and Canada, without colonial continuity, have nevertheless established aid programs and bureaucracies. Germany has recognized this function with a cabinet ministry and is supporting programs in some forty countries.

The International Institutions of Aid

In addition to the individual countries, there are the international institutions which engage in aid activities. The broadest in membership is the United Nations — with its Special Fund to help nations make surveys of resources and projects; its Technical Assistance Program carried out by all its agencies in such fields as health (World Health Organization — WHO), education (United Nations Educational, Social, and Cultural Organization — UNESCO), and agriculture (Food and Agriculture Organization — FAO); the World Bank (International Bank for Rehabilitation and Development — IBRD) which makes "hard" development loans, and its subsidiary, the International Development Association (IDA), which makes "soft" development loans.

Then there are regional international aid organizations. The European Economic Community (the Common Market) is halfway between a nation and a region. Even though its member countries have aid programs of their own, it has established its own Overseas Development Fund with three quarters of a billion dollars to be spent, largely in Africa, within a five year period.

The Colombo Plan Organization includes countries of the Pacific and South and Southeast Asia, Australia, New Zealand, Canada, the United States, and the United Kingdom — both developed and developing nations. This is not so much an operating entity — except for a small technical assistance program — as it is an annual forum for an exchange of views on common problems, and a device for the better planning and administration of aid.

The Alliance for Progress, a partnership agreement involving the United States and nineteen other American Republics, also has its institutions. Under the sponsorship of the Organization of American States, development planning is both aided and assessed by a Panel of Experts. The Inter-American Development Bank, financed by both the United States and the other Republics, is engaged in development lending in accordance with the basic principles of the Alliance.

Finally, there is a unique organization of countries in Western Europe, Canada, the United States, and Japan dedicated to the increased quantity, quality, and coordination of assistance. It is the Development Assistance Committee (DAC) of the Organization for Economic Cooperation and Development.[2] This Committee does not have funds of its own but it seeks to influence the level and the use of the funds of its members. Originating in 1960, it is the concrete evidence of the will of Western Europe and Japan that the time had come to join hands with Canada and the United States in the serious business of helping less privileged nations develop in freedom. In a sense, this is the ultimate achievement of the Marshall Plan. The very countries which were thought to be lost causes in that remote Senate debate of 1948 have now banded together for a task immeasurably greater.

The Size of Aid

The DAC nations account for well over 90 percent of free world aid — both bilateral and multilateral. Since 1956, their official aid to developing countries has almost doubled. During 1961 and 1962, it had reached the level of about six billion dollars

[2] The Organization for Economic Cooperation and Development, with headquarters in Paris, arose out of the earlier Organization for European Economic Cooperation, which was Europe's response to the planning requirements of the Marshall Plan. With Canada and the United States now being members, it provides a forum for policy discussions on trade, monetary and fiscal policy, as well as aid.

a year. This compares with an estimated Sino-Soviet Bloc disbursement of about $450 million in 1962.

Of the free world aid total, the United States contributed $3.6 billion, and our allies in aid, $2.4 billion. This ratio is exactly 60:40. So is the ratio of gross national product: 60 percent for the U.S., 40 percent for our DAC partners.

Is the burden being shared fairly? The answer is, "No, not yet." On the surface it may seem so. By 1961, the other nations were contributing in official aid expenditures an average of about .71 percent of their gross national product. The figure for the United States was .66 percent. Since 1956, we had increased our level by 71 percent, while they had increased 112 percent. France is currently supporting aid programs at a level over twice that of ours in terms of per capita percent of gross national product. The United Kingdom, Portugal, and Belgium are also carrying higher per capita burdens.

This picture, however, is not a complete one. The United States is paying about 9 percent of its gross national product for defense. The average for our industrialized partners is about 5 percent. And yet our defense expenditures are for free world security as well as our own. Therefore it cannot yet be said that the free world has struck a fair balance of total burden.

But there is one other factor which complicates the analysis. It is the level of the standard of living. In the United States, in 1961, the per capita income was $2823 a year. In the DAC countries of Western Europe the average, $1200, is 43 percent of this amount. How far can one go in applying percentages? If a citizen of the United States, earning $2823 a year, pays $273 for defense and aid, and a European, earning $1200, pays $69, how are their respective burdens measured? The graduated income tax recognizes that one's level of wealth is a factor to be taken into account in attempting a fair distribution of burden.

Still another way of looking at the burden of assistance is in the form of surplus agricultural commodities. In fiscal year

1962, Food for Peace shipments reached a record figure of $1.6 billion, while the total funds expended for other kinds of development assistance amounted to $1.8 billion. In other words, almost half of what we properly call "aid" was surplus food — tremendously valuable to the receiver but not outstandingly sacrificial for a nation fighting the problem of farm surpluses.

All of this does not argue for accepting the current levels of aid from other countries as satisfactory. Clearly they have not reached that point. The long-term upward trend, interrupted in only two of the past seven years, should continue. But self-righteous fingerpointing is neither a persuasive nor constructive way of helping organize the wealth and diversity of the free world to live up to its obligations and opportunities in the fateful years ahead.

The Quality of Aid

Total figures on the flow of aid do not reveal the wide variations in the helpfulness of assistance. "Aid," as it has been used in the computations of the Development Assistance Committee, includes governmental grants of funds or food, official loans for periods of over five years, and contributions to international agencies. This umbrella definition would include, at the extremes, a six year loan repayable in hard currencies at 6 percent interest, as well as an outright grant. The question, therefore, "What kind of aid?" is fully as important as "How much?"

Only recently has the quality of aid been faced as a vital issue. The staff of the World Bank has dredged up the disturbing fact that the external debt of thirty-two developing countries more than doubled in the six years between 1956 and 1962. Some nations have reached the danger point where their ability to continue to pay back their loans and interest is in question.

Continued development can take place only if the debt-servicing capacity of developing countries is not strained beyond the breaking point. This fact is gradually being recognized. The profile of the quality of aid is showing substantial — and quickening — improvement.

Already, two thirds of free world aid places no burden on debt-servicing capacity, being in the form of grants or of loans not requiring payment in foreign exchange. This proportion holds true also for the United States. Although the United States has taken the lead in making its dollar repayable loans on very liberal (up to 40 years) terms, what is easily overlooked is the high proportion of grants made by other countries. For example, Belgium, France, Canada, the Netherlands, Norway, and the Common Market's Development Fund made three fourths of their 1962 aid commitments in the forms of grants. The United Kingdom provides over half its aid in grants. Germany, Italy, and Japan, however, are long on loans, short on grants.

There has recently been encouraging movement toward realistic interest rates and longer periods for repayment. In 1961 over 70 percent of DAC country loans carried a rate of 5 percent or more; in 1962, only 40 percent carried such high rates. Loans for twenty years or more rose from one third in 1961 to over one half in 1962. While both results were heavily influenced by U.S. liberal development loan policies, Germany, Japan, Italy, and the United Kingdom have moved toward reducing interest rates, lengthening repayment periods, or both. Much more progress needs to be made, and the Development Assistance Committee has already, through a working party, a report, and a formal resolution, begun to attack the problem.

Aid through People

Funds and food account for most of the money value of "aid." The transfer of skills and the building of institutions — em-

braced by the bland label of "technical assistance" — account
for 10 percent of the total bilateral aid flow, or about $600
million. But these are the funds which finance people to work
in developing countries, to transmit what they know, to leave
behind them, when they depart, trained teachers, administrators, and other specialists; new ways of cultivating fields, taking
censuses, keeping accounts, and planning for development; and
new laws, cooperatives, credit unions, banks, trade unions, housing institutes, schools and hospitals.

The Communist countries maintain over 11,000 experts in
some thirty developing countries. The nations who are members of DAC maintain 60,000. The Communist countries sponsor the studies abroad of 15,000 students. The DAC countries
officially sponsor some 40,000 students and trainees, with 100,-
000 more under the auspices of non-governmental institutions.

In terms of the involvement of people abroad, the United
States is clearly a minority partner. Even if the 5000 volunteers
in the Peace Corps are added to the U.S. total, United States
representatives are only one seventh of the 70,000 field personnel
working on development assistance.

The variety of institutions, training, languages, and experts
offered by this collection of resources is and can increasingly
be a solid foundation for confidence in removing the roadblocks
to development.

Aid Coordination

A measure of the serious and deepening involvement of other
free nations in aid activities lies in the attention now being
given to the coordination of aid. The question is no longer:
Why don't other nations help? It is: How can the efforts of all
these nations go forward without overlap and duplication?

Some observers long for the neatness and simplicity of one
superorganization to administer all aid. Most agree, however,

that while nations will hopefully increase their support of the United Nations, and the World Bank, they will continue to insist on their own bilateral aid programs and relationships with other countries.

The Development Assistance Committee has been the pragmatic response to the need to increase the level, the quality, and the coordination of free world aid. It is not an operating unit with decision-making power, funds, or a huge bureaucracy. It is like a three-way electric socket: a way of exchanging information, plans, and experience among the aid-giving countries; a way of bringing together developing and industrialized countries to engage in either general background discussions or to make detailed decisions to join in a collective assistance effort; and finally, it is a way of linking officials representing national programs with officials representing the great international development institutions — the World Bank, the International Development Association, and the Inter-American Development Bank.

This committee is not, however, merely a forum for talk. Each year all member nations subject themselves to a critical examination of their own aid programs. Through these Annual Reviews and through studies and reports on such questions as interest rates, periods of repayment, restrictive procurement policies ("tied aid"), the programming of aid, and technical assistance, the committee is slowly building standards for effective free world aid. It has initiated both discussion and working groups on such diverse areas as Latin America, the Far East, and East Africa.

The peak of coordination is reached when many nations unite in a common effort directed to support a large and significant project, such as development of the Indus Basin, or the development of a particular country, such as India, Pakistan, Greece, or Turkey. Such efforts or consortia are organized either under the leadership of the World Bank, as in the case of India and Pakistan, or with its cooperation and backstopping.

When this happens, there is a powerful joining of the financial resources of a number of nations and of the international lending institutions, and the skills of many analysts and experts, both national and international. The result is a carefully worked out multi-year program of grants, soft loans, harder loans, and commodities, all furnished by individual nations and institutions, but within a framework of amounts, timing, and conditions understood by all. In such cases, the free world demonstrates its ability to mobilize itself for a specific purpose.

Here again the reservoir of skills and material resources of the free and industrialized nations learning constantly how to work better together is both incalculable and unrivaled.

Allies in Mufti

In meeting the demands of the age of development, the free world possesses other resources than its financial ability, its skilled people, its national and international organizations. It has a vast army in mufti. It consists of entrepreneurs — those willing to take a risk in industry, finance, and commerce. It also consists of nongovernmental enterprise running through the entire fabric of modern society: universities, foundations, labor unions, cooperatives, credit unions, savings and loan associations, philanthropic and religious organizations, trade and professional groups.

In pursuing our purpose of helping bring about development within the framework of an open society, we are immeasurably supported by the immensely diversified products of the world's most successful open societies.

In material terms alone, the net flow of private capital from DAC countries to the developing world amounts to about two and one half billion dollars a year — five and one half times the flow of resources from the Communist countries. The flow of physical resources from other nongovernmental groups has not yet been estimated, but must be of a magnitude of hundreds of millions of dollars.

In nonmaterial terms, the total impact of the knowledge, techniques, and attitudes of the allies in mufti cannot be measured. They are the environment of freedom.

*   *   *

As we complete this survey of our allies in aid, some things lend themselves to measurement. Comparisons of the free and the Communist worlds lead to a set of ratios.

In comparing the two worlds, these are the ratios:

	Free World	Communist World
GNP	2.5	1
Official aid	13	1
Aid plus private capital	19	1
Purchases of exports from developing countries	14	1
Experts working in developing countries	7	1
Students and trainees from developing countries	9	1

What cannot be measured is the quality of free world assistance, actual and potential. The improvement of national programs, the constant and increasing exchange of views, the continuing search for common standards, the resources and experience of the international institutions, the broader and deeper involvement of private and nongovernmental enterprise — all are the raw materials for a sense of confidence.

But they are only raw materials. There is no victory in ratios, no achievement in mere potentials. Strength and opportunity must be realized, seized, and acted upon if the promise is to become fact.

CHAPTER 15

View from the Kremlin

The socialist commonwealth . . . renders the liberated countries steadily expanding economic aid, the importance of which is determined by its nature and in conformity with the tasks of the contemporary stage of the national liberation struggle. If imperialist loans serve the cause of colonial expansion and enslavement of underdeveloped countries, socialist aid is called upon — and therein lies its principal significance — to promote the economic liberation of the Asian, African, and Latin American countries from the bonds of foreign monopolist capital . . .

Excerpts from two-page spread on Soviet aid
Pravda, August 7, 1963

IN AN era of restraint in the use of arms, aid will increasingly become a principal instrument of policy. Military forces are no longer the chessmen of international affairs. Words alone are hollow. Aid has emerged on the modern scene as an inevitable instrument serving the policy of great and not-so-great powers. We may dispute this fact. The Communist countries do not.

In the issue of *Pravda* cited above, aid as an instrument for "the destruction of imperialism" is proudly described, both in its purpose and in its application in many countries. Ironically, the thrust of the issue was aimed at the Chinese Communists as the foremost critics of Soviet aid.

For too long a time we have looked at Communist aid through a glass darkly. We have tended either to dismiss it as token assistance, maladroit and ineffective, or to exaggerate the smooth efficiency with which monolithic machines can work their will.

Between these extremes, we have missed the essential facts. It is folly for us to continue to do so.

Kremlinologists recognize that aid has increased the influence of Communist nations and has given them a presence in strategic areas. It has challenged and diminished Western ability to influence the outcome of some critical political issues. It has helped identify Communist countries with the aspirations of the developing world for a better life. It has been a vehicle for attempting the demonstration of the Communist way as a model for achieving rapid economic growth. And, in latter days, as *Pravda* states, it provides a concrete means to the Soviet Union for proving its practical ability to help poorer nations — no mean counter in its ideological contest with Communist China.

Communist aid, therefore, has its purposes. It is real. It is serious. And it will persist so long as the purposes are served. In this arena of inevitable comparison, if not competition, how shall we fare?

We have immeasurable advantages. The first is our purpose — not to impose system or dogma but to help build free nations. This is the common objective — of ourselves and of those we help. As Secretary of State Dean Rusk has put it:

> It is not for us to fear the great winds of change that are blowing today. They are the winds we have long known and sailed with, the winds which have carried man on his unending journey, the winds of freedom.[1]

There are other advantages — the quantity, quality, and variety of material resources and human skills, from within and without government. We need not fear either comparison or competition in the complex task of nation building.

Merely asserting these propositions sounds unconvincing and self-serving. In this period of wavering and self-doubt, it would be a useful exercise to place ourselves in the position of those

[1] *The Winds of Freedom,* Selections from The Speeches and Statements of Secretary of State Dean Rusk, January 1961–August 1962, ed. by Ernest K. Lindley. Boston: Beacon Press, 1963, pp. 9–10.

who would, as Khrushchev said, "bury us" in the arena of peaceful economic, social, and political competition. How does the world look from the Kremlin?

To perform this exercise credibly, we shall need to transport ourselves to a meeting of the Soviet Presidium of the Council of Ministers. We shall have to assume that this is a closed session, one where the participants are forced to speak with candor. Testifying before the Presidium are the Chairman of the State Committee on Foreign Economic Relations, the equivalent of our A.I.D. Administrator.

This is an extraordinary hearing convened to assess the record of eight years of Bloc overseas economic assistance since 1955. A number of recent events have provoked questions and the Presidium has instructed its staff counsel to ask hard questions and tolerate no easy answers.

The Chairman of the State Committee on Foreign Economic Relations takes the witness's seat at the table.

Q. Comrade Administrator, as you know, the Presidium has scheduled this special review of our aid programs. Unlike the United States, we do not do this every year, but eight years seems like a long enough time to see what has been accomplished. First of all, can you tell us briefly how our aid program got its start?

A. As you recall, in 1948 we refused to participate in the European Recovery Program. In retrospect this has not seemed wise. Europe — Western Europe, that is — recovered remarkably well without us, and we lost what once appeared excellent opportunities to exercise some influence. In the same year we saw another effective use of economic and military aid when, unhappily, untimely aid to Greece and Turkey upset the hopes of our Party in those two countries. It didn't help matters when Comrade Tito closed his borders to reinforcements.

Q. This is not the time to criticize our ally. Please confine yourself to my question.

A. In any event, by 1954 it began to be apparent that we

could no longer discount the effectiveness of aid. To denounce it as neocolonialism carried very little weight. We had to have something more concrete than words to offset the tangible benefits of American capital and technicians. To be sure, there was ferment in the developing countries, but to exploit it we had to identify ourselves with their desires for a better life. We also had to offer something if we wanted to encourage neutralism and loosen ties to the West. There was little choice but to compete. It was at this time that Comrade Khrushchev and Bulganin made their celebrated tour through South and Southeast Asia. They came back with many requests and a number of promises — some of which we are still working on.

Q. Since 1954, what have we done? How much money? How many people? How many countries?

A. We and our sister People's Republics have committed some $5 billion for economic aid and $3 billion for military aid. We have programs in about thirty countries. There are over 11,000 of our technicians abroad working on economic aid projects, not to count those in Cuba.

Q. If I have my facts straight, this means that we have more employees abroad in these countries than the Americans. Aren't we trying to do too much for too many, too soon?

A. Well, Comrade, those are very good questions. We do have more government technicians in the field but this is because the Americans, like the British, Germans and others, do much of their work by contract with private companies. Sometimes when I think of the Aswan Dam, I wish we had a few private companies to —

Q. Comrade!

A. Sorry. As for the number of countries, it is very hard to say "Nyet," particularly when so many of them are already receiving help from the United States or from some European countries. It almost seems that being a great power and giving some kind of aid go together. And we want to be considered a great power by all countries. The picture, however, isn't quite as confusing as one would think. Actually, we haven't spent more than 30 percent of the amount we have promised.

Q. Doesn't this cause us problems with the other countries?

A. Yes, I'm afraid there has been a lot of grumbling over our delays. Part of it is their fault but you can't say so. In Indonesia, our economic aid commitment runs to about $645 million. We're going to build some steel and fertilizer plants, but we haven't yet found enough raw materials. We're also supposed to build some four hundred miles of roads in Borneo by 1964. But, Comrade, road building in Borneo is no simple task. We've had to cut the mileage by about one hundred miles and postpone completion by two or three years. We haven't moved much on actual construction. We also planned to do a large agricultural project in the same area, but I'm afraid much of our equipment is just rusting and rotting on the docks.

Q. (Aside) I knew this should be a closed session . . . Tell me, how do our technicians get along? At least no one has written a book on "The Ugly Russian."

A. We've had our problems. Not many of them know the local language. They don't even know English or French, which is spoken in many places. We have had growing complaints that our technicians cost too much. We've had to renegotiate some of our contracts, in Ghana, of all places. Sometimes some of our people are indiscreet. We had to recall our Ambassador in one country. They suspected him of trying to make trouble with some groups of teachers. Several of our people were caught smuggling diamonds in bags of coffee. Occasionally, some of our young men get into difficulty with native women. Recently we had a case the other way around when one of our female schoolteachers became too involved with the native men. She had a great deal of empathy. Other times, they get into difficulty by advocating nonassociation. We lose either way. The other countries are bothered by such little things.

For example, some of our workers in Egypt have run into problems because when they go to the markets all they buy is small items like — of all things — secondhand American clothing. And they are not good tippers.

Q. What about our student training program?

A. That is going ahead very well. At our new Patrice Lumumba Friendship University and other universities and factories we have over 12,000 students and technical trainees.

Q. Hasn't there been some difficulty lately? Hasn't there even been something in the newspapers?

A. Unfortunately, yes. There have been protests over both accommodations and curriculum at Lumumba. And at Sofia in Bucharest there was that embarrassing protest by the students against racial discrimination. As a result a substantial number of them have returned to their homeland. I must also report that we have had difficulty filling our scholarship quotas. The better students seem to have a preference for training in the capitalist countries.

Q. You said that we and our sister Republics had committed about $5 billion in economic aid since we began our programs. Where has most of it gone?

A. Ninety percent has gone to twelve countries. Each of these has received commitments of at least $100 million. Here is the record of the principal countries:

Latin America: Argentina ($104 million); Brazil ($180 million); and, of course Cuba, where I don't really have a current total, but I'm told that we may be putting in as much as a million dollars a day.

Africa: Ethiopia ($114 million); Ghana ($200 million); Guinea ($127 million); Mali ($100 million); and lesser amounts to the Somali Republic and others. As you know, we have recently concluded a $100 million agreement with Algeria.

The Middle East: Iraq ($218 million); Syria ($193 million); and the United Arab Republic-Egypt ($715 million).

Asia: Afghanistan ($500 million); India ($982 million); and Indonesia ($645 million).

Q. I assume, Comrade Administrator, that these countries were chosen because they presented us the best opportunities to serve our cause.

A. Yes. We picked these countries to serve one or more of three objectives: to enlarge our influence; to erode Western influence; and to speed the movement toward Marxist socialism. We've tried to pick others. But so much depends on how receptive they are.

Q. We would like to have you tell us how far we have accomplished these objectives. Begin, please, with Latin America.

A. Brazil is a new venture for us. Our European colleagues have extended some credits for machinery and commodities. We don't yet know what they will be.

Argentina has frankly been disappointing. Perhaps this was not a good choice to begin with. It is really one of the wealthiest Latin American countries. Capitalist activity seems to be increasing, not decreasing. We had high hopes, however, that the continued influence of Perón might have kept things boiling long enough to pave the way for significant Party progress. But Argentine elections last year came off quite peaceably and the country seems to have settled down under a middle-of-the-road government. We were particularly disappointed when Argentina voted with all the others to exclude Cuba from the Organization of American States. It also voted — again with all the others — to join the embargo against Cuba. One of our problems was that we didn't have much leverage because of our aid. When we began to deliver oil machinery under our hundred million dollar agreement, it seemed to be so unsuitable that Argentina canceled the whole transaction.

Cuba, however, is a happier story.

Q. Yes, we all agree. But, Administrator, there are some who question whether even here we are getting our rubles' worth. Our figures show that, counting our military and economic aid, we have put in over $1.5 billion. How does this come out on a per capita basis?

A. Well, there are seven million people in Cuba. We've given our aid over the past three and a half years. This works out to $61 per capita each year. This is, admittedly, a large drain — in fact, three times larger than what the United States has put into Laos and Vietnam together. That works out to $18 per year per person. But this, of course, was a political problem. My concern has been ironing out some of the problems in administering our aid.

Q. What kinds of problems?

A. Equipment has given us some difficulty. If the equipment is poor, the Cubans protest. If it is our best, our own technicians grumble because it is better than they see at home. We have the usual problem in meeting delivery schedules. And we face a peculiar problem with our technicians. Most Cuban professionals have been trained in the United States. Our experts — say, from Bulgaria — have had trouble getting their advice accepted by the Cubans. But these, I'm sure, are only growing pains.

Q. How long must we continue aid on such a scale?

A. I'm afraid I can't answer that question. This will be a decision for the Presidium itself.

Q. Well, after all, Latin America is not even in our hemisphere . . . yet. Would you come closer to home and discuss our progress in Africa?

A. Africa has proven very difficult to understand. We start, of course, with far fewer resources than the capitalist countries. Our commitments to our four largest recipients have totaled over $700 million since 1959. France alone gives over $700 million of aid a year in Africa. The Western countries together channel about one and a half billion dollars each year into Africa. This doesn't count their private investment. We have trouble competing against this.

Although we recognized this, we did feel that we had a great asset in anti-colonialism and the desire of the new leaders not to depend wholly on the West.

Q. How have we done in the four countries you named?

A. Well, we can discount Ethiopia. We have done some good work there such as building hospitals, but Ethiopia seems far more interested in developing an African regional organization than in any anti-Western activity. Perhaps we should not have expected much from an old man who is, after all, an emperor. We had much higher hopes for a promising threesome — Guinea, Ghana, and Mali.

Guinea, as you recall, presented an excellent opportunity for us when it broke off with France on gaining its independence in 1958. Not only did we send aid missions there but so did Poland, Czechoslovakia, Bulgaria, and China. From then on, we ran into fantastic problems. Through some error we shipped so many screwdrivers that the natives took to using them as daggers. A shipment of cement was left on the shore and ruined by rain. Because of delays in scheduling, a load of bananas we were to buy rotted on the docks. Naturally we decided not to buy them, and this seemed to irritate the Guineans. We were particularly annoyed when the Guineans thought our Ilyushin Transport planes were too expensive to operate and replaced them with American planes. To add insult to injury, they use the airport we built at Conakry.

Q. What explains this fiasco?

A. A combination of events. The Guineans expected too much from us in economic assistance and too little in indoctrination activity. As you know, they expelled our ambassador and are replacing many of our teachers. The whole fiasco, as you put it, is partly due to our own shortsightedness in saying "Da" to every project request that came along, whether it was feasible or not. In any event, the present outlook is far from favorable, either politically or socially. Guinea is now seeking

French cooperation and is apparently being welcomed. It has applied for membership in the capitalist International Monetary Fund. Western countries will probably develop the bauxite deposits at Boke — and these are one fourth of the world's reserves. Although Guinea is still largely state-controlled, it has passed laws to entice private capital and is even liberalizing some state-controlled sectors.

I would not want to leave the impression that we have not achieved results in Guinea. We still have many teachers and technicians there. We are still working on a number of projects. And we still have the opportunity to exercise influence. Guinea is by no means a closed book. It is a most important country for us.

Q. What about Mali and Ghana?

A. Not so bad a story there, Comrade. But Ghana, too, is trying to attract capitalist investment and has even created an investment bank to make loans to businessmen. Mali, like Guinea, seems to be trying to settle its difficulties with France and may also join the International Monetary Fund. These trends are discouraging when we look back on over $200 million of aid for these two countries.

Q. I agree that Africa is an enigma. Perhaps we ought to be more careful in the future.

A. I should point out that Africa is not entirely without hope. Angola, Southern Rhodesia, and South Africa will give us excellent opportunities. So long as colonialism lives — not to mention Apartheid — we have much to look forward to. We are also encouraged by prospects in the horn of Africa and Yemen. In Yemen particularly we have made very good progress recently in airport construction. We are very hopeful about expanding our aviation service across Africa.

Q. Would you now discuss the Middle East? Adding up your figures, I judge we have given over a billion dollars in economic aid to Egypt, Iraq and Syria.

A. That's correct. And of course more than that in military equipment and training. Over a billion dollars for Egypt alone.

Q. Our big coup, of course, was the Aswan Dam.

A. Yes. This, we hoped, would do a number of things for us — give concrete evidence of our technical ability, show our friendship for the people, and enlarge our influence in the country. The Dam is going ahead very well. We have some eight hundred technicians on the spot. But not all the advantages we had hoped for have come to pass.

Q. What do you mean?

A. As in the case of Cuba, some of the Egyptian engineers are Western trained and are sometimes critical of our experts and techniques. We have had — as is bound to occur in any large project — trouble with some equipment. Some of our drills broke down and were replaced by some from Western Europe. Trucks and tires have worn out quickly. Our power shovels have been too small. These, however, are some of the frustrations we must expect. More disappointing has been our difficulty in making propaganda out of this project. Most Egyptians think this is their project. Those who know that we have something to do with it assume we are minor suppliers and contractors. Try as we will, the story seldom seems to come across.

Q. But surely the officials know. They must realize on what side their bread is buttered.

A. I wish I could say so with better assurance. The fact is that they apparently think their bread is buttered on both sides. I even wonder if there is any butter on our side at all. There is, of course, President Nasser's insistence on putting many of our comrades in jail. This is very hard to explain to our people here at home. Then there are other disturbing signs. Egypt has taken the wrong position on a number of issues in the United Nations — the Congo, the Cuba revolution, support for India in its difficulties with China (perhaps, Comrade, this was not a wrong position), and nuclear testing. Its actions at the so-called Cairo nonaligned economic conference in 1962 were not at all helpful to us. Moreover, it has recently shown some vaguely capitalistic notions. It has applied for membership in GATT (the General Agreement for Trade and Tariffs); it has signed the multilateral long-term textile agreement; it has executed a civil aviation agreement with the United States; and it has even entered into an investment guaranty agreement with the United States. All of these steps are confusing to us, Comrade. I might almost say they are evidence of opportunism, not to mention ingratitude.

Q. It does seem a small harvest for a billion dollars. Have we a better record in Iraq and Syria?

A. We were doing well in Iraq until the revolution in 1963. We may have bet on the wrong horse. It's too early to tell. Our relations are somewhat strained. Syria is somewhat better. Both our trade and aid are rising. But the government is wary. We have a lot of technicians there, but they still like capitalism.

Q. Then I suppose we are to assume that the Middle East is as enigmatic as Africa. Suppose we go to more familiar territory — our own back yard, so to speak. Here in Asia, you've told us, our largest economic aid commitments have gone to Afghanistan, India, and Indonesia. Together, they total over $2 billion. Can you give us an appraisal of our success here?

A. In Afghanistan, we have committed over half a billion dollars, a good part of it in fifty-year, interest-free loans. This, of course, has been much appreciated. But Afghans are a stubborn people. They have welcomed Western and particularly American teachers and education experts. More disturbing still, they are talking about enacting a democratic constitution. Unfortunately, it has apparently patched up its differences with Pakistan. For a while, this dispute seemed promising. Of course, this is, as you say, our own backyard — but it has proven a very expensive one.

India has been given or promised about a billion dollars. Our biggest monument there has been the Bhilai steel mill. This is operating well and our three hundred technicians are trying to double its capacity. As for our influence, our aid over eight years, large as it has been, was only half the yearly amount India receives from the Western nations. In any event, the whole picture has been muddied up by the action of the Chinese along the Indian border. That particular action has cost us considerably. But it has also been an opportunity. We've increased our military aid substantially. We're also considering building the steel mill the Americans turned down. We stand very well in India. But for all our help, India's private sector investment was twice as great in its second plan as in its first, and it is planning on greater, not smaller, private sector activity in its third five-year plan.

Q. I take it you are saying that despite all our aid India is still . . . India?

A. I'm afraid that's exactly it.

Q. Our last major client is Indonesia. Here, you say, we've given about $645 million. Is the picture any clearer there?

A. Perhaps. We've given almost twice that amount in military aid. They use our military equipment, have sent personnel to our schools for training, and work with our technicians. But Sukarno, for all that, has not proven himself very reliable . . . or grateful.

Q. Go on. Tell us the details.

A. Well, we've had project difficulties, the same as in other places, only more so. We sent down 4000 jeeps — but the windshield wipers twisted in the tropical heat and steering gears wouldn't work. Our aircraft had take-off speeds which were too slow and landing speeds which were too fast. A sugar mill built by the German People's Republic has been anything but sweet. Our earth-moving equipment doesn't hold up too well in the tropics. The Indonesians had to supply U.S. equipment. All of this was awkward. However, these are really insignificant items. Indonesia could prove to be an excellent investment. It all depends on President Sukarno. He disappointed us in settling with the oil companies and accepting the West Irian compromise so easily. Then he was encouraging when he opposed Malaysia. It's too early to tell how it will all come out. But we do have good access to a number of high Indonesian officials and we have trained many key people.

Q. I must say, on behalf of the Presidium, that this record leaves something to be desired. What, in your opinion, has gone wrong?

A. I wouldn't say that we have been unsuccessful. We have been able to open many doors that otherwise would be locked. We have some influence in many parts of the world. Without our aid, the capitalist countries would have had a much easier time. But, to answer your question, all of these nations seem to be unsophisticated in their political thinking. They think exclusively of themselves. They are not at all alert to the world struggle between capitalism and socialism. What strikes a chord with them is the division between the rich and the poor nations. This is not good Marxism, as you know. Moreover, they consider us as being rich rather than being one of them.

Q. Don't we use trade as a weapon along with aid?

A. Yes, indeed. Part of my responsibilities include barter deals. It is a great advantage to be able to take payment in goods, at any price we choose. Here again, since we are in closed session, I shall have to tell you that there are disadvantages. In the first place, the trade between us and the less developed countries — even though it has increased — is still less than 5 percent of their total trade. In the second place, even though we have been critical of the capitalist countries for taking in trade mostly raw materials, the fact is that we take no smaller percentage, and we are able to take only a small fraction of their manufactures. Finally, the chicken sometimes comes

home to roost as it did when we took Egyptian cotton in payment for arms, and sold it in Europe at a discount. The Egyptians complained that we were stealing their markets. This is,
I say once again, a difficult business.

Q. Don't think we don't sympathize with you. We have our
problems too. Some of them are our allies. Are they helping
share the burden?

A. All things considered, yes. In fact, they feel they are doing
too much. Overall, the Soviet Union has given about 70 percent
of our total aid, Eastern Europe 22 percent, and China 8 percent. In 1957 we in the Soviet Union were carrying 80 percent
of the load. More recently Eastern Europe has had a larger
share, but we probably still will have to shoulder the major
load. Most of the countries are facing their own economic
problems. They are beginning to balk in the Balkans, if I may
be so free . . . sorry.

The Czechoslovakians are a case in point. They have extended the largest amount of credits of any of our Eastern
European neighbors. They used to be one of our most prosperous partners. But now they complain of power shortages,
railways in need of repair, failure of their third five-year plan,
high food prices, trouble with their agriculture. Despite these
conditions, their exports to less developed countries have increased in the past three years. But they are hurting. When
riots broke out between Czech and African students, it was not
racial discrimination. It was, we understand, simply the feeling
that aid was keeping the Czechs from a better standard of living.

The Rumanians are unhappy with us because they feel, to
use their words, that we want to make their country just a raw
materials colony. The Bulgarians and Hungarians oppose our
plans because they think their industrial development could be
blocked.

The Poles have talked about pulling out of aid entirely. But
I question this. They really have been very active recently, in

Morocco, the United Arab Republic, India, Brazil, and Syria. But you know the Poles. They have their own ideas.

Q. What about China?

A. We've had a special task force working on this problem. Since the recent unpleasantnesses, we've had to recast our whole approach. Under the present circumstances we have been forced to recognize that our immediate competition is not only with the capitalist countries. That, of course, will be with us for a long time. What is at stake in the next year or so is the loyalty of the Party — in Asia, Africa, and Latin America. The chief threat to our leadership is China, which not only challenges our doctrine but insists on calling us both "rich" and "white."

Our strategy, we have concluded, is not to argue theory or ideology, but to demonstrate through our aid what we can do to help other countries. China is not in a position to do much. We are. Our capital, our experts, our commodities are living proof of our effectiveness. Perhaps you have seen our two-page spread in *Pravda* on what we have actually done in developing countries and how these countries feel about our aid. We have actions; the Chinese have only words.

That is why, Comrade, we are seeking a larger program next year. It is the key to our global leadership.

Q. I quite agree with you. Indeed, I do not see any alternative. This has been a highly informative session. I think, Comrades, that we ought to be particularly careful about the information we have had today. I see that some of you have been taking notes. The secretary will collect those notes for safekeeping. We all ought to recognize the merit of our way of doing things. Just think what would happen if this were a session open to the press and public. There are some things that are just too . . . sensitive.

PART VI

A Climate for Perseverance

The question for our times is whether there can be perseverance in a fixed design so complex in its operations, so remote from daily life, so uncertain in its immediate results as assistance to far-off peoples.

The portrait of aid has now taken shape — its operations, its uneasy image, the annual agony of decision; the past development of policy; the national purpose of aid; and the basic attitudes of realism and confidence which are preconditions to any sustained support for this function of national policy.

What further is needed — beyond a sense of history, of purpose, of realism, and of confidence — if the United States is to be able to persevere through the critical, difficult, frustrating years of an age of development? Since a democracy does not function through curtained chancelleries vested with continuing power, the people themselves must come to a working consensus and commitment.

The consensus must be broader and deeper than it has been in the past. The areas of agreement must encompass the broad ends and means of aid. There must be a more general understanding of the limitations, problems, opportunities, and achievements of aid. The areas of disagreement must be confined to those of specific policies and operations. And the temperature of controversy must diminish.

A national sense of commitment must somehow manifest it-

*self in a new and unfamiliar steadiness in the face of reverses,
a tolerance for strangeness, a heightened ability to discriminate
between major and secondary issues.*

*How does a nation of over 190 million people come to
broader agreement and steadier commitment? There is no
cheap and easy way. New studies, new committees, new forms
of organization will not do the job for us. The most serious
studies of aid for nearly a decade have agreed on basic principles and on the need to perfect in practice what we have
preached as doctrine.*

*The proposals which follow, therefore, are not a merchandis-
ing attempt to create "a new look." They will be aimed at two
kinds of objectives: increasing the competence and effectiveness
of U.S. aid operations, and removing some artificial and un-
necessary obstructions to the attainment of both a deeper consensus and a steadier commitment.*

*As has been suggested there are three partners in aid — the
executive branch, the public, and the Congress. There are
moderate and attainable objectives which can be pursued by
all three.*

*A better three-way partnership in aid policy and program
among the operators, the lawmakers, and the public involves
some contribution from each partner: from the operators — a
higher level of professionalism; from the lawmakers — policy
making and funding geared to the unique requirements of overseas assistance; from the public — understanding, maturity,
steadiness.*

*No set of proposals, by themselves, will equip the United
States to carry out its assistance role on the level of competence
which the times require. But they can help create a more
favorable climate for the kind of partnership among the executive branch, the Congress, and the public on which our ability
to "persevere in a fixed design" finally depends.*

CHAPTER 16

A New Professionalism

OUR HISTORY of striving for effective aid operations has been a search for a latter-day, secular Holy Grail. This has led to new forms of organization, new kinds of assistance, or new principles to govern aid. The steps taken over the past decade in this search have equipped the United States with the instruments to do a professional job in the complex tasks of planning and administering overseas assistance: a single organization with clear lines of responsibility; legislative authority for extending many different kinds of aid, tailored to different situations; and the guiding principles of country programming, long-range development, self-help, emphasis on loans, selectivity, and co-ordination with other nations and institutions.

Everything has been provided except the concept and goal of professionalism itself. This word has been taboo in discussing problems of assistance. The assumption has always been cultivated that aid was a transient phenomenon which would shortly be terminated. Each year saw renewed calls, sometimes backed by legislative exhortation, for phasing out assistance. In such a climate, talk of professionalism was out of place. It was folly to think in terms of "career development" for personnel; they had been borrowed from other careers to which they would soon return. There was no incentive to dig deeply into the experience and problems of the development process, or to invest months and even years in trying to improve the methods and procedures of administering assistance.

In retrospect, looking back over nearly two decades of major aid activity, we may well conclude that our blindness to the need for a concept of professionalism has been immensely costly. But whatever may have been our justification in the past for treating aid as a short-lived phase of national policy, there is no longer any reasonable basis for being content with less than the excellent in people, standards of analysis and programming, and methods of operations.

One of the unheralded advances in our national approach to aid has been the acceptance of a longer time span as the framework for serious effort in development. President Kennedy in his first message on aid to the Congress in 1961 dramatized "A Decade of Development." The Alliance for Progress was also envisaged from the start as a ten-year joint effort. The United Nations unanimously voted to launch its own Decade of Development. None of these decisions evoked criticism that too long a time involvement was being contemplated; the major dissent has been from those who have cautioned that the decade will end with much still to be done.

The concept of termination of aid has not been abandoned. Indeed, it is receiving greater emphasis today, but in the realistic and practical sense of termination for particular countries as they reach the point where continued development can reasonably be expected from their own savings, trade, and more normal commercial credits.

Under these circumstances, it is not only permissible to think how maximum effectiveness can be achieved; it is imprudent not to seek excellence. The importance of the task, its many dimensions, its cost, its minimum time span — all point to the obvious truth that we should no longer be content with less than the best in people, knowledge and methods.

Developing Professionals

People are the starting point. No matter how sophisticated our knowledge of the processes of development or how adequate our methods, the effectiveness of U.S. aid depends upon the quality, competence, and sensitivity of the men and women working on aid in Washington and in the field.

Their competence, staying power, and dedication are of a much better quality than it is the fashion to recognize. One of the tribal rites practiced by casual observers, visiting inspection teams, and Congressional travelers is to return from the field with two observations. The first is that the quality of aid personnel should be improved. The second is that the individual employees with whom the visitor talked were unusually deeply motivated and competent.

The biblical irony often applies to our field personnel: they are often not without honor except in their own country. They frequently are viewed with greater respect by people in the country where they work, or by officials of the United Nations or of other countries, or by representatives of universities and foundations than by their own Congress, press, and public. In one country, the people thought so highly of the work of the aid mission (which used to be called the United States Operations Mission — USOM) that they named one of their valleys "Usom Valley."

In Washington, officials who entered into aid work directly from business, industry, universities, or other agencies of government are frank to say that they have been impressed with both the quality and the quantity of work turned our consistently under pressures which would elsewhere be considered abnormal, if not excessive and unreasonable. In August 1963, the Civil Service Commission study of personnel management, while critical of management techniques, said, "AID's employees are loyal and strongly motivated by the vital foreign aid mission . . . It is clear that, on an overall basis, AID has a dedicated, competent work force."

That aid personnel have so often reached and sustained high standards of performance is more a tribute to them as individuals and to their sense of service than to any system or concern for the development of their careers. They have been recruited over the past fifteen years under varying conditions of urgency, under varying sets of standards, to serve varying concepts and purposes — depending upon the current leadership, the latest form of organization, the most recent area of Congressional concern, the major recommendations of the last Presidential commission to report its findings. Some personnel were undoubtedly recruited in haste to mount some of the early programs. Today we too easily forget the magnitude of that task to recruit quickly agricultural, health, and educational advisers who would be willing to forego their careers in government agencies or universities at home to undertake strange work in remote places.

Although Congress has not positively promoted the concept of professionalism in aid personnel, it has on two occasions reflected its concern for excellence by enacting "purge" legislation. The assumption was that if all civil service protections were shunted aside, the aid director or administrator could winnow out all those whose performance, competence, suitability, or dedication were lacking. These were naïve attempts at "instant professionalism." In the process half a thousand employees deemed marginal were separated from aid service. Many more left on their own accord because of the suspicion, criticism, and uncertainty which seemed to haunt aid personnel and programs.

Some of the most gifted workers in aid's vineyard have understandably moved on to more lucrative, respected, and secure positions in industry, in the academic world, or in other government agencies. Each such transfer represented the loss of an immeasurable investment of time, money, and experience. This waste of human resources has not gone unnoticed. In 1961 aid officials commissioned a study on the career development needs of aid personnel by Brookings Institution. In 1962, a citizens' committee, appointed by Secretary of State Dean Rusk, under the chairmanship of former Secretary Christian Herter, recommended career status and opportunities to aid employees as part of a "family of compatible services," together with officers of the Foreign Service and United States Information Agency.

The root concept is that of a career service, as opposed to hiring to fill a particular position for the period of a limited tour of duty. Implied in such a concept is systematic recruiting of gifted college graduates, young professionals, and Peace Corps Volunteers who would like to continue working in developing areas on a career basis. Also implied is a first class career development system within the Agency for International Development, with more thorough orientation courses for new employees, more frequent training courses in languages and economic and social development for junior and middle level employees, specialized and refresher courses at universities for senior employees, and — most important of all — the opportunity to serve the United States abroad not only in a top aid position but, in senior posts in the Foreign Service when merit justifies, even as Ambassador. Key elements in such a career system are fair and meaningful methods of evaluation of work, promotion based on achievement and potential, and — the reverse side of the coin — selection out of the service not merely for misconduct and incompetence, but for marginal performance and lack of potential for professional growth.

Another resource for professionalism is the rich reservoir of our pluralistic society. What is needed is to build a relationship between government and society so that talented specialists in the academic world, in business, in labor unions and cooperatives can be drawn upon for limited but fairly regular tours of duty abroad without prejudice to their home careers in the university, in the plant, the union, or association. In other words, what is envisaged is a career alternating between refreshing one's roots in his home institution and serving several tours overseas. In this way, U.S. aid would not be pyramiding a huge bureaucracy but would be drawing upon an increasingly seasoned cadre of specialists from whom service abroad would not be a diversion, a sabbatical, or a possible dead end, but rather part of their career's main stream.

Although much can be done administratively to build a new professionalism, a vital ingredient is strong Congressional support. In the past Congress has tended to boggle at talk of career systems for aid personnel. There was the unpleasant connotation of perpetuity. Members of Congress who yearned for the day when overseas aid was a thing of the past could hardly be expected to be enthusiastic about institutionalizing a profession which, it was hoped, might not long be necessary. To this point of view there are two compelling answers. The first is that so long as the United States supports assistance — at even the present level — nearly $5 billion a year, if food is included — investment in the best kind of professional and administrative attention is called for by any standard of prudence, self-interest, and common sense. Indeed, we can look back with a wistful eye on over $100 billion of assistance we have spent since World War II and wonder how much better a record we could have written if we had always insisted on a high degree of professionalism.

But there is another answer for those who are concerned about stimulating gifted people to enter a career which might — in their view — disappear after a decade or so. Regardless of the realism of this concern, there should be no doubt that the future relations of the United States with the other nations of the world will increasingly have an economic coloration. Those who build careers in the field of economic and social development assistance will always find their services in demand. To assure the United States a reasonable supply of such people is a blue chip investment, long overdue.

Professionalism in Knowledge

If there is a need for developing a spirit and a tradition of professionalism among those inside and outside government who work on assistance policy, programs, and operations, is there anything for them to be professional about?

The challenge to professionalism in knowledge about development constantly haunts the top professionals in the Agency for International Development, as they race against deadlines preparing for tomorrow's testimony for the Congress, or for the budget review of next year's programs. They know, better than anyone else, the extent to which they lack answers, answers which time and effort might provide . . . if only there were the time for the effort. Their sense of frustration over the problems with which they wrestle is eased when they look back over the distance they have traveled, even in the short space of two or three years.

The program guidance manual for development diplomats in the field is a vast improvement over the fragmented and unrelated instructions which used to be the sole source of help for the harried technicians overseas. Already valuable case histories are being collected, with a start made on their analysis and evaluation. Already studies of various countries in unprecedented depth are being made, using the skills and approaches of many different disciplines. More and better statistics, reports, and records of experience are becoming available from other nations, international agencies and financial institutions. Even the developing countries themselves are reaping the initial rewards of technical assistance in the taking of censuses and the organization of economic and financial data.

But there are still virgin areas where experience must be probed, experts trained, guidelines established, and action programs launched. Some of these are the problem fields of political development, monetary crises, trade, debt-servicing capacity, and technical assistance.

For example, how, in the process of economic development, can political development be stimulated without involvement in internal politics? If assistance is not to result solely in materialistic gains, how can fundamental values be transferred?

Here again we have scratched only the surface of knowledge how to use goods and services to advance toward the intangible goal of the irreducible values of a free society.

Another "skill gap" is the highly technical field of monetary policy. There are today increasing numbers of a new breed of economist — the development economist. Working for governments, foundations, universities, the United Nations, the World Bank, they shed increasing light on what must be done to stimulate investment, savings, and growth. They are still in short supply but their need and value are recognized. They are everywhere in demand. Not yet so widely recognized or so eagerly sought is the monetary economist, the expert whose advice is needed in the stabilization crises faced by so many countries as they attempt to set the stage for sustained development. Questions of currency devaluation, single or multiple exchange rates, import controls, organization of central banks, control of inflation — these are the issues which call for prompt, decisive, informed action. The lack of timely and authoritative advice on such matters can be infinitely costly in delaying both the chances and the hope for orderly development.

Another looming area requiring the expansion of competence is that of the trade problems and opportunities facing developing countries. Those charged with the administration of aid programs cannot solve all the problems arising out of the movement of the terms of trade. But they must conduct their operations in the light of their implications on trade. Aid poorly planned can increase the production of surplus commodities or stimulate the manufacture of substitutes for the major exports of hard pressed countries. Aid well planned can help countries diversify their products and assist a group of countries in a region to develop complementary products and markets. Aid can provide technical assistance for trade analyses and projections, for studies of trade policy, of schemes for commodity stabilization and crop reduction, and compensatory financing.

It can help in the search for new sources of revenue, for new uses and new markets. At the moment, knowledge of the trade implications of aid programs is in its infancy. This is another priority item on the agenda of the Agency for International Development.

In these first years of the age of development, almost exclusive attention has been paid to increasing the amount of aid and the number of countries participating in aid efforts. During these years, short-term, high-interest suppliers' credits were offered and accepted as "aid." In the past two years concern has mounted over the predicament which more and more developing countries face, with payments of interest and repayment of principal accounting for an ever larger share of their foreign exchange. If the pattern of aid were not to change, wholesale international bankruptcy would some day ensue, resulting in debt repudiation, chaos, moratoria, and diminished confidence in the usefulness of development assistance.

Part of the answer lies in the current effort of such international institutions as the Development Assistance Committee and the World Bank to encourage nations to extend aid on increasingly liberal terms. But there remain other avenues of attack. The developing countries themselves must muster the discipline to refuse aid if it imposes too great a burden on repayment. International aid groups, or consortia, must be prepared to exclude short term, high interest credits. Definitions of aid in such international forums as the Development Assistance Committee must rule out such credits in their comparative reporting.

The United States itself faces a vexing problem. On the one hand its objective is to help particular countries reach a self-sustaining basis as soon as possible. On the other, it cannot long tolerate being in the position of most lenient creditor, with its long term, low interest loans being used, in effect, to help repay the "hard term" creditors. As we participate in group efforts to help particular countries, our strategy is to realize both the goal of adequate aid and that of equitable terms. But further knowledge of both tactics and techniques is needed.

For all these reasons the work on debt-service capacity launched by the World Bank needs not only to be continued, but top policy attention to this problem must be given by all countries and international groups engaged in aid.

Finally, technical assistance itself presents a major challenge. Technical assistance is today much more than the planning and carrying out of programs in the various functional specialties such as health, education, public administration, and agriculture. Formerly each mission felt obliged to have personnel and programs in each of ten technical fields. Today much more analysis is demanded if we are to know when technical assistance is needed, how much, in what specialties; how it should relate to capital development projects; how planning can be approached in terms of goals or objectives, involving a number of separate skills; and when technical assistance should be done by outsiders and when by host country personnel.

The building of key institutions and the training of critical manpower are the primary new objectives of technical assistance, rather than the carrying on of many productive but unrelated programs. To develop doctrine which will both serve this objective and be concretely helpful to the administrators and technicians in the field is of the higher priority. Technical assistance will always require the services of many professions but, in its basic concept and planning, it must develop a new kind of overview — a professional approach to the use of many disciplines.

A special mandate within the field of technical assistance applies to what is called community development. As was clear from the discussion of the population problem, the organization of community workers in health, medical services, and education will be needed on a massive scale, whatever may be the nature of action programs. This immediate need points to a re-examination of assistance for community development efforts. A.I.D. and its predecessor agencies have long given such assistance, with greatest success in India and the Philippines. In other countries the record has been mixed, leading some experts to discourage assistance in this field because of towering administrative problems — involving organizations and training on many levels, from nation down to small village. But if the effectiveness of any effort to achieve regulation of fertility consonant with national development depends upon trained workers in the villages, "community development" assistance should speedily be given increased attention. Because of the population problem, this kind of assistance may well undergo a renaissance of interest, analysis, and organization.

These are some, not all, of the knowledge gaps which must be filled if developmental aid is to reach the professional standards demanded by the problems of development. This is not to say that help in nation building can ever be reduced to a formula or a set of rules. But it is a master profession in the sense that it involves a host of professional skills. We cannot hope for the most from our expenditures unless we bring to bear unremitting intellectual discipline of the highest order.

Professionalism in Operations

The call to higher standards is as insistent as it is invisible in the interstices of aid operations. Good work is marked by the distinction of being unnoticed. Poor work leaves behind it a trail of loose ends, frustrations over delay, and a reputation which blankets aid operations in general. The goals of operations are inherently inconsistent: to move with speed; to be thorough and precise in planning, documentation, accounting, and reporting; and to attain both speed and thoroughness with minimum numbers of personnel. To move more rapidly, with as lean an organization as possible, without sacrificing sound planning and accounting, requires the highest degree of professional competence and organization.

For a year and a half the officials and employees in A.I.D. have labored at a massive, arduous, and unspectacular task appropriately called "The Implementation Project." This has been no less than an attempt to overhaul the ways of doing things that have developed over at least a decade and a half. Hundreds if not thousands of rules, regulations, and customs have been reexamined, brought up to date, simplified, and made consistent.

Methods of procurement, contracting, hiring specialized services, overseeing capital projects, providing commodities, maximizing procurement in the United States, reporting essential data, organizing statistics — these have been the major targets of effort.

The three arenas of operations are the field, headquarters, and coordination with other organizations participating in or affecting aid programs.

The challenge of professionalism in field operations lies in such questions as: How big should a mission be? What kind of a table of organization should it have? What skills should it maintain in its permanent complement — and what ones should it obtain by contract, special assignment, or detail from other agencies? What are the minimum necessary reports to insure adherence to sound standards, without threatening suffocation through an excess of red tape?

For A.I.D. headquarters some of the questions are: What kinds of management reports are necessary? What decisions should be delegated to the field? How can contracts with firms and universities be simplified? How can uniform standards of programming and evaluating technical and capital assistance be enforced among four regional bureaus with widely differing country problems?

In the realm of coordination, new horizons have been added with the increase in aid-giving countries and institutions. Coordination must take place on at least seven levels: with the Department of State of which A.I.D. is an integral part; with other agencies and departments of government; with the international financial institutions (the World Bank, the International Development Association, the Inter-American Development Bank, the International Monetary Fund); the Development Assistance Committee in Paris and its member nations; the United Nations, its specialized agencies, and its Resident Representatives in the field; such regional organizations as the Colombo Plan, and the Organization of American States; and the private business firms, foundations, universities, and other organizations with operations in developing countries.

Of all these levels of coordination, the first is of paramount importance. A.I.D.'s predecessors had been wholly or partly autonomous organizations. In 1961, the new Agency was brought under the roof of the Department of State, with its administrator having the rank of an Undersecretary of State, and its key officials having the rank of Assistant Secretaries of State.

The basic concept was simply that aid policy and foreign policy were not separate and distinct areas. For each to be most effective, there must be constant interchange of information, plans, and influence. This does not mean a condition of subservience of aid policy to overall foreign policy, even though the latter must remain paramount. The equality of rank given senior aid and State Department officials symbolizes and was intended to establish a parity of weight in the making of critical decisions.

The progressive development of close and constructive relationships based on mutual respect is part of the unfinished business of both A.I.D. and the Department of State. Increased interchange of personnel, the adjacent location of State and A.I.D. offices dealing with similar areas, combined administra-

tive services, uniform rules and regulations have all been initiated. Aid has long been an important tool of foreign policy;
it is now taking its proper place in the workshop itself.

*   *   *

The steps outlined in this chapter for the increased effectiveness, competence, and professionalism of U.S. aid activities are
in most cases being taken. They do not depend on any major
overhaul of concept, leadership, or organization. Indeed, they
depend for their full fruition on a moratorium on "new looks"
for a significant period of time. They depend on stability of
organization, continuity of leadership, persistence in refining
and carrying out existing concepts. The work being undertaken is not spectacular, nor immediately productive of increased public respect. It is the hard, honest work of doing a
difficult job as well as it can be done. This, however, for a
public jaded over reorganization and investigation could be
the basis of fresh confidence and support. In the long run it is
the only basis.

CHAPTER 17

Changing the Dance

IN THE TASK of building a better partnership, the executive branch, particularly the Agency for International Development, has the full-time job of improving the professional quality of its personnel and performance. This effort is the foundation for both increased effectiveness of aid policy and better relations with Congress and the public. But without Congressional participation and initiative, the task will be immeasurably more difficult and less certain of success. Critical years will have been lost.

What is needed is to change the dance — the time-consuming, tedious, and often fruitless minuet which now characterizes the annual decisions on aid. It is time to view critically the cost of our manner and style of decision in terms of delay and uncertainty in operations, the time and energy of key personnel which could be devoted to better administration, the tedium and irritation in Congress, the agitation of the public, and the cynicism of the very peoples we seek to help.

The obvious question is: Ought we not subject the processes of decision to the same hardheaded examination that we apply to the substance of aid programs? Are there feasible improvements which can cut this kind of cost?

The annual routine, with its apparatus and folklore, is the result of growth and accretion over a decade and a half. It represents the efforts of Congress to deal with a field of policy and program which is inherently different from all others. There has been no attempt to step back, take a fresh look, and see if Congress is being well served by its existing methods of overseeing aid. Indeed, responsibilities of both House and Senate are spread among so many committees that any attempt at reappraisal may founder on jurisdictional questions.

Yet the inescapable conclusion one draws from observing each year's routine is that, apart from other disadvantages, Congress itself is not well served.

The key objectives of Congress are to obtain the significant facts, to assure itself that policy is being carried out, to make necessary changes in policy, and to make sure that administration is as honest and efficient as possible. The present apparatus, for all its exhausting detail, falls far short of these objectives. Congress asks for and receives so many facts that it can with difficulty distinguish the trees from the forest. Amidst the welter of facts on the military and economic assistance programs in some ninety-five countries, there is too little time or occasion for the orderly consideration of policy issues. The desire to curb inefficiency frustrates itself either by added procedures or by large blanket cuts in appropriations. The procedures all too often result only in compounding delay, requiring new personnel, and multiplying reports. The large cuts, as a device for Congressional control, are as effective as a chain saw for a lobotomy. The actual results are often the reverse of what Congress desired. The hard necessities of the cold war must be met. Excessive cuts mean that progress in development is slowed down. Instead of getting rid of marginal personnel, cuts mean laying off the newer employees whatever their competence.

Anyone venturing suggestions in the field of Congressional practices ought to realize it is one strewn with hidden mines. The wary sapper knows enough not to attempt to remove or alter some of them. Moreover, he ought to be under no illusion that any outsider can speak with persuasive authority. Any realistic proposal can at best minimize irritations and sharpen decision-making.

Re-examination of Responsibility

Aid was never envisaged by the founding fathers as a function of government. Their chief concern was the proper ordering of domestic affairs. In these the President could propose, and Congress, holding the purse, could dispose. To the President they gave the conduct of foreign affairs. These were not foreseen as substantial. Indeed the Department of State was so named, in preference to a Department of Foreign Affairs, because it was thought unlikely that foreign affairs alone would be enough to occupy a separate department. For over a century and a half the two areas of policy remained separate and distinct. With the increasing involvement of the United States in aid activities, the traditional allocation of responsibilities between the President and Congress was no longer possible. Aid was unquestionably in the Presidential field of foreign affairs. But it also heavily involved the Congressional purse strings.

Both Congress and the President felt their way into the aid field through sharply focused and special purpose programs. Postwar relief, Greek-Turkish aid, the Marshall Plan. All of these involved the uses of funds in conjunction with a few, clearly outlined issues of foreign policy.

In the mid-fifties aid broadened in its geographic coverage, in the tools available, and in its versatility as an instrument of foreign policy. The consideration of each year's proposed aid programs touched upon a vast range of foreign policy issues. But Congress and the executive branch have adhered to the pattern established in earlier and simpler days.

Aid has emerged as a major, and sometimes dominant, instrument of foreign policy. What once was a weapon of limited use and range has become an intercontinental economic missile of incalculable significance in the relations among nations. To some extent it has replaced the sanctions and incentives of traditional diplomacy. Recognition or nonrecognition of a country may on occasion be considered a lesser use of power than granting or terminating aid. Diplomatic protests may carry less weight than threats to suspend or cut down aid. Treaties of friendship and commerce may not pack the incentive power of a multi-year aid commitment. The building of a dam or factory may well be more effective than the visit of a fleet or high officials.

A strange irony is apparent, not foreseen by the Founding Fathers. The treaty-making power, once thought of as the pinnacle of involvement in foreign affairs, is subjected only to the advice and consent of the Senate. The entire range of aid policy, because of its dependence upon appropriations, has become subjected, in detail, to the judgments of both Houses of Congress. Through aid legislation, Congress now exerts at least a co-equal influence on the wide spectrum of foreign policy affected by aid.

In short, aid is a major weapon. And it is loaded. Both facts must constantly be borne in mind. The constant hazard is that, as members of Congress consider the past, present, or proposed aid programs for particular countries, they understandably may be influenced by their own information, biases, preconceptions, or pique over specific statements, actions, or personalities associated with such countries. Not infrequently, an individual Senator or Congressman possesses the power to push through an amendment which can change radically the relations of the United States with a foreign country. This power can be sufficient to override the collective judgment of the President, the Secretary of State, the National Security Council, and all the judgments of Ambassadors and supporting staffs in the field and in Washington. Such a power is not confined to senior members of the foreign policy committees of the House and Senate. It is not even confined to members of these committees.

Sometimes an amendment aimed at a country will be accepted by one of the foreign policy committees because the members are convinced that if some kind of amendment is not adopted in committee, a much more sweeping amendment will be offered and passed on the floor of the House or Senate. Sometimes such an amendment will be offered, debated, and defeated in committee, only to be offered again and be passed in floor debate. Indeed, sometimes an amendment is rejected by the foreign policy committees and by both houses of Congress after full debate on the authorizing legislation, only to be inserted as a rider to an appropriation bill and, without much further debate, become the law of the land.

Not only are decisions so arrived at sometimes prejudicial to the conduct of foreign affairs; there is another unhealthy by-product. It lies in the resourcefulness of executive response. If Congress has written into law conditions which it intends to block or limit aid to a particular country, the executive branch may deem it necessary to construe the prohibitions narrowly, to utilize the general waiver authority of the President, or to make the best of a confused legislative history. When this happens, no matter whether the original restriction was the result of the deliberations of the policy committees or a hastily contrived floor action, Congress feels that its intent has been frustrated, its authority challenged. It increases its distrust of "downtown" and proceeds to tighten the screws and plug up the loopholes. What might have begun as a "sense of Congress" amendment becomes, in a year or so, a rigid requirement with no room for executive discretion. This hardening process happens, year after year, not with one but with a dozen or more issues; the result is a serious case of angina. And the relations between the two operating branches of government become steadily more estranged.

All of this is not to say that the executive branch is infallible in its judgments in the field of foreign policy or that the Congress should not participate fully in the process of decision on aid issues, whether they involve a particular country, the conditions governing the extending of aid, or the standards to be followed in administering aid.

The point is that such decisions should be made solemnly, with full consideration of the complex issues of foreign policy. Major amendments affecting our relations with individual countries ought not to be capable of easy adoption. Whim, caprice, the pressures of time, the mood of a large body of harried legislators ought not to govern major decision-making involving incalculable, serious, and often irreversible consequences.

Is it possible to strike a better balance in the exercise of power in foreign relations, without jeopardy to Congressional prerogative? Congress itself provides a precedent. In the exceedingly complex and technical field of taxation, the House of Representatives has recognized the absurdity of its Committee on Ways and Means arriving at an informed judgment on a tax bill after weeks of arduous hearings, reaching a delicately balanced judgment, only to face a flood of special interest amendments in floor debate. Accordingly, the House has an unwritten custom honored by the Committee on Rules that proposed tax legislation issuing from the Committee on Ways and Means will not be open to amendment on the floor. The House imposes extraordinary trust in its tax experts on this committee and extraordinary restraint on the powers of noncommittee members. They have two opportunities to work their will — by appearing before and expressing their views to the Committee or its individual members, and by voting for or against the proposed legislation. This arrangement has worked well. Indeed, without it, sensible and balanced fiscal legislation would be almost impossible and fraught with interminable controversy.

Should not similar ground rules be adopted for policy legislation on aid? Is not the same degree of complexity present —

and the same hazard of ill considered action? If the members of the Senate Committee on Foreign Relations and the House Committee on Foreign Affairs, in their judgment, with their accumulated experience and exposure to executive branch officials, and other witnesses, including members of Congress, accept or reject proposed policy changes, neither the executive branch nor disappointed legislators ought to have a second time at bat. Should the two committees misjudge the will of Congress on a major issue, the remedy would lie in recommitting the legislation for further consideration. What power would be sacrificed by this kind of voluntary restraint would be more than compensated for by more orderly decision-making, greater stability of policy and more deliberate judgments on international relations.

Focus on Policy

If the Congress is to increase its participation in the orderly deliberation of policy questions, a second change is warranted. It is a change which requires only the action of the two policy committees — the Senate Committee on Foreign Relations and the House Committee on Foreign Affairs. Here are the experts of Congress in foreign affairs in general and aid programs in particular. From them should be expected wise judgment, mature appraisal, and sensitive initiative. Particularly if the first proposal in this chapter were to be adopted would their policy judgment and leadership be critical.

But the irony is that these committees often have too little time for orderly consideration, in depth and in breadth, of policy issues. The reason lies in large part in the custom of fixing annual funding ceilings for aid programs. Except in cases of starting new programs or stopping old ones, or of making major changes in magnitudes of aid, setting ceilings bears little relation to policy. The ceiling has no real meaning since the final decision on funds is made by the appropriations committees, subject only to floor action. Nevertheless, these two policy committees find much of their time diverted to haggling over figures that often serve no other purpose than creating one additional layer of cuts, doubling the decibels and duration of debate on the levels of aid.

It would seem in the interest of these committees, without giving up jurisdiction to make changes at any time, or the right to insist on full reviews of programs, to absolve themselves of the yearly figure exercise by voting either continuing or multi-year authorizations. The former method would not involve figures at all; the latter would authorize a ceiling for several years' activity. The historical argument against this is understandable. It is that by so doing, the committees "give up control." But the initial cuts at this level bear little relation to the final action of Congress, and the real potential for constructive control lies in the use of the time of the two Committees for systematic discussion of policy and programs.

Legislative Housecleaning

A point of beginning for a new emphasis on policy would be a restatement of the purposes, policies, standards, and procedures contained in the Foreign Assistance Act. This is now, through the accretions of time, an ungainly and confusing document. If it is true that a clearer sense of national purpose needs to be articulated, the Act itself should lead the way.

If the Senate Special Committee to study the Foreign Aid Program was correct in 1957 in calling for the separation, the refinement, and the restatement of the objectives of aid, the point is doubly well taken today. But who will bell the cat? The executive branch has the initiative of drafting legislation to send to Capitol Hill. It very properly takes the attitude of causing as little commotion as possible. Usually the marching orders are to seek only the minimum number of legislative changes. The Congressional Committees, on the other hand, deal with the draft legislation as they receive it from the administration.

The President's message on aid is sent up to Congress in March or April, after the appropriate phase of the programming process has been reached and figures have been carefully reviewed for the entire program. At that point, there is quite enough grist for the legislative mill, without attempting a complete writing of the statute.

What is needed is a cooperative undertaking, wholly separate from the annual consideration of future aid programs. It should involve the Congress, represented by the House Committee on Foreign Affairs and the Senate Committee on Foreign Relations, and the executive branch, represented by the Agency for International Development. It would begin by informal discussions in the summer, while Congress is still in session, and after these two committees have finished their work on the current legislation. Two subjects would be explored: whether a restatement of aid legislation would be valuable; and what should be the general principles governing the redrafting.

If agreement can be reached on these two points, the executive branch would mount an effort in the fall of the year to do a complete job of rewriting the legislation to clarify the principal objectives, the secondary objectives, the standards, and procedures of aid operations, drawing in the committee staffs as part of the task force. This effort would be quite separate from the normal, ongoing programming and presentation effort.

The next step would be a presentation to Congress shortly after it reconvened, before the committees were burdened with their usual chores. At this point of time, they would not be concerned with figures and could focus on the thrust and structure of the new legislation. This would not mean another reorganization of the aid agency nor a redirection of policy or

of program, but an attempt to restate in the simplest and clear-
est terms those things which it is necessary to formalize in legislative language. Later on the committees would consider, as
always, the President's annual request for funds.

Such a joint effort is timely and necessary if the people of the
United States are to clarify their own thinking about aid and,
indeed, the role this nation should play in the world of today
and tomorrow.

A New Cycle

Another Congressional contribution to the effectiveness and
continuity of operations would be adoption of the practice of
legislating for a two year period. Each Congress would act, but
not each session of a Congress. There would, however, be regular annual committee reviews. Such a proposal was made in
1957 by the Fairless Committee. While this is consistent with
other, more basic proposals concerning the reorganization of
Congressional procedures, it has a special urgency and justification for overseas assistance projects which require both extensive lead time and some assurance of reasonable continuity.
For the executive branch, such a cycle would liberate an incalculable amount of time in Washington and in the field for
concentration on operations. For Congress it would provide a
more significant debate, with greater opportunity to measure
progress and assess policy.

A variant of this proposal, already in use for some programs,
is that Congress make forward year appropriations. Instead of
acting for the fiscal year beginning on July 1 during the current session, it would be fixing the appropriations for the year
following. This would mean that by the fall of any year Mission Directors and Ambassadors would know what they would
have to plan and work with during the succeeding year and a
half, instead of the next nine months. This simple device

would contribute substantially to sound planning, more thorough execution, and elimination of uncertainty and delay.

Whatever the methods used, it is time that Congress realize the unique requirements for engaging most effectively in aid policy and program, and that it construct new ways of dealing with this relatively new function of government. The elastic capacity for invention which the Congress has often demonstrated may prove de Tocqueville wrong in his judgment that a representative democracy is incapable of persevering in a fixed design.

The Essential Cadre

There is another dimension to the potential of adequate Congressional management of responsibilities on issues relating to aid. It is divorced from changes in procedures or custom. Without it procedures will accomplish little; with it, even awkward procedures will be workable.

This vital ingredient is the development and encouragement of a cadre of aid generalists in both Houses of Congress, equipped with knowledge in breadth and in depth of aid policies, problems, and programs. This demands more knowledge than is gathered from participation in committee hearings or occasional travel. There are all too few interpreters of aid in either house. Indeed, it is a thankless task, with hours of labor unrewarded by the gratitude of constituents.

Such a cadre implies two commitments; the commitment of such Congressmen and Senators to invest time, to dig deeply, and to maintain their interest in a subject which has only the national interest to recommend it; and the commitment by the executive branch to consult frequently and seriously with such persons on the same basis of confidence as if they were administration colleagues. This consultation would be a continuing one, with special attention being given to the planning for the coming year. In this way, there could develop an atmosphere of shared responsibility which would do much to displace the present general attitude of the lawmakers, who look on the annual aid legislation as an unwanted baby deposited on their doorstep.

There is no incentive for the development of such a cadre except concern for the national interest. However, this concern exists and there are Senators and Congressmen who would welcome a deeper understanding of the workings and problems of aid.

*   *   *

These suggestions imply a greater degree of mutual cooperation and confidence between the two branches of government. No mechanical changes will achieve the increased understanding so urgently needed on the part of the Congress and the public. Nor will they have great value without such understanding. But, to the extent that our processes of decision have created artificial barriers, such changes in the dance would be welcomed by all.

To the extent that the Congress can solemnize its decision-making, clarify our purposes, concentrate on the assessment of policy, contribute to the stability of operations, and interpret the achievements and problems of aid, it will contribute to the building of national consensus. In turn such a consensus will greatly ease the task of Congressional decision.

CHAPTER 18

The New Dimension of Citizenship

This is the first generation of Americans to be . . . deeply
involved with the outside world . . . But the strain of this
involvement remains. We find ourselves entangled with apparently unanswerable problems in apparently unpronounce-
able places . . . In world affairs as in all other aspects of life,
the days of the quiet past are gone forever . . . And if this
nation is to survive and succeed in the real world of today, we
must acknowledge the realities of that world . . .

President Kennedy, Remarks at
the Mormon Tabernacle, Salt Lake City,
September 26, 1963

HOW DO WE as a nation bridge the gap between the international facts of life and a set of shared ideas adequate to cope
with these facts? The President can propose. The Congress can
dispose. But the boundaries of tolerance of any policy, domestic or foreign, are fixed by the knowledge and attitudes of
citizens. These boundaries are not immutable. They can be
broadened or constricted by individuals, groups, and institutions which influence public attitudes. Not the least among
these are the President and the Congress. But, at any given
time on any given issue, the range of leadership policy and
action is limited by these boundaries.

It was this interaction between the leaders and the led in a
democracy that persuaded de Tocqueville to conclude that such
a country as the United States could not expect, in the field of

foreign policy, to "persevere in a fixed design" or to await its consequences with patience. That this is still the critical test was underscored by President Kennedy, who concluded his 1963 aid message to Congress with these words: "This, for the American people, is a time . . . for patience . . . We have dared to label the sixties the Decade of Development. But it is not the eloquence of our slogans, but the quality of our endurance, which will determine whether this generation of Americans deserves the leadership which history has thrust upon us."

These were measured words. To speak of "the quality of our endurance" was to recognize that there is a difference between uncertain, uneasy, and unconvincing acceptance and confident, determined, and steady commitment. To speak of the leadership thrust upon us compels an awareness of the great forces moving in our time. It raises the question: How well are we prepared to exercise the enduring leadership demanded of us?

It is sobering to reflect that fully half the population of the United States came to maturity before there was a consciousness of the developing world, before aid was a recognized instrument of national policy, before the United States found itself playing a leadership role in peacetime, before Europe had emerged from devastation, before the Communist world was engaged in assistance at all, and before nuclear weaponry radically changed the ground rules on the use of force.

The carefree twenties, the depression, the postwar relaxation — all were periods when a citizen of the United States could ignore the world. World war, or the threat of war could and did engage our complete attention, but in time of peace we would leave the world to experts. What the past decade and a half have done to us, whether we like it or not, has been to add a new dimension to our citizenship. Good citizenship once meant knowledge of and participation in affairs of the community, state, and nation. It now embraces the world.

It now matters deeply to us how India is doing, what tariff

levels are being considered by the Common Market, what actions are being taken by the United Nations, whether the Congo is settling down or erupting into violence, how affairs are progressing in Southeast Asia, and whether a government falls in Latin America. Trade, defense, political stability, orderly development, our image and influence, those of the Soviet Union or Red China — these now claim our interest and our opinion. We are becoming world-minded.

The adding of this dimension has crept upon us. We were not conscious of the process. We have read as we have run. Our intake of information, particularly that concerning aid, was bound to be in imbalance because of the very nature of the subject. The fields of action were remote. Coverage was spotty. Trouble made news. Progress and success did not. Charges of waste and corruption were graphic and long lived. Explanations, qualifications, and denials were too technical, too long, too dry, and too late to be readable or newsworthy. Even the English language conspired at imbalance, with the words of condemnation far outshining those of justification; witness "giveaway," "boondoggle," and "rathole." No alert, interested, informed, and articulate domestic constituency existed to interpret, defend, counterattack, and set the record straight.

It is small wonder that we have backed into this new and extraterritorial dimension of citizenship grudgingly, querulously, being both confused and opinionated. Is it possible to imagine going through school without having studied the Supreme Court, the Bill of Rights, and the federal system, and, upon entering adult life, reading news mostly directed at criminals set free, burdens laid on private property, and restrictions imposed on states as the result of Court decisions? Such a preparation would strain our capacity for good citizenship. But this is the kind of preparation we bring to meet the demand that we be broad-gauged citizens, mindful of a world calling on our country to play a leadership role.

Does the answer lie in a more balanced flow of information? In 1959 the Draper Committee called for "a major, sustained effort to make available to the public all the facts about the [aid] program." In the same year both the Senate Committee on Foreign Relations and the House Committee on Foreign Affairs made the same plea.

Providing more "information," however, is difficult to accomplish. Congress has traditionally been alert to any effort that might be said to cross the indefinable line into "propaganda." Moreover, even with a more liberal interpretation of "information," the hard fact is that interpretation, explanation, and description in depth is not news. It cannot claim headlines or news broadcast time.

The need for a better balance in the flow of information lies at the deeper levels of description and interpretation. The public seeks insights and understanding about the progress being made, the difficulties faced, the way in which funds are being put to use. Such a need calls for functional and area studies for organizations; films showing aid and other activities abroad combatting specific problems in a specific setting, for theaters, citizen groups, and television; feature stories in depth for magazines and newspapers; tailored case materials for seminars, schools, and colleges; assistance in providing speakers and materials for meetings and conferences; periodical reports for interested citizens, editorial writers, commentators. Should there be doubt that such activities might be considered "propaganda," Congress should clear the air and give a mandate that these services be provided. This would seem to be a minimum, if the public's right to know is to be respected in substance rather than only in form.

Attitudes ingrained by half a lifetime, however, will not easily change. The greater opportunity to realize a climate of perseverance lies with young Americans.

What is required beyond information is a concept of education designed to qualify us to carry out the responsibilities of the new dimension of our citizenship. More than the layering on of additional courses in world affairs is at stake. Our basic equipment should consist of attitudes adequate to deal with the world as it is — attitudes shorn of arrogance and excessive expectations, free of neurotic self-doubt, realistic as to the problems that lie ahead, and radiating confidence in our ability to make reasonable progress if we but persist. The shaping of such attitudes involves the demolition of prejudgment, bias, and unquestioned assumptions. This is a long run, basic, comprehensive task of education for all age groups. Structural changes, reappraisal of curricula, reshaping of materials, developing seasoned and sensitive teachers — all may be involved. The task is no less than helping America come of age.

President de Kiewiet of the University of Rochester has sketched the magnitude of the task:

> America's consciousness of its world must undergo the same transformation that occurred in Western Europe in the sixteenth and seventeenth centuries as a result of the great voyages of discovery . . . To a degree we do not yet recognize, with an unparalleled speed, we are discovering a new world . . . Our educational habits and practices have of necessity been deeply influenced by Western Europe . . . Yet there simply must be room in general education . . . for the opportunity to bring into focus the new world . . .[1]

In 1960 the Committee on the University of World Affairs (of which both Secretary of State Rusk and Senator Fulbright, Chairman of the Senate Committee on Foreign Relations, were members) stated in a report of major significance:

> To a greater degree than ever before, world affairs are American affairs, and American affairs are those of the world.

[1] Quoted in *The University and World Affairs,* report of the Committee on the University and World Affairs, New York: The Ford Foundation (477 Madison Avenue, New York 22), 1960, p. 11.

These are matters not alone for the specialists. They are a dimension or whole new set of dimensions of the problems with which all American students and all American universities and colleges are or should be vitally concerned.[2]

One of its principal conclusions recognized that: "A first-class liberal education in the second half of the twentieth century should unquestionably include an effective international component. Few universities or colleges have yet organized themselves to meet this standard." Both the achieving of faculty competence and the reshaping of curricula to give adequate place to world affairs were seen as tasks that still lay ahead for most universities and colleges.

This is a delayed action fuse. If, in 1960, most institutions of higher learning were doing a less than effective job in preparing students to be citizens in the world of today, what about the youth in secondary schools?

The U.S. Office of Education estimates that today almost 4.5 million students are enrolled in colleges and universities. There are over 12 million students in grades 9 through 12. Of those who will graduate from high school, 43 percent will enter college on a full time basis, 10 percent will attend part time, and 47 percent will not go on to college at all.

Roughly half of tomorrow's adult citizenry, therefore, must depend solely on secondary education for initial understanding of the world and the role of the United States in that world.

Ideally, secondary education should convey an optimum number of disciplines and skills. It should impart a broad range of learning with the aspiration to pursue further knowledge. And it should develop attitudes and values relevant to living in the modern world. Consciousness of the world beyond our borders should be a part of these objectives.

Increased world awareness is evident in the courses in many

[2] Ibid., p. 11.

schools on Problems of American Democracy and U.S. History, in several excellent student and teacher periodicals, and in special study materials. Widening and deepening attention to this new dimension of citizenship in some 30,000 secondary schools of the nation will be formidable tasks. Today's high school curriculum is as tightly packed as a tin of sardines. The demands on qualified teachers are already at the straining point. And the very nature of the problems confronts the teacher with the same question facing the Senator or Congressman: How far can one go beyond the established attitudes of a community?

Most discussion about aid and public understanding revolves about the issue of "selling aid." This leads down the alleys of special promotions, conferences, and efforts to persuade Senators and Congressmen to support aid requests. All of these have their place. But emphasis on education has not yet seized the imagination of many of the makers of educational policy. There seems to be a lack of intensive joint exploration of the task of organizing for the new dimension on the part of those charged with carrying out U.S. foreign policy and those charged with keeping education in touch with the times. This lack of exploration is understandable. The preoccupation of the executive branch and the Congress with each year's aid legislation has shortened the perspective.

But all these problems must be faced and overcome if there is to be an adequate effort to develop an understanding of the international facts of life and the range of our response to these facts. This is an educational effort of the first magnitude. Upon this effort will depend, to a large extent, the quality of our endurance during the demanding years that lie ahead.

CHAPTER 19

The National Interest

THE KEY LINK in the chain of reasoning about aid policy is a conviction that it is in the national interest to pursue that policy with perseverance. Awareness of the realities of aid in action, appreciation of historical achievement, insight into our deepest purpose, self-conscious cultivation of realistic attitudes, increased confidence from the efforts of ourselves and others, and efforts to improve performance, the making of decisions, and public understanding are all vital elements to national consensus and commitment. But they all remain academic exercises without a recognition of the relation between aid and the national interest in today's world.

"National interest" is a pragmatic term. It embraces philosophy and history but goes beyond. It speaks to the here and now. It cannot be argued in abstract terms. It takes its life from the world in which we live. Only after a perceptive look at that world does the nature, scope, and magnitude of our national interest take on meaning.

To achieve some sense of perspective about our national interest, we shall measure it in two dimensions. The first is a geographic *tour d'horizon;* the second is a view of the major forces moving the world of today. Our purpose will be to link aspiration and reality.

One of the most appealing recent doctrines of aid policy — and one of the most misunderstood — is that of selectivity. It appeals because it says we should not spread ourselves too thin, by trying to do "too much for too many too soon." No one would disagree with this admonition. Aid should not be distributed on a per capita basis, without regard to our objectives, the limitation of our resources, the possibility of maximizing accomplishment. But the label of selectivity often masks the proposition that the United States should confine its assistance to only a few selected countries "where a real job can be done."

Such a plea appeals to our fear of numbers but it ignores the extent of our basic interest. Both the fear and the interest require deeper scrutiny.

In 1963 the United States was engaged in economic aid relationships with 76 of the countries of the world and four dependencies. In 1963 there were 38 nations outside the Communist sphere not receiving either capital or technical assistance. Economic aid (excluding military assistance, food programs, and Export-Import Bank loans) was being extended to two thirds of the world's free countries. Ten years ago, when there were 80 countries counted outside the Communist world, we were aiding 60, or three fourths of all free nations. Our percentage has declined while the number of aid recipients has increased.

Numbers themselves are neutral. This is a world of almost 130 nations, over fifty of whom have reached independence in the past two decades. The pattern of our aid efforts has been termination in 14 European countries, recent relationships with the new nations of Africa, and almost no change in the number of countries in Latin America, the Middle East, South Asia, and the Far East (41 in 1953 and 44 in 1963).

These numbers conceal the high degree of concentration or selectivity of aid which already exist.

The facts about the current distribution of assistance are that 80 percent of economic aid goes to twenty countries, with 60 percent going to eight countries. Most military assistance, 80 percent, is concentrated in nine countries. We already have a pattern of concentration of the bulk of assistance, with smaller programs, accounting for a minority share of aid, in most of the countries.

Is such a pattern consistent with our national interest? What is the scope of that interest? The way to answer this question is not to philosophize but to look at the map.

In this hemisphere there are three areas of concern — Central America, the islands of the Caribbean, and South America.

Mexico and the smaller countries of Central America are part of the ring containing the Gulf of Mexico and the Caribbean Sea. They are close neighbors of Cuba. Their orderly development and political stability are of high importance to us. The same can be said of the chain of island communities projecting southeasterly from Florida. One Castro is one too many. And while Great Britain and other Commonwealth countries such as Canada may legitimately be expected to assist former and present British dependencies, we have an immediate interest in the harmony, progress, and trade of this entire area.

This is a generalization. Does it stand analysis? Of our interest in a stable Mexico, sharing our 1500-mile border, there can be no doubt. A look at the six smaller countries of Central America and British Honduras shows not only the strategic importance of the Panama Canal, and the threat of Cuba, pointed like a saber at the Yucatán Peninsula, but the obvious impossibility of containing prolonged disorder, chaos, or externally financed Communism within any one of the countries. This small intercontinental bridge is an interdependent region. Should it develop constructively, it will be a source of hemispheric solidarity. Should it become an area seething with subversion, the hemisphere can be effectively severed, with a beachhead for operations both north and south.

As to South America, there is no nation toward whom we should be indifferent. All of South America is in flux and, although historically old, the entire continent is set on the goal of modernization. The efforts, abilities, and determination of these nations vary. What each country does affects all. A nation which makes demonstrable progress under the banner of the Alliance for Progress will be a bellwether for the others. But a nation which rejects this approach in favor of a completely controlled economy will not only distort commercial relationships beyond its borders, but, by its very example, substitute incessant ideological controversy for concrete progress in planning and action. South America would be rent asunder in philosophy rather than united in progress. An old saying is that a rising tide lifts all the boats. It is just as true that an ebbing tide lowers all.

U.S. aid will vary in amounts among these countries — depending mainly on their ability to use it wisely. But our posture is and should remain that of readiness to respond generously to good plans and difficult self-help measures. When countries develop political leaders able and willing to commit their energies to backing such plans and measures, our help should be unstinting. We — and they — need the kind of successes that breed further successes.

Our posture ought also to be one of steadiness, for progress will proceed at an irregular pace. There will be relapses, monetary and political crises, trade negotiations with Communist countries and criticisms of U.S. intervention in domestic affairs. Some assistance will be given to cope with short-term problems. Not all of it will be well used. Some plans and reforms will not proceed on schedule. But our interest lies in the long-run evolution of social and political democracy and the stable prosperity of the nations of this continent. This is also their long-run interest. We must let no event, crisis, or frustration distort or divert that interest.

The Middle East presents a wide spectrum of problems. Greece and Turkey are struggling for both stability and rapid economic growth. They are both members of NATO. Lebanon has now reached the point of being independent of external aid. Iraq is determined to achieve internal political tranquillity. Jordan, having chiefly depended on outside aid from Britain and the United States, shows progress in its long slow climb toward being a viable nation. Should it fail, it would be a hotly contested prize for all its neighbors. Israel has made itself almost a developed country in a short decade and a half, but sits under the cloud of Arab hostility. Syria and Egypt are beset with problems of internal development, and intraregional tensions. The Arabian peninsula, site of oil and sheikdoms, is a constant target for outside threats and internal revolt.

The basic aid interest of the United States is to extend varying degrees of assistance in an effort to focus attention of each country on its own serious problems of national development. One essential fact stands out. Despite the Aswan Dam and other Communist aid, there is no satellite in the Middle East. And difficult though it sometimes is to deal with the forces of nationalism, it is not impossible. Genuine national development offers a foundation for increasingly constructive relationships, while satellitism does not.

Going eastward on the map brings us to South Asia, to Iran, Afghanistan, Pakistan, India and Nepal — all bordering either the Soviet Union or China. In India and Pakistan alone are almost 600 million people, one half of the independent developing world, with more than the population of Africa and Latin America combined. With able governmental services, well-advanced plans, and multi-nation financing, these two nations are in the midstream of a great experiment in the compatibility of open societies and economic development, an experiment challenged, in the case of India, by a continuing threat from Communist China.

Our concern for and interest in Iran and Afghanistan can be seen by visualizing their location. Each lies between Pakistan and the Soviet Union. Iran is flanked by Turkey, the Soviet Union, Iraq, the Persian Gulf, the Arabian Sea, West Pakistan, and Afghanistan. A similar point can be made about Nepal, separating some 500 miles of Indian border from Communist-occupied Tibet.

Were the United States to decide to abandon all its aid to any of these countries, the cost of such action would be immeasurably greater than the savings of dollars. The cost, though not capable of a dollar measurement, would lie in increased Soviet or Chinese penetration, frontier threats, interruption of transportation and communication, the diversion of greater economic resources to military forces to counter external threats, a substantial slowdown in development, and, above all, doubts as to the depth and reliability of the interest of the United States.

Following the Chinese border eastward, into Southeast Asia, we enter an area that has been a caldron for over a decade. First comes neutralist Burma, sharing a 1300-mile border with China — a country which could give Chinese troops easy access to India just as the Burma Road carried General Stilwell and his troops to China in World War II. Next comes the Indochina Peninsula, with Thailand, Laos, Cambodia, and Vietnam — whose fertile deltas and rice fields are a constant magnet for the Chinese to the north. To the south sprawl 3000 miles of the Indonesia archipelago — the fifth largest nation of the world and still not a Communist satellite despite huge Communist credits. Together the peninsula and the archipelago surround the new Federation of Malaysia; all but surround the Philippines; and thrust close to the shores of Australia and New Zealand. The pattern of geography is repeated farther north where the Korean Peninsula almost touches the southern tip of Japan.

The area is still in crisis. No end is clearly in sight. Many critics look upon U.S. involvement in this part of the world as folly. But there are two questions which should be answered. The first: What has been accomplished? The second: Is there a better alternative?

The accomplishments are impressive, given the difficulties of remoteness, of ancient civilizations facing the problems of modernization, of the proximity of a huge and implacable foe.

South Korea, still beset by instability, has recovered from the war. It has shown its capacity to develop agricultural productivity rivalling that of Japan. It requires a period of financial discipline and political quietude to make real progress. The free Republic of China on Formosa has converted a barren refuge into a viable economy and society which will soon be self-sustaining. Malaya, through the persistent help of the British, staved off the threat of Communist subversion and now provides the cornerstone for the new Malaysia. The neutralism for Laos prescribed by the Geneva Accords hangs constantly in the balance. A nation is not yet saved, but neither is it yet lost.

The cost of all that we have done in military and economic assistance, including food, in the five countries of Burma, Cambodia, Laos, Thailand, and Vietnam from 1946 to 1962 has been about four billion dollars. This is one billion dollars more than U.S. citizens pay each year for fishing licenses. Clearly this has been costly. Equally clearly, there is something to show for the investment, ranging from the success story of Taiwan to the buying of time — a valuable purchase so long as there is hope for ultimate success.

The harder question is that of alternatives. To withdraw from any country in this troubled area, unless it is clear that such country no longer is committed to its own independence, is to issue a declaration of noninterest in one of the five developing areas of the noncommunist world. It would create a power vacuum, inviting Peking to extend its hegemony to one vast semicircle, from Manchuria to New Guinea, cradling the Philippines, Formosa, and Japan.

Africa perhaps presents the most difficult test of U.S. aid purposes. Here is where the proponents of withdrawal may feel they have the strongest case. It is tempting to say that the U.S. interest, apart from aid associated with a few military facilities, should be confined to one or two countries, such as Nigeria, which have the administrative equipment to develop and implement a sound plan. Africa, in a phrase, should be out of bounds. Such thinking ignores history, the nature of our aid programs, and our deepest national interest.

The fifties saw the sleeping giant, Africa, not only awaken but become significant — politically, economically, socially. At the same time, Western Europe revived, gained strength, and lengthened its economic stride. Revisionists with a passion for neatness would have liked — indeed, would still like — to see all of the political, social, and economic lines run between Europe and Africa. The modern apostles of spheres of influence are at least a century too late. The increasing interdependence of the world in trade, in science, in culture, in politics is an inescapable fact. For the United States to declare Africa beyond its field of interest and influence would be a thinly veiled act of withdrawal from a continent which, according to forecasts, will contain almost 700 million people by the year 2000.[1]

The United States responded to the new family of African states by acting promptly to offer its assistance. In the overwhelming majority of cases our assistance has been modest, far less than that of European countries. It has been chiefly in the field of teaching skills and helping to build institutions. The advocates of withdrawal seldom trouble themselves to see what kind of aid programs make up what they view as shocking totals. All of Africa accounted, in 1962, for only 10 percent of our current economic aid. In ten countries our programs were less than $1 million; in twenty-one countries they were less than $5 million.

A hundred years ago, if we had wanted to establish a relation of friendship and influence with a new country, we would have had the choice of diplomatic recognition, special trade arrangements, or protection through standing military forces. In today's world, the latter two approaches would be both inordi-

[1] *The Population Dilemma.* The American Assembly, Columbia University. Englewood Cliffs, N.J.: Prentice-Hall, Inc., 1963, p. 21.

nately costly and contrary to the international order: the former is of little weight. What is available to us is the sensitive and selective use of aid, a constructive instrument of far greater utility than its cost in creating and sustaining a mutually helpful relationship between nations.

Africa is not one problem. There is a growing spirit of pan-Africanism, but this does not obscure the wide variation in problems, opportunities, and capabilities among all the countries. The U.S. objective in some nations is more obvious than in others. Some countries are immediately important for their strategic location. Some are important to us because they have first relied on Soviet assistance, found it less than satisfactory, and have opened their doors to the West. Some have every prospect for making dramatic progress in development and should be made examples of success in orderly growth. Some are so situated that chaos and disorder might lead to subversion, military adventurism, with resulting threats to neighboring countries. Finally, some are new countries, with small populations, massive problems of health, literacy, and poverty, and with a scant administrative apparatus to grapple with these problems. These countries usually receive substantial budgetary assistance from their former metropole power. France, for example, spends twice as much on overseas aid, per capita, as the United States. What is the United States to do in such a case?

If the decision were to be made solely in terms of an immediate threat, it could be that of total abstinence from aid. No immediate adverse effect on the United States could be measured. But the future development of Africa will inexorably be determined by the choices open to nations in their most tentative, groping, critical years of development . . . and the conditions under which choice is exercised.

African nations must seek external resources. These are essential to accelerated development. Sometimes these efforts to obtain outside help are criticized as unprincipled acts of cynical opportunism. But sovereignty and diversity of sources of help go together. It is a fact of life that an elected leader cannot long urge his country to rely completely on its former colonial master for assistance, no matter how generous it may be. Apart from such exclusive economic dependence being a continuing affront to nations proud of their new independence, metropole aid will simply not be enough — either in quantity or quality. Development means partly a growing interest in certain kinds of training, institutions, and capital projects which no one country has the material or human resources to supply. Even in the United States, miners and textile workers as recently as a few decades ago found that the company store was not only a mark of semi-dependence but limited in variety.

Conditions under which the searching for assistance takes place are of crucial importance. If, in addition to substantial metropole aid, there are skills and some capital available from the United States and other free world countries, the availability of Communist credits and technicians poses no great threat. Such assistance is merely another resource, not the critical key to development. The African country can solicit and accept assistance under conditions of dignity. It can compare, complain, and cancel. The free and developed countries need not fear the results.

But if assistance from Communist countries is the only source of aid supplemental to that of the metropole, it assumes an unnecessarily high value. It then becomes — or appears to become — the critical margin of development. The African country stands in a different position. It must agree to conditions and arrangements, however onerous or unwise, for there is all the difference in the world between a country which can choose and a country which must submit. And the aid necessary to preserve the former condition is one of the best investments we and other free nations can make.

These are the first and most precious years for the new countries of Africa. They, for the most part, are not asking for massive aid. The opportunity is to step in at this early moment of their national life with some kinds of assistance which the United States is well equipped to supply, which they desperately need, and which do not compete with the aid they receive from others. It may be training in crop diversification, in forestry, in public administration. It may be a capital project, which would be vital to the sprouting economy, visible to all, without creating excessive expectations as to continuing annual aid at the same levels.

To create a relationship of confidence in the early stages of nation building could be worth much to the United States and to the free world. Willingness to give limited assistance to small countries would go far beyond the impact on these countries themselves.

The United States, insofar as Africa is concerned, should be known as one of the earliest, stoutest, and steadiest supporters of African development in freedom, not because of a fear of a future conflict between races, but because of the realization that, in the world community of nations, Africans will increasingly develop both a voice and an influence in world affairs. It is of crucial importance to the kind of world in which we wish to live that both the voice and the influence are based on an attitude of friendship and cooperation. This is not the cheap goal of "buying friends" for a specific purpose or vote. This is the large goal of creating a friendly neighborhood.

What has emerged from this *tour d'horizon* is a concept of U.S. interests that is not "cribbed, cabined and confined." The United States has an interest in every part of the uncommitted, developing world. We should not be afraid to acknowledge this. Other free and developed nations should share this interest. They are increasingly sharing it. We should stimulate their interest and welcome their participation. But what we do, we do because of the kind of world we want — for ourselves and

our posterity. This is our business and our purpose. It is also
theirs. But it is no less ours because it is also theirs.

The other measure of national interest is not space but time.
We live in time. Our interest must always be related to the
times. Our policies, to serve us well, must be responsive to the
great forces that move these times.

A look at the world, piercing the haze of daily events, reveals
five of these major forces or conditions of international life
today which carry a profound significance for the United States
as it seeks to define its interest and its role.

First, we live in a time of mutual restraint on the use of
major military force. To the extent that international tensions
are relaxed by such agreements as the Test Ban Treaty, other
instruments of policy will play a larger role. For there is no
relaxation in the basic contest between ways of life. In this
era of muted conflict, aid takes on new importance as a major
vehicle of leadership, of influencing by doing, showing, and
helping.

Second, we live in a time of nationalism. Half a hundred
new nations and almost as many older nations are seeking complete sovereignty, free of political and economic dependence
on any single major power. The present decade is the formative decade for most of these nations. These are the years when
timely and effective assistance in helping meet their problems
can crystallize internal patterns of conduct and external relations for years to come.

Third, we live in an age of development. The one craving
of all people in the developing world is to make measurable
progress, in their time, toward a better life. This surging aspiration can result in false starts, frustration, chaos, the repression of individual liberty, and bloodshed. Or, by generous,
wise, and sustained assistance, it can lead to sound economies,
responsible governments, and progressive societies, enriching
not only themselves but an increasingly interdependent world.

Fourth, we live in an era of rapidly expanding free world economic strength. Helped by our first great aid effort, the nations of western Europe and Japan have joined Canada and the United States in making available to developing countries an increased flow of resources on improving terms. Here is a phalanx of material wealth, human skills, and liberal values of incomparable potential. The continued momentum of this accelerating free world assistance movement could be the critical factor in helping bring about the kind of peaceful, mutually prospering, trading world which can benefit all. The role of the United States in strengthening this partnership ought to be one of steady leadership, not abdication or Hamlet-like vacillation.

Lastly, we live in a period of dissension within the Communist world. This fact should not mislead us. The Communist nations still hold faithfully to the conviction that capitalism "moves toward inevitable ruin." They are still pledged to a "world system of socialism." But a new motive has been added. Both Communist China and Russia, and their respective supporters, see aid as a weapon in their internecine strife. To the extent that China seeks to wean the support of the Communist apparatus in the developing countries away from the Soviet Union, it will engage in strategically selected assistance programs. As for the Soviet Union, aid is now more essential than ever as a vehicle for retaining its global Party leadership.

On the issue of ideological purity, Communist China can claim stricter adherence to classic doctrine. On the highly charged racial issue, she wastes no opportunity to link herself with all peoples of colored skin. On the issue of material well-being, Russia is set apart as a "have" nation, with China being a fellow suffering "have not." In the face of this formidable forensic battery, the Soviet Union has recourse to its weapon of economic assistance. This can be a powerful one if it can convince developing nations that Russia's way has not only worked well for Russia but can render concrete, effective assistance for others. Her hope is that deeds can speak louder than dogma.

Just as an East-West relaxation of tensions elevates aid as an instrument of policy, so does a Communist schism. We should not underestimate this new implication. If both sides of the Communist world increase use of aid as a weapon, whatever may be their internal or external purposes, we can look forward to an increasing thrust of attempted influence throughout Asia, Africa, and Latin America.

All of these forces — the relaxation of tensions, the strivings of nationalism, the surge toward development, the gathering free world effort, the split in the Communist world — set the stage on which the United States must play its role. If to these global facts is joined a view of the United States as determined, in its own ultimate national interest, to advance free societies, a working consensus on aid adequate to the task would consist of these elements:

– A deeply held conviction that aid is an increasingly important instrument of a foreign policy unwaveringly dedicated to the enlargement of freedom in the world — the only final assurance of the blessings of liberty to our own posterity;

– An insistence on improving the quality of aid personnel, knowledge, and operations, with the recognition that there is no crash program, or scheme of reorganization that can be a substitute for solid and sensitive professionalism;

– A continuing effort to search for and draw upon the best nongovernmental resources, in business, in the educational institutions, and in the wide variety of associations making up our society;

– A recognition of the need to develop a practice of Congressional decision on aid issues that will strike the best possible balance between legislative responsibility, operational continuity, and overseas sensitivities;

– A set of realistic attitudes — of what aid can reasonably be expected to accomplish in a striving and complex world; of humility and patience; and of measured pride in our efforts and a solid confidence in our ability to succeed in the most complex enterprise we have yet undertaken.

With such a consensus, we would have equipped ourselves to deal effectively with a world turning its attention from military confrontation to other uses of power; to respond to the universal drives toward nationalism and development; to sustain our leadership in realizing the full potential of the combined efforts of the free world; and to cope calmly and constructively with the diverse thrusts of the contesting branches of the Communist world.

*   *   *

Most of the great domestic problems of the times pose challenges to positive action and new initiatives. The field of foreign affairs often poses an additional kind of challenge — that of steady perseverance in policies, programs, and attitudes whose fruits are slow in ripening.

Such is the deep demand of the age of development. Its call to the people of the United States is to endure in sustaining their historic efforts to assist in the evolution of free, responsible, and prospering nations.

It is a levy on the American spirit, understanding, and will. It is a call to this generation to sense a new extension of the spirit of the Declaration of Independence in an interdependent world. In responding to this call, the people of the United States will be doing far more than giving this nation the ability to endure in its leadership. They will have rediscovered their national purpose. They will be serving their deepest national interest.

INDEX

INDEX

Africa, aid to, 260–64; development of, 180–81

Agency for International Development, administration of, professionalism in, 221–29, 230–34; as development broker, 27–29; establishment of, 85–86; headquarters operations and case study of, 19–27; "Implementation Project" of, 232–34; Mission Directors of, 6–13, 18; organization of, 86; planning of program, 13–16, 46–47; personnel overseas, number of, 132–33

Agricultural commodities, grants or sales of surpluses of, 15

Aid, achievements of, 175–88; alternative approaches to, 166–68; characteristics of U.S. program, 18; committees to investigate program, 42–44, 77; Communist program of, 197, 200, 201–16; comparison of free and Communist world programs, 200; consensus on: gap in, 89, 93, growth of, 80–89, need for, 75–80, 219; consequences of discontinuing program, 140–42; coordination of national programs, 197–99; cost of program, 134–40; criteria for choosing recipients, 37–38, 117, 119, 124–26, 127; decision on giving, making of, 29–35; diplomacy of, 6, 12, 16–18, 35; forms of, 15, 38; history of U.S. program, 66–74, 82; investment nature of, 163–69; as percentage of GNP of recipient countries, 122; phasing out of country program, 34–35; public attitudes toward, 36–37, 40, 76, 117, 122–23, 126, 129–32, 143; purposes of, 13, 37, 39, 93, 95–99, 101, 104–11, 121, 127, 145; selectivity of program, 254–55; suspension of, 33; see also technical assistance

Alliance for Progress, 73, 124, 125, 181, 185, 186, 192–93; Inter-American Committee for, 185

Ambassador, relationship of with A.I.D. Mission Director, 8

Asia, South, aid to, 258–60

Ball, George W., 85
Barkley, Senator Alben W., 69
Barratt, George H., 157
Bell, David E., 87, 152–53
Bogotá, Act of, 72–73
Brazil, aid to, 31–32

Catholic Church, role of, in Latin America, 186
Central America Free Trade Area, 187–88
China, Republic of, economic development of, 179

Churchill, Winston, 59, 68
Clay Committee, 43, 87–89
Colombo Plan, 192
Committee of European Economic Cooperation, 68
Communist countries, aid program of, see Aid, Communist program of
Comptroller General, 42
Congress, action on 1963 aid bill by, 55–56; effect of aid debate: on Communist world, 79–80, on other donor nations, 79, on recipient countries, 78–79; formulation of aid legislation by, 46, 47–56, 99–100; supervision of aid programs by, 41–42, 45, 77, 78, 123–24, 235–36, 238–46
Cuban revolution, significance of, 72

Decade of Development, 73–74
Developing countries, capital requirements of, 148–49; increases in per capita GNP of, 146–47; political instability in, 152–53; relative increase in poverty of, 143–45, 149–51
Development Assistance Committee, see Organization for Economic Cooperation and Development, Development Assistance Committee
Development grants, 15
Development Loan Fund, absorption into A.I.D. of, 86; establishment of, 82
Development loans, 15
"Diplocracy," 19
Draper, William H., Jr., 43, 82
Draper Committee, 82–83, 87

Eisenhower, President Dwight D., 72
European countries, aid programs of, 191–94; see also European Economic Community Overseas Development Fund; Organization for Economic Cooperation and Development, Development Assistance Committee
European Economic Community Overseas Development Fund, 192
European Recovery Program, see Marshall Plan
Export-Import Bank, 66

Fairless, Benjamin, 43
Fisher, Joseph L., 155
Foreign aid, see Aid
Foreign Assistance Act of 1961, 74, 87, 96–99, 101
Free world, GNP of, 189
Fulbright, Senator J. William, 56

Gant, George, 85
Gray, Gordon, 43
Greece, development of, 178
Green, Senator Theodore Francis, 81
Guinea, aid to, 31

Hamilton, Fowler, 86
Harriman, W. Averell, 43
Herter, Christian W., 43, 224
Hoffman, Paul, 148

India, development of, 177–78; military aid to, 30
Institute for Inter-American Affairs, 66
Inter-American Development Bank, 72
International Bank for Reconstruction and Development, 66, 83, 199
International Cooperation Administration, 86
International Development Association, 83, 88
International Monetary Fund, 66

Israel, development of, 178–79

Japan, economic success of, 179
Johnson, President Lyndon B., 55
Johnston, Eric, 43

Kennedy, President John F., 73, 85, 86, 88
Krug, Julius A., 43

Labouisse, Henry R., 85
Laos, support of, 32
Latin America, aid to, 72–73, 256–57; development of, 181–88; private investment in, 186–87; see also Alliance for Progress
Latin America Free Trade Association, 188
Lebanon, development of, 178
Lippmann, Walter, 93
Lorimer, Frank, 157–58

Marshall, General George C., 68–69, 81
Marshall Plan, 67–70, 95, 146
Middle East, aid to, 257–58
Millikan, Max, 85

Niebuhr, Reinhold, 116
Nigeria, aid to, 31
Nourse, Edwin, 43

Organization for Economic Cooperation and Development, Development Assistance Committee, 193–99
Organization of American States, 72

Pakistan, development of, 178
Passman, Representative Otto E., 50, 53–54
Philippines, economic potential of, 179
Point IV, 70–71, 72, 176
Population problem, 154–60

Potter, Neal, 155
Punta del Este, Charter of, 73, 181–82

Randall, Clarence, 43
Rockefeller, Nelson A., 43
Rosenstein-Rodan, Paul, 148
Rusk, Dean, 202, 224

Schlesinger, Arthur M., Jr., 59
Senate Committee on Foreign Relations, studies by, 81–82, 95; view of aid objectives, 95, 101
Supporting assistance, 15

Task Force on Economic Assistance, membership of, 85
Tannenwald, Theodore, Jr., 85
Technical assistance, challenge of, 230–31; Communist program of, 197; first U.S. program of, 66; free world program of, 196–97; see also Point IV; United Nations Technical Assistance Program
Tocqueville, Alexis de, 3
Toynbee, Arnold, 154
Truman, President Harry S., 66–67, 81
Truman Doctrine, 66–67

Underdeveloped countries, see Developing countries
United Nations Relief and Rehabilitation Administration, 66, 81
United Nations Technical Assistance Program, 70, 192

Vandenberg, Senator Arthur H., 69–70
Vietnam, U.S. commitment to, 32

Ward, Barbara, 128
World Bank, see International Bank for Reconstruction and Development